THE BATTLE
FOR
JERUSALEM

AVAILABLE NOW

THE BATTLE FOR JERUSALEM

By Lt. General Mordechai Gur
Translated by Philip Gillon

ibooks
new york
www.ibooks.net

DISTRIBUTED BY SIMON & SCHUSTER, INC

An ibooks, inc. Book

Ibooks, inc.
24 West 25th Street
New York, NY 10010

The ibooks World Wide Web Site address is:
http://www.ibooksinc. com

Original Hebrew title: *Har Habayit Beyadeinu*

Editor: Dwight Jon Zimmerman
Cover Design: J. Vita

ISBN: 0-7434-4488-4
First ibooks printing June 2002
10   9   8   7   6   5   4   3   2   1

Share your thoughts about *The Battle for Jerusalem* and other ibooks titles in the new ibooks virtual reading group at www.ibooks.net

"None can read Gur's book without savoring a deep sense of its locale. This, after all, was a battle being fought in and for Jerusalem, by men whose forebears fought on this very site three thousand years before and in the centuries thereafter. It was being fought by men with a profound sense of history and a deep sense of mission. Unforgettable was General Gur's own history-making moment when, after two days of fighting, he stood upon the summit of the Mount of Olives and looked down upon the magnificent esplanade of Temple Mount where King Solomon had constructed Jewry's Temple in the 10th Century BC. Taking the signals' microphone into his hand, the transmitter set to 'network', Gur gave 'all battalion commanders' the final objective: 'The Temple Mount, the Western Wall, the Old City. For two thousand years our people have prayed for this moment. Let us go forward—to victory.' And unforgettable is Gur's account of it."

—Moshe Pearlman, Israeli journalist

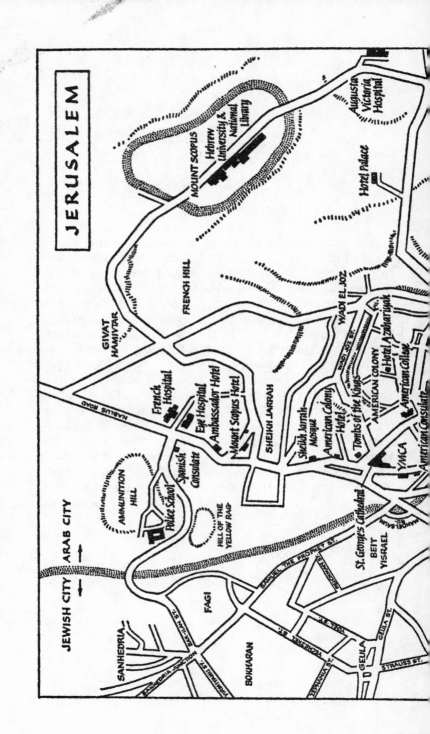

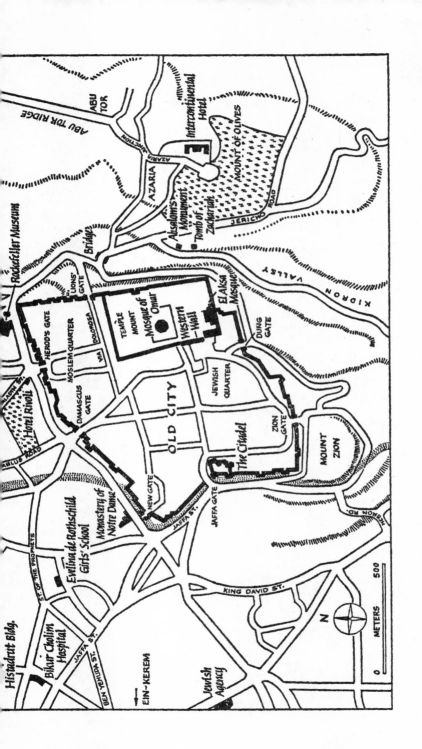

Chapter I

STANDBY

Monday, June 5, 1967

At 0712 the noise of the planes warming up came over from the airfield. We were sitting at the table of "Moshe-and-a-half." Then we heard the jets roaring away.

Yesterday they had offered me a position at General Headquarters. But I preferred to be here with the brigade. I dozed a bit last night on a camp bed in Moshe-and-a-half's room. I sent members of my staff to the units to deal with a few matters.

We held a short discussion to coordinate transport problems to the airfield in preparation for the parachute drop. Then the planes stopped taking off. I wondered if something had gone wrong. But at 0752 I heard more planes taking off.

The war had begun.

At 0745 Colonel Yaakov informed us that the outbreak of the war would be announced at eight over the radio. There was no other way of telling all the troops on standby that the waiting was over. It was possible that at that very moment a great battle was being fought in the skies over the airfields of Egypt. We heard planes taking off from both the runways, but did not hear whether any planes had returned or what might be happening to the war in the air over Egypt.

It is a strange feeling to begin a war like this ... writing a diary far in the rear of the battle. Will we, or our children, ever live here in peace?

At 0700 the brigade had gathered at the rendezvous point in the citrus groves of Givat Brenner; the men, having arrived in the middle of the night, were confused as to exactly where they were. Parachutists, cars, war equipment swarmed among the orange trees while Dr. King, the brigade doctor, satisfied that nothing was really going on, decided to shave—to set an example.

They heard the roar of planes in the distance, and the experienced parachutists could tell each other, "They're warming up the engines." But no one was sure. As Dr. King hurried to finish his shave, a pale youngster suddenly appeared. "My name is Nathan Schechter. I have just arrived in Israel from Italy. I'm a medic. Please give me a job." Compared with the sunburned fighters, Nathan seemed even paler than he really was. Dr. King sent him to Battalion 28.

The forces organized for breakfast, opening cans and boiling water. The noise of the planes increased. Some could not resist going to the borders of the grove to watch the planes taking off. One after the other, they zoomed aloft, then joined in formations and flew west and south. Quite a few men stayed close to the deep antibomb trenches ("Better to play safe."), their ears glued to transistors. They wanted to hear whether the war had started, having no doubt that we would not permit the Egyptians to surprise us. According to the number of planes taking off from the field, it would seem as if the war had really begun. Then at 0800 the radio announced clashes on the Sinai border.

Now there is no doubt. The war was on!

There were more orders. We waited, listening anxiously to the radio for news. The battalion doctor went on a tour of inspection. In one of the kitchens he spied a tub full of chopped meat that the cook said he planned to use for lunch. The doctor smelled it and ordered them to bury it immediately. "That's all we need now—parachutists with ptomaine poisoning in the air . . ."

While we were still listening to the news on the radio at eight o'clock, Colonel Davidi informed me that the "Grapefruit" force was leaving us and would serve as reserves to regional General Staff Headquarters. I sent a note to Battalion Deputy Commander, saying that even without these forces we could carry out our mission as planned.

Fifteen minutes later the supply officer returned and demanded ten extra buses for transporting troops to the airport. I talked to Major Sasson, and said we could execute the plan even without Grapefruit. We checked the parachute soldiers' equipment and added items we might be short of in view of Grapefruit's departure. Major Gaon examined the loading schedules with me.

We heard that two Egyptian planes had been brought down and that their airfields were closed. One of our Oregons had fallen and the pilot had parachuted into the sea where a helicopter had gone to rescue him.

Suddenly parachute instructors appeared, bringing new parachute equipment.

The Commander ordered: "Fall in by platoons and companies!"

Everyone asked anxiously: "Where are we jumping?"

No one yet knew where he was going, though rumor was that it would be El Arish. The paratroopers double checked the ammunition they needed for their weapons. Nerves taut, they scrutinized every detail of their equipment—the ropes, the loops, the locks. Their lives hinged on the equipment being flawless.

Because the excitement had upset the soldiers' concentration, instructors passed among the men giving professional, expert advice, calming them and making them realize how crucial the next hours and days would be.

The supply man marked out positions for the units and erected signposts on the roads to the airfield. Each unit had to go to a particular plane by a specific route. The officers checked the lists to be sure they made use of every place on the plane, and at the same time didn't break up the regular framework of the units. We had to be certain where every single man was. Otherwise we'd lose men in jumping and wouldn't even know that they were killed, wounded, or captured.

Men whose equipment had been checked sat down to rest—and wait. Many took the opportunity to write what might be a last letter home before going into action, maybe even the last letter of all. Some wrote on their knees, others on crates of ammunition or cans of food. They wrote with pen or pencil; on writing pads or on scraps of wrapping paper, anything at hand. Still no order came to fly. So they waited. And waited.

At 0930 Kotik was asked how many buses he needed to transport the whole brigade. He didn't understand the reason for the question and wondered if headquarters had decided to change the original objective. But it wasn't the time to grumble about inadequate orders—we'd have something to say later. For some reason, we did not believe that the war would be short.

At 1000 Davidi sent orders that we were to guard the airfield that night, for the Arabs had assigned Hussein of Jordan to attack the fields. It was certainly an essential task to guard the fields, but it wasn't one our group had expected or wanted.

At 1030 we held a staff discussion. Davidi reported that about one hundred and twenty Egyptian planes were on fire. A chief paratrooper officer from headquarters reported that twenty Ilyushins were burning in Abu Svir. Some of our planes were also missing. First losses.

We wondered suddenly how the Egyptians would treat those who became POWs.

At noon I learned from Davidi that Raful and Shmulik were

4

completing the conquest of Rafiah at that very moment, and that the discussion on operations would take place at General Headquarters and the decision made as to who would jump, and when, and where. We were given permission to announce the plan of action to the soldiers and asked the companies to gather round the improvised notice boards, covered with maps and aerial photographs.

The place: El Arish. The method: to jump by night, to move on foot and by helicopter. To get right inside the town and the surrounding positions. The aim: to gain a bridgehead with which the infantry coming from Rafiah would link up later.

The enemy had many tanks, masses of artillery, including enormous coastal guns, and large numbers of soldiers.

It wasn't going to be a picnic. But nobody had any doubt that we could establish our bridgehead. But afterward, we would have to entrench ourselves so that we could withstand counterattacks by tanks. When would our troops arrive from Rafiah?

The moment would come when each man had to stop thinking about the general objective in order to concentrate on his own problems and specific objectives: jumping; landing safely; running with heavy equipment through the deep sands of the dunes; signaling helicopters; finding the right house inside the town—the police building, the hospital, the government house, the road to the airport, the bypass road that was covered with sand . . . His life and the lives of his friends would depend on his not making a mistake.

The photographs were good, but were small and it was hard to make out details. Each soldier craned closer to memorize every detail.

The antitank corps were particularly worried, but they felt good that they were doing a real job at last, after all the waiting. Antitank cannon, missiles, and bazooka corps—they were proud of the responsibility; pleased that they would have a chance to do their job. On the other hand, it was dangerous, very dangerous.

But they smiled, banished their fears, at least on the surface. The main thing was to be patient and to keep cool. To let the tanks go past—and then hit them. True, the infantry accompanying the tanks would then hit back, but they would be in turn a target for our men in the rear . . .

The commanders of the battalions and companies finished what they had to do. Platoon and Special Forces commanders summoned their men to quiet corners and continued to brief them.

Then they checked the equipment, again and again . . . added a few more grenades, extra bandages, canteens. Some brought sweets to moisten the mouth.

The engineering corps studied the area thoroughly. They would be in an isolated position and did not know how much time they would have or if the transport would arrive in time. They only knew things would be very hot for them.

The reconnaissance corps was disappointed. Practically all its equipment was with Grapefruit.

Then experts on antigas warfare arrived and told the units how to behave under a gas attack: put on gas masks and give themselves injections.

The gas masks and injections were unfamiliar, and therefore all the more frightening. The gas people were supposed to be concerned only with the rear. Women and children. We were not prepared for a gas attack. We hadn't contemplated parachuting with gas masks on. In films, we'd always seen soldiers throwing off their masks.

But as suspense mounted, our morale rose. It was a relief finally to be going into action, going to jump at last. From Brigade Headquarters good news reached us about the number of Egyptian planes hit. We ate and remembered other meals before retaliation raids: cans of meat and rice. Somebody described the battalion diarrhea during one raid and everyone laughed.

Our mood was high. But Moshele, the Deputy Brigade Commander, was worried: Would they give the "red background" award—the paratrooper emblem—to men who had landed from helicopters and hadn't jumped? He described to the men what would happen: "Here we are in a helicopter. In the distance we see the coast. Ready. The helicopter lands. I get out. Stand still. Look around. Adjust my equipment and begin to shoot . . ."

Many were worried about the enemy bombing our cities. Our children would be in shelters, but there was concern that these might not be adequate.

A man wrote a short letter home: "I'm O.K. Don't worry. Look after yourselves." Some youngsters worried that the war would end before they had seen any action. The "adults" intervened: "Listen, war isn't so pleasant that it's worth running after just in order to take part in it . . ."

At 1430, suddenly, everything changed. I received an order to send one battalion to Jerusalem. Drawing lots, Yossi Y.'s battalion was selected. Then I spoke to Colonel Arik Regev at Central Command and he said that according to Brigadier General Uzi Narkiss, two battalions would have to go up to the city.

I picked up Amos, Orni, Arik, and Ziklag, and we went to the headquarters of Central Command for our new orders, wondering if it would be our fate to liberate Jerusalem.

At Central Command we were told that only one battalion would go to Jerusalem. It was Moshe-and-a-half, commander of the Parachute School, who informed us.

Yossi Y.'s battalion was ordered to return its parachute equipment, for ordinary transport would take it to Jerusalem. There was a lot of grumbling.

"What are we—Civil Defense? For this, we trained all the time? For this, we're parachutists?"

"Jerusalem or not Jerusalem, we want to jump! Let them send somebody else!"

Morale dropped. But some among them were Jerusalemites

and they were pleased. "We're going home. We'll fight near home." Other paratroopers were secertly glad that the jump had been canceled, and that they wouldn't have to tackle struggling through the sands; still others were worried about the prospect of war with the Jordanians. In the past, Jordan had had the best of the Arab armies.

Men from the other battalions jeered at those who wouldn't be jumping. Some were ashamed of feeling relief that the jump was canceled; others were disappointed. The men loosened their parachute belts and threw them angrily on to the ground. The officers cursed—but were already preparing for the journey to Jerusalem, explaining to the men: The breakthrough in Rafiah had gone so swiftly and successfully that they didn't need them there.

The battalion commander was worried: A great part of the battalion equipment was already packed up and prepared for the jump. Now he had to reorganize for a completely new mission.

By 1600 the whole brigade was on its way to Jerusalem—its mission the conquest of the Holy City, with the first objectives the Police School and Mandelbaum Gate.

I asked Uzi Narkiss if we could start with the Rockefeller Museum and the Old City rather than Ammunition Hill. He agreed. Both of us understood the importance of this historic battle, and Uzi agreed to give me a free hand in the battle for the city.

When I left him, I bumped into the command chaplain, who embraced me. I promised: "We shall liberate Jerusalem for you!" He answered: "Keep a place for me there!"

Then I asked the head of engineering of units attached to Central Command, Colonel Y. Dori, to work out the best way for us to break into the Old City, and to prepare explosives for such an attack.

We passed columns of armored corps—loaded trucks, jeeps, half-tracks, fuel trucks, tanks. We wondered if we would manage to achieve as much as the airmen had. We passed more half-tracks, filled with soldiers. I doubted if the commander of the brigade would really be able to attack as planned at 1730. But it seemed to me it wasn't the hour that was so important as the actual decision to take Jerusalem. We passed an armored infantry battalion and our feeling of confidence and strength was enhanced by the vision of hoisting the flat of Israel on the Temple Mount.

Chapter II

UP TO JERUSALEM

Our Oldsmobile struggled up the steep, winding Ramat Raziel road, the first step toward the Holy City. Below us were the coastal lowlands. On the left, smoke rose from the chimney of the Bet Shemesh cement factory, still working despite the outbreak of war. Further toward the coast, similar smoke rose from the other cement factory at Ramle. Opposite us were the slopes of Tsora and Eshtaol, clothed in pine forests.

Amos, a staff officer, took out the photograph of Jerusalem that we received at Central Command and spread it on his knees in the back of the car. We supplemented the information contained in the photograph with what we remembered from pre-1948 days of the parts of Jerusalem held by the Arabs. Amos marked with arrows on the photographs the suggestions emerging from our discussions in the car.

We had been in the Israeli-held sector of Jerusalem a week before, on May 30, to discuss various contingencies if war were to break out. At that time it seemed certain that the fighting would be in the south against Egypt, that war with Jordan was out of the question. The Jordanians, we thought, were too vulnerable to attack us. But the possibility did exist that they might try to prevent convoys from going up to Jerusalem. They could do this either by staging an ambush—in 1948 they had ambushed a convoy of Hadassah doctors and nurses—or by announcing that the road had to be closed.

These assessments had led us to concentrate, at the time, on the northern Jordanian sector; we had looked for a springboard from which we could join up with the police garrison on Mount Scopus. Now that Hussein had elected to join in the war and had attacked us, the objective had changed: we were thinking suddenly not only of Mount Scopus, but of the liberation of the whole of Jerusalem. So, as we traveled to Jerusalem in the car, we were trying to improvise a completely new operational plan.

The previous plan had tried to solve two basic problems: to break through the Jordanian fortifications, and to open up traffic for our armed forces to rescue the isolated unit on Mount Scopus.

The correct solution offered the richest of all prizes. In one stroke we could capture a vital area of Arabheld East Jerusalem and acquire a convenient springboard for the conquest of the Old City, so that the Jews could occupy the Temple Mount for the first time in millennia. At the same time, we also had to make sure that we did link up with the troops on Mount Scopus.

All our thinking led us to the conviction that we must first conquer the northern part of Jerusalem—the sector of the Police School and Sheikh Jarragh. This would allow us to link up to Scopus and approach the Old City from the north—the direction, incidentally, from which all attacks have come since Titus first looked down from Scopus on Jerusalem. As far as the broader strategic aims of Central Command were concerned, action by the paratrooper brigade would complement an encircling movement by the armored brigade on the Nebi-Samuel-French Hill ridge from the north, and operations by the Jerusalem battalion aimed in the direction of the UN headquarters in the south.

We arranged to rendezvous in Jerusalem. It was important for the three battalion commanders to get a chance to see the battle-field while there was still light. We were used to short retaliation raids, but this was real war—and we were going to fight in the most difficult sector of all, the built-up areas of Jerusalem. The Police School, Sheikh Jarragh, Ammunition Hill, the Ambassador Hotel, the Rockefeller Museum—and then the Old City.

I knew that Yossi Y.'s battalion had gone on ahead of us in buses. He had been told to travel on the main highway from Shaar Hagai, but had asked for this order to be changed since the enemy lines overlooked the road, which was also the place where many convoys had been ambushed in 1948. He was also worried that his buses might become entangled with armored columns of the Harel Brigade.

When Yossi's battalion reached the Shaar Hagai intersection, the armored-forces men called on him to halt, because there was shooting beyond Dir-Iyov. But Yossi did not stop. His men were fired on at close range by the enemy, armed with heavy machine guns, but the drivers raced through and no one was hurt.

The Jordanians added mortar fire. From the ridge of villages they held, and Nebi-Samuel, they subjected the battalion to heavy fire all the way into Jerusalem.

In the meantime, forces of the armored brigade took up positions in the area around the Castel and opened up artillery fire on enemy positions at "Radar" and at the Legion Housing Estate at Sheik-ibd-Aziz.

Central Command put medium machine guns into action against the batteries of Jordanian artillery, which were shelling Jerusalem. As soon as the Jordanians identified the armored forces at the Castel they directed their fire there, and before long shells began to drop in the fields, among the houses of the settlements in the neighborhood.

To the paratroopers, the road seemed very long indeed. They

didn't know exactly where they were going or what was their objective.

Music helped them. In the beginning the radio played songs of the Negev; but when Hussein attacked Jewish Jerusalem, the songs were all about the capital: "Bab-el-Wad," "From the Summit of Mount Scopus," "Jerusalem the Golden," "Israel Will Endure Forever." Some paratroopers sang along softly. Others were quiet, dreaming . . . Bar-Ilan opened the Bible and read verses about Jerusalem. When he stopped, the men shouted to him to go on—"More!"

Toward evening, the drivers stopped. The religious prayed "*Maariv*" . . . The rest broke out into conversation or got some exercise after the long trip, some jumping, some walking around. Shells exploded nearby and there were exchanges of machine-gun salvos. Jerusalem had been under fire since morning. Paratroopers, used to action, were compelled to stay in the closed buses, their survival out of their own hands and up to chance.

While some units were still climbing slowly on the road to Jerusalem, other commands were already in the thick of the fire. Yossi Y. and his men had arrived at the Schneller compound, the rendezvous point, but had not found anyone there. He was told that the command of the Jerusalem Brigade had moved over to the Evelina de Rothschild Girls' School. Quickly and under shell fire they went there, only to find that, except for "Moshe Commando," a veteran paratrooper officer who now served in the local brigade, there was no one at the school. Moshe Commando told them the war room was still at Schneller, the original rendezvous point.

Impatient, cursing, the officers turned to leave. Then they met Lieutenant Colonel Hagi, the deputy brigade commander of the Jerusalem Brigade, who, though he knew nothing of the mission assigned to the paratroopers, placed his driver at their disposal to show them a shortcut back to Schneller.

There they found the commands of the two other battalions and also an extra paratrooper officer—Amos Neeman—a general staff officer of the Jerusalem Brigade. He reviewed the events of the day and outlined the development of the various battles. But he had neither maps not photographs. The boys were still talking with him when a runner came to call them outside to me.

We had been delayed on the way by our "luxury car"—the Oldsmobile—which, on the ascent to Ein-Kerem, had heated up and begun to boil. While our driver tackled the problem we got out to observe the enemy shelling Castel. Some time passed before we could continue on our way.

When we finally arrived at Schneller, we were all in a fury. Watching the enemy shelling, hearing the thunder of bursting shells among the houses of Jerusalem, and waiting for the car to cool was a most frustrating experience. At the entrance to the Bet Hakerem suburb, a civil-defense barrier halted us. The headlights of the car had to be painted blue and we were instructed on how to behave in a city under shellfire.

The prolonged shelling by the Jordanians did not succeed in making Jerusalemites take to the shelters. People were still wandering warily in the streets. But the nearer we got to the center of the city, the fewer people we saw, and there were hardly any vehicles, while the thunder of the shells steadily increased. The artillery fire was concentrated in the direction of Schneller, and the explosions became worse and worse as we drew nearer. We parked our car not far from the gate and I sent a runner to find the battalion commander.

A salvo of shells dropped near us—two shells in the grounds of the camp, two over the road in the adjacent yard. We ran to the cars and put on helmets as a second salvo fell not far away. Then we heard a whole salvo exploding inside the compound and the first cries of "Medic! Medic!"

Tanks began to assemble in one of the streets, though we still didn't know if they had been assigned to work with us. Captain Rafi, their commander, came with the operations officer of the Jerusalem Brigade, who told Rafi that he had to join with us in the breakthrough into Arab Jerusalem that very night. We kept close to the high stone wall of the camp, for we realized that the enemy were shelling us with 25-pound field guns. These shells had a particular shriek with a short explosion, bright and light.

There was no great danger from these shells, especially in a build-up area, because the course of their flight was flat: They struck the houses and high walls but did not reach the streets. Their ability to destroy, in a city built of stone like Jerusalem, was minimal and a stone wall served as efficient protection against them.

At 1700 the commanders of the three battalions arrived on the run. Together we constituted the Command Group of the whole brigade. We all crowded under cover and I told them to put on helmets. We began to exchange explanations, but the frequent shells disturbed us and we felt like sitting ducks for the enemy artillerymen. I ordered them to jump into their cars and follow me to the corner of Zephaniah Street, from which point we could study the breakthrough sector. As we drove, I looked around. The surroundings were very familiar to me. In these streets I had spent many happy childhood years. Before me, stretched Geulah Street, where I used to eat wonderful *falafel* in a great thin *pita*. We turned left and came to Amos Street which had a sign—No Entry. We stopped for a moment and then continued on. War is no respecter of traffic regulations. Behind us followed a long line of cars—each unit with at least two vehicles. We passed a house where my family had lived once, for about two years. A doctor and his wife had had the rooftop apartment and we loved their wonderful wolfhound, Aza, whom we called Azit at first, thinking him a her.

Here we had played marbles and ball games. What a child I was then! The balcony rail got pretty hot on bright summer days, and once when I noticed a shadow fall across part of the rail, I hastened to sit on it, only to leap up as though bitten by a snake. Everyone laughed at me, and I could not understand how a place in the shade could be so hot . . .

We came to the Zephaniah Street intersection with Bebman's grocery store on our right. Later on we lived there, in the house of "the madman." On the roof we used to crush green olives, which Mother put into jars.

We turned left at the entrance to another house we had lived in. It was at the time when I was going to Rachel's Nursery School Kindergarten and was in love with a little girl, Drora; we played Esther and Ahasueras at Purim.

When we arrived at the intersection of Zephaniah and Bar-Ilan streets, I stopped and the convoy halted behind me. The thunder of the shells sounded farther away; we could only hear echoes of explosions from inner areas of the city. Apparently it was a good idea to stick so close to the enemy—they were afraid to bombard this area for fear their shells might land on their own men . . . Instead there was the rat-tat-tat of machine-gun volleys and rifle shots, for now we were near to the border, the boundary line between the two Jerusalems, Jewish Jerusalem and Arab Jerusalem.

To the north we could see the Hirbat Talliah position, from which the enemy began to direct their fire at our intersection. We wondered if they could see us, and I asked the men to wait a few minutes while we, the Brigade Command, went up on to the roof to find out if we could spot the enemy lines. But we could not.

We ran across Bar-Ilan Street and climbed on to another roof.

From here we got a better view, but I was still dissatisfied. The inhabitants of the building regarded us with joy mixed with apprehension. We rushed back to Zephaniah Street and were again met with volleys of shells. The soldiers were sticking close to the row of houses to the east so as not to be hit by a stray shell.

At 1730 I summoned the battalion commanders to give them their orders. To my regret I had not been given as many photographs as the orders required. Everything had been decided so quickly that Intelligence had not managed to prepare the material for us. I tried to explain our mission in a few words, and outlined what the battalions should do according to the plan we had evolved in the car on our way to Jerusalem.

We decided to wait for the arrival of better photographs. Arik, an intelligence officer, had contacted Central Area Command and had asked them to send all the photographs to Jerusalem. They would have to come soon, for it was nearly evening.

Then Arik suggested that he race over to the Jerusalem Brigade and bring the photographs back from there. I authorized this and he rushed off. I had given the two photographs that I had to Battalions 66 and 71. I suggested to the commander of Battalion 28 that he go to the top of the Histadrut House, from which point he could get a good view of his sector. It lay in a valley and could not be seen at all from the border itself. I promised to come to him with extra material the moment we got some.

I suggested that Battalions 66 and 71 not approach the border in full daylight, but instead that they should work out a provisional plan based on the photographs they had, and on what they could see from the Histadrut House. I asked them to present the plan to me for confirmation, and afterward, with the last glimmer of light, they should go down to the border to study the area from close quarters. The commanders of the two battalions followed my instructions and soon Arik returned with the intelligence material.

We then set up our headquarters in the apartment of the Alisian family, at 72 Zephaniah Street. There was a table at the entrance of the apartment: On this the men spread out the maps and photographs, and prepared to distribute them. Arik brought with him from the Jerusalem Brigade Sergeant Avi, who was an expert on every Jordanian position and trench, and was ready to brief the commanders about the Jordanian units facing them, down to the last detail. (Later, after the battle, we were to discover tunnels and positions about which we had known nothing, despite Sergeant Avi's efforts.)

Residents of the neighborhood welcomed us with cakes and hot drinks, throwing their doors open wide and inviting us to come in and work comfortably at their tables by electric light, even though the enemy were only a few hundred yards away. From time to time, people turned up who had been caught in the shelling while at work or out visiting, and had arrived home with great difficulty. Suddenly a group of children also appeared. The paratroopers found themselves helping the youngsters to cross the street in safety, just like policemen in peacetime.

Strange people. The city was at war, the border a few hundred yards away was aflame, with their own eyes they saw paratroopers preparing for an attack across the nearby border, and they—instead of evacuating the members of their families to safety—returned with their children to their homes on the border.

Members of the Alisian family offered us the use of their telephone. It was brand new, a white luxury instrument, installed only the day before. The number was 85200. Our secretariat took up its position beside it, and at once contacted the headquarters of central command to give them our new number and address.

The commander of Battalion 71 and his officers moved up to a roof in Yirmiyahu Street to make further observations. They decided that it was still too far from their assigned breakthrough area, part of which was concealed in a little valley. So they went across to another roof, nearer to the border. One by one the officers raised their heads above the rail on the roof to observe their sector. But the Jordanians spotted them, and shots from 81-millimeter mortars and long-range Jordanian fire fell near them as the Arab gunners tried to get the range.

The officers continued calmly to plan their attack as salvos of bombs and bursts of bullets came closer and closer. The battalion commander decided that the surroundings were a little too hot for comfort, so he brought his men down from the roof. But instead of retreating westward from the border, to put some distance between them and the fire, they advanced eastward toward the frontier. They executed this advance swiftly, keeping close to the walls, crossing Samuel the Prophet Street at a run and hugging the wall opposite the Garden of Abramoff. They advanced all along this wall up to the trenches, which had been designed as positions from which the enemy could be pinned down at the time of the breakthrough. From this spot they completed the final plan for the breakthrough, down to the last detail, determining the exact location of each force. Then they reported back to me.

Meanwhile, the officers of Battalion 66 had climbed onto one of the roofs to observe their assigned sector. The high buildings made observation of the breakthrough area difficult, but the objectives could be seen, and so they worked out their plan.

Yossi decided that Company B, Dudik's, should effect the breach in the minefields and fences, but that the duties of the other companies would be decided only after the overall plan was confirmed. Since dusk was about to fall, Yossi came down to present the plan to me. I ruled out the other alternatives and confirmed Yossi's plan—a breakthrough along one axis from the "Evacuees' Houses" to beyond the Police School. In preparation for a tour of the breakthrough area, Avi, the intelligence sergeant who joined us, briefed the battalion and company commanders.

Rafi, the tank corps commander, arrived at headquarters. We

explained the plan to him and outlined the task of his tanks. He attached himself to Battalion 66 for reconnaissance of the area. The sectors assigned to the tanks, the positions they would occupy, and the roads they would use were all determined.

At 1900 dusk fell. The extended group of Battalion 66 commanders and tank commanders rolled down the slope of Bar-Ilan Street in their own jeeps, in the direction of the Evacuee Houses. Enemy fire did not cease for a moment, and the area was lit up every now and then by exploding shells. We could see the explosions of bombs dropped by our Air Force, attacking the Jordanians in depth to the east. These flashes intermingled with the light of searchlights and tracer shells.

When the officers reached the extensive grounds of the Evacuees' Houses, they parked their jeeps in the shadow of one of the houses and rushed across to the observation point. The enemy seemed to be shooting wildly, not aiming at specific targets.

The houses in the immediate vicinity of the boundary had been prepared in advance as battle sites. On every roof positions for weapons had been constructed. Now we found that the iron gates to the roofs were locked. The rapidity with which the battle plan had evolved made it impossible to coordinate all necessary details, and the men with the keys couldn't be found.

The officers got into one of the apartments facing no-man's-land, and from there observed the breakthrough area. The light shed on the area every so often by shell bursts helped them to identify the objectives without any particular difficulty. Later they went right up to the point from which they would have to breach the enemy barricades of barbed wire and minefields. Silently the officers approached the corners of the houses from which they would launch the attack, and pinpointed the fences situated a few meters from them.

When the company commanders were positive that they had

identified the places for action accurately, the group returned to Bet Hakerem, where the battalion was waiting.

Rafi, the tank corps commander, felt that he needed to go down to the breakthrough area with the commanders of his sections so as to determine the precise location of each tank with accuracy. He went to Zephaniah Square, but did not find a single top-ranking paratrooper officer there. He was told that they had gone to the Evelina de Rothschild School.

The commander of the engineering corps, Yod-Bet, had stayed with his commanders in the area, after he had correlated with Yossi and Rafi the role of his engineers in clearing a path for the tanks through the minefields. He gave the necessary orders to his deputy commanders, and allocated specific tasks to each engineering team.

The fact that his force would be operating between the tanks and the Police School made precise timing essential, or his men would be hit by fire from the rear when the barricades were breached.

At 2000 in the open square on the corner of Zephaniah Street a kind of hush reigned, broken from time to time by the sound of exploding shells and bullets. At headquarters, we summed up the situation: Most of the forces were already in Bet-Hakerem.

We had come a long way since we left the orange groves that morning, but we were still only at the beginning of the long day's work.

On their way to Jerusalem, Moshele and Kotik of Central Command had coordinated the urgent dispatch of new ammunition to replace that packed for the drop, since there had not been time to unpack and send what they had.

Now we decided to go to the command post of the Jerusalem Brigade and try to obtain from them vital items which he must have to complete our requirements for battles in a built-up area.

Outside it was absolutely dark. Instinctively, we lowered our voices and talked in whispers. We got into our cars, Arik—who had already been there during the day to collect the intelligence material—leading the way. The darkened headlights gave almost no illumination.

The streets were empty. We passed the Mekor Baruch neighborhood, and cut through Mahane-Yehudea. I wanted to tell Arik what route to take, for it seemed to me that he was going in a roundabout way. After all, I knew this area well, from the time I was a Boy Scout. But I let him lead us rather than waste time discussing routes.

Although several shells burst near us, we reached the command post safely. There we left the jeeps parked at the curb, with one wheel of each on the sidewalk.

The battalion policeman allowed us in without any trouble. In the yard, a lot of people were milling about. We walked into the inner yard, where we heard many voices from every quarter—talking, giving orders, laughing.

We entered the command post, finding the crowding rather pleasant. The electric lights were full on and, with the windows blacked out and closed, the air was full of tobacco smoke. It was good to come in from the darkness into light, and to pass from oppressive silence and the thunder of shells into a world of light and companionship.

In the command bunker all the men were old acquaintances. There were handshakes and cries of "Shalom!" and "Long time no see!" We sat down to work.

Rafi (the tank commander) came in, delighted to find us at last. He explained the problem of his tank locations to me, and asked for permission to go down to the battle area with his deputy commanders. I agreed, and he left for the frontier.

* * *

A heavy pall of smoke hung over the Evacuees' Houses, where Rafi and his section commanders and intelligence sergeant took their jeeps, zigzagging to avoid snipers' bullets. There, on the roof of one of the buildings, the tank men worked out their final plans.

Rafi himself, with Shaul's platoon, would start the action from between the olive trees to the northwest of the Police School, giving support to the attack on the school and on Ammunition Hill. Arzi's platoon would be positioned among the Evacuees' Houses, right next to the front, to support the breakthrough into the Police School. Gilboa's platoon would be placed in the Garden of Abramoff to the southwest, to support the attacks on the Police School and the breakthrough area of Battalion 71 in the Arab suburb of Sheikh Jarragh.

When the plan had been worked out, the commanders moved on foot to their chosen positions. There they worked out the exact location of each tank, as well as the road by which it would come and its fire sector. They decided that the platoons of Shaul and Arzi would go down Bar-Ilan Street, while Gilboa's would come through the Bokharan suburb from Yechezkel Street straight to its location.

At the command post of the Jerusalem Brigade, we continued trying to coordinate the organization of equipment. Suddenly Colonel David came in, brimming over, as always, with energy and smiles. We got up to greet him and to shake hands. He radiated happiness and joy. With him was his adjutant, Yigal.

David was the oldest in years and the youngest in spirit of the officers in command: he had a fertile mind, an inventive imagination, a warm heart. As usual his answers sounded slightly confused: "*Nu*, yes, of course—what do you expect?...But of course—we'll bomb...everything—we have everything..."

Behind us we had years of working together. Long ago he and I had planted charges of explosives to undermine the wall of the Old City, hoping that some day we would have a chance to set them off.

Now the great day had come. Dozens of times we had discussed ways of breaking through the wall of the Old City. Every unit which had ever planned to fight in Jerusalem had turned to David for advice. Each time he had invented new ways of taking the Old City, each plan more ingenious than the one that went before.

"Bangalores" (technically a *bangalore torpedo*, this weapon is a long sectional tube packed with explosive, used to make a breach in a barbed-wire barricade), bazookas, hand grenades, 81-millimeter mortar shells . . . we had a long list of needs. The men of the Jerusalem Brigade were in a quandary: They were themselves going into battle, and might need the ammunition themselves. But they conceded that our assault must get preference.

In the end, they promised us maximum help.

At our request, Lieutenant Colonel Nehemiah, commander of the battalion of the Jerusalem Brigade holding the City Line, came to discuss with us the coordination of the entry of our forces into his sector. We also wanted to get his assessment of the enemy, and to find out how his force, which had been operating since the Jordanians opened fire in the morning, could help us.

Nehemiah gave us details of the Jordanian positions and explained how his battalion was disposed. He suggested using his 81-millimeter mortars to help our attack. We decided that we would send the relevant orders through him. The place selected by David was far from our communication points, and we agreed that a runner from Nehemiah should carry orders to him. Because of this improvised arrangement, it was agreed that we would pass on the order to go into action to Nehemiah half an hour before zero hour. This was the only way we could be sure that the order would arrive in time.

We were still discussing the problem when General Uzi Narkiss arrived. I outlined the plan of action to him and told him about the administrative problems. I estimated that we could begin the operation between 2300 hours and midnight. He approved of the plan and we arranged to meet again on the roof of the Histradrut House, which was serving as a command post for Colonel Amitai, commander of the Jerusalem Brigade. There we could coordinate the action of the two brigades.

A special problem arose about the artillery. Ziklag, commander of our support company, received certain orders at Command Headquarters, but when he arrived in Jerusalem, he found that the artillerymen still had not heard about his orders. The organization of the artillery would be complicated enough, since three brigades had to operate together. The armored Harel Brigade had been in action since 1730, and now, at 2030, it still needed most of its artillery. The Jerusalem Brigade had not yet finished the battle at Zur-Bachar; they too could not release their artillery. Ziklag was not satisfied; he wouldn't accept the idea that nothing could be done. He communicated directly with the units in the field in order to find the ranges, and set out at once for the observation post on the assumption that when the time came he would have all the artillery he needed. He carried out the rangefinding with the help of the searchlights.

To our surprise, it now became clear that the artillery liaison officers in our battalions had not participated in the officers' reconnaissance tour earlier and did not know the area and the plan of action. When the brigade had set out from the plain for Jerusalem, they had not been with the battalions but, since time was pressing, had been left behind with the units. Only one liaison officer, Carmi, had arrived, and Ziklag attached him to Battalion 66 because the fiercest fighting was expected in their sector.

The absence of the liaison officers was not so serious, however, because the artillery attack was to be launched in the Police School sector only. We planned to concentrate two 81-millimeter mortar platoons in Sheikh Jarragh. The location and rangefinding for these would be worked out by the commanders of the companies and the commanders of the mortar platoons.

Only at 2300 hours, when the two brigades had accomplished their first breakthroughs, would almost all the artillery in the area be placed at our disposal.

The lull before the storm—we sat a few minutes longer. Sandwiches and hot tea were served to us, and very welcome they were. Not that we went short of tea and coffee throughout the afternoon hours. The residents of Zephaniah Street provided liberally for us. But when would we be able to sit back again and relax over a cup of hot tea?

We crammed as much as we could into us, and got up. We shook hands with our friends of the Jerusalem Brigade. Their eyes were anxious. They wanted to go with us, for there is nothing harder than to send comrades into action while you yourself stay behind. True they too were ready for battle, but at this moment we were going and they were staying . . .

We hurried outside the room and leapt up the narrow stairs. In the brightly lit corridor we heard again the din of voices and saw crowds of people. Then we went outside, where we found absolute darkness except for the flashes of exploding shells. We had managed to forget them for an hour. It was not bad inside there . . .

At 2130 we split up. Moshele and Amos went off to Bet Hakerem to make final arrangements to bring our forces into action. I asked whether they would find the way in the dark. They didn't even bother to answer the question.

We set off for Histadrut House and this time I drove. The streets were deserted. Ussishkin Street, the Rehavia Gymnasia, the Jewish Agency, King David Street, Jaffa Street, Bikur Cholim Hospital—places as familiar as our hands—now seemed strange and eerie in the blackout. A bus in the middle of the street blocked the road. We decided to walk a bit and let the drivers find parking places.

We jumped out and passed a few cars before entering Histadrut House. The elevator wasn't working and the stairs had been blocked, requiring people to leap over the first few steps. In the halls soldiers were stretched out, some lying, some sitting. They seemed bewildered. They had already been through a day of war.

"Where is the advance command post?" We were directed up, up, through unfamiliar doorways. In the past we had always used the elevator. We panted heavily—there were many storeys. At last we reached the iron door leading onto the roof, where a cool breeze greeted us. We heard voices coming over the communications instruments. In the center stood Uzi Narkiss and Lezer, the brigade commander, discussing what was happening on the battlefield. We came up to them to learn that the men of the Jerusalem Brigade had just completed the conquest of Zur-Bachar. We stretched out our hands. Congratulations. What next?

The brigade commander was delighted with the victory his men had won. It was good to know the stars of his team, with whom we had to deal: Micha Paikas, a veteran paratrooper who fought with us in the Sinai Campaign and took part in the last retaliatory actions as a battalion commander of the Golani Brigade, was especially close to me, because we were friends in the Youth Movement. His brother was a new recruit serving under me in Nahal, and his father had been my commander in the Hagana. Svika Ofer was also a former paratrooper who had seen action in retaliation raids. He was a veteran combat soldier with ginger hair. We had met again in the Golani Brigade, where he served as intelligence officer. In the attack on Nukeib he excelled as a reconnaissance officer and received a citation for bravery from the Chief of Staff. I also knew Asher Dreisen and Nehemiah Oz personally. We had not happened to fight side by side in the past, but we were pleased to be doing so this time. Lezer himself was a member of Palmach, and fought in Jerusalem during the War of Liberation. A veteran fox in battle. Lezer's deputy, Hagai Hefetz, served under my command when I was battalion commander in Golani. Quiet, straightforward, solid.

Lezer gave us a brief outline of the day's fighting in Jerusalem. He explained his aims, leaving no doubt that we were to conquer the whole of Jerusalem. At that very moment, the armored brigade was moving swiftly over the Nebi-Samuel ridge, and there was a reasonable basis for the hope that this important chain of mountains would be in our hands by dawn. Their presence there would do away with any threat of a Jordanian attack on Mount Scopus and would make it possible to consider maneuvers northward to Ramallah, eastward to Jericho, and southward against the Old City. The Jerusalem Brigade would act in southern Jerusalem, and we, the paratroopers, would fight in the north, our eventual aim being the conquest of the Old City.

We fixed clear sector boundaries between the brigades, and I told Lezer that we had already met Nehemiah at his chief command post and had coordinated all arrangements for the breakthrough.

Everything seemed clear.

Beside us, every now and then, searchlight beams helped artillery find the range. Shells and salvos from the Jordanians were attracted to the searchlights like moths, and fell with a whistle and thunderous explosion. The men crouched below the walls and beneath the roof railing. Anyone not needed to plan the attack went inside. From the north we could hear the artillery of Uri Ben-Ari's Harel Brigade.

Lezer told Uzi Narkiss that Asher, the battalion commander, had been wounded for the second time that day, and someone must be found to take his place.

Colonel Yehoshua Nevo, who had returned from Africa especially for the war, had joined our brigade and was standing next to us. In the past he had served as a Battalion Commander in the parachute corps. We had been friends since the War of Liberation. He wanted to take part in the drop on El Arish, so he chose to be with us and now had arrived on the roof of Histadrut House. When he heard that a battalion commander of the Jerusalem Brigade was wounded, he immediately volunteered to replace him, even though his rank was so high. His offer was accepted with enthusiasm. Within minutes we parted with a warm handshake—he beaming with joy because he had been given a chance to lead a battalion into battle.

At 2230 I asked for permission to return to our command post in Zephaniah Street as zero hour was approaching and I knew I was needed there. Uzi agreed.

We went down. Opposite the entrance to the building was a signboard: *Sokolow High School*. Here I had studied for seven years, from first to seventh grade, and here my military career had begun. Angry with the school administration, which for financial reasons had failed to supply us with sport equipment, I organized a group of pupils and friends and one night stormed the school with a hail of stones, smashing windowpanes, so "they" would have to pay for the damage . . . Next morning we saw that we had succeeded. On the next night we arranged another attack, and this time our victory was total—not one pane was left whole . . .

I hoped that this time the windowpanes of the school wouldn't be damaged.

In the meantime, the street had been cleared and our cars were parked next to the house. We drove down the slope of the street to the Geulah intersection, and arrived at Zephaniah Street and the command post.

Here we found that our men and the people living in the house had become one group. The interior of the apartment was dimly lit—and men, women, and children were crowded together near the stairs, sitting or lying down and trying to sleep. Some of them made tea and did all they could for us. Our girls, Stella and Ninutchka, sat at the telephone. The Intelligence people were still busy preparing material for further distribution.

Outside in the street, silence reigned. All movement had stopped. Enemy fire had weakened. We didn't know if this meant they were finally succumbing to our artillery fire or not. On the frontier between Arab Jerusalem and Jewish Jerusalem, activity had also decreased. We wondered if our brigade had already out-flanked the enemy to the north and south, compelling them to withdraw. It was difficult to believe. It seemed more likely that they had decided that there would be no major attack tonight.

The time was nearly 2300.

A telephone call came from Moshele saying that events were running behind schedule. The ammunition promised us that afternoon had not yet arrived. We had to distribute the ammunition among the units according to the plan, and found it difficult because so much was still missing. Moshele didn't think we could go into action before midnight, possibly not before one o'clock.

If Moshele said he couldn't do it, it could not be done.

"Can we help you with anything?"

"No, no. Everything is O.K.—it just takes time."

"O.K., Moshele—try to rush it. Let me know. I'll report to Uzi."

"See you."

I reported the difficulties to Uzi Narkiss. He agreed that we should postpone zero hour and, incidentally, told me how well the armored brigade was doing.

Until now, there had been complete understanding between us, both as to the Old City, and as to the details of implementation. He had made all the decisions about the overall program, but left me wide powers of decision as to how my brigade would operate. I decided to lie down for a while—to think, and to snatch a little sleep. In my head, I staged a kind of miniature war game: what would happen if . . . ? How should we act if . . . ? The more I thought about it, the more convinced I was that our plan was a good one. I was satisfied with the deployment of my forces and I knew I could rely on my people.

I looked around me. I was lying in a small room, furniture in barrels and crates heaped up in a corner. To my left, on a mattress spread on the floor and covered with a woolen blanket, lay an old man. On my right, light filtered in through the door to the passage. I turned round to the left and curled up, covering my eyes with my hand, hoping to doze off . . . but plans and more plans kept whirling through my head.

The brigade was in a fever of preparation—the briefing . . . the distribution of equipment . . . columns organized for deployment. When Moshele had arrived at Bet Hakerem at 2130, the units were scattered all along the main streets in the vicinity of the Supermarket. Yossi Y. and Uzi were already with their battalions, but Yossi P. was still at the advance command group of the Jerusalem Brigade, on the roof of Histadrut House. We had decided earlier that he was to wait there till we came, but under the pressure of events we forgot about him. Since his battalion was not one of those scheduled to make a breakthrough, we had not noticed his absence. All through the evening hours he had tried in vain to locate us. The communications officer, Orni, who, after completing the communications coordination had arrived at the Command Headquarters, also waited with him there. They spent the time getting reports about the enemy strength and the terrain from the Jerusalem Brigade communications officer. Precious hours passed.

When Moshele got to Bet Hakerem and realized what had happened, he contacted Histadrut House and asked Yossi and Orni to join him at once. Kotik gave Sergeant Major Nitzan, the ammunitions officer, the list of items that the Jerusalem Brigade had agreed to give us, and sent him to fetch them. Kotik himself remained to wait for ammunition that had been promised at Headquarters for 2100 hours, but which had not yet arrived, and also to check and recheck the distribution of the ammunition available. Hand grenades and bangalores were the main items missing; these were essential to breach the barricades.

Moshele and Amos briefed the commanders on the arrangements worked out with the Jerusalem Brigade. Amos fixed the boundaries of the sectors between the battalions and gave the finishing touches to the plan of operations.

At 2300 the brigade doctor, Dr. King, arrived at Bet Hakerem with his unit; he had another ten ambulances and additional medical equipment. After correlating with the brigade sergeant, he sent out medical units to take up positions in the Fagi neighborhood, and beyond Mandelbaum, according to a plan worked out together with the medical officer of Central Command. Dr. Kahanski and Dr. Leventhal took their unit to the Fagi neighborhood while Dr. Yossi Zach and Dr. Zvi Friedman took theirs to beyond the Mandelbaum Gate.

On the way to Fagi, Dr. Leventhal, who knew Jerusalem well, passed a pharmacy in Ben Yehuda Street and added some needed items to his equipment, later distributing some of his aquisitions among all the sectors. He also went by Magen David Adom and warned them to prepare to receive wounded.

The sections took up positions in the houses indicated. The Orthodox, long-time residents of the area, with their long experience of crises, seemed to be completely tranquil. They explained to the doctors exactly where the enemy was located: "Over there, opposite us, on the third floor." In order to black out the light coming from our house, they hung their black frock coats over the windows.

When Yossi, commander of Battalion 66, returned to Battalion from a reconnaissance tour of the breakthrough area, only Dudik's company knew what their job would be—breaching the barricades. No decision had yet been made as to what the others would do. He sent the company commanders to their companies to be sure that everything was ready for the attack, while shutting himself up in one of the rooms to put the finishing touches on the plans. Captain Dudik, commander of Company B, began organizing the company into teams of bombardiers and groups responsible for pinning down the enemy. Realizing that he was short of bangalores, he ran to the command post of the battalion to get more—only to be told that his company's task had been changed. The battalion commander had finalized the entire plan and reallocated the jobs. Captain Giora, commander of Company D, would command the breakthrough, while Dudik would clean up the trenches of the Police School as far as Ammunition Hill.

In Giora's company there were only eight bangalores. Collecting other bangalores from the companies had involved difficulties: nobody was willing to give up those he had. But there seemed to be many missing. Micha, the deputy company commander, sent the company sergeant major to check the ammunition column for the missing bangalores, and there the bangalore vehicle was found and emptied swiftly, and the all-important bangalores were distributed among the teams.

A similar process was carried out in Lieutenant Eilat's Company B in Battalion 71, which was to go to Sheikh Jarragh. In accordance with the number of barbed-wire fences, the company commander prepared sections of barbed-wire cutters and of bombardiers for each fence.

The engineering company was split into two. The company commander, Captain Yod-Bet, reported with half the company to Battalion 66. Their task was straightforward: to clear a path through the minefields for the tanks. Lieutenant Avi, the deputy company commander, with the rest of the engineers, reported to Battalion 28. They didn't know exactly what their mission was, perhaps breaking down walls and into houses during the advance. They had already changed the equipment they were carrying several times. Each sergeant had a set of demolition materials—bricks, detonators, fuses. There were five-kilogram charges of dynamite and there were bangalores, and it was hard to decide what to take, so they took everything. They pushed the charges into their pockets, or held them in their hands, or put them in the haversacks. Then they sat beside the supermarket and waited. They noted the address—84 Herzl Street—to remember to tell the residents of the house later on.

The owner of a car came out and said to Yiftach: "You see, the car was hit by a shell. Only half an hour ago."

Avi, the deputy company commander, got an order from the commander of Battalion 28: The force would split into three subforces, each attached to a company. The assignment: to help break through walls and ramparts at the time of the advance, to barricade streets in order to prevent an outflanking movement, and to blow up houses when necessary.

Major Katcha, commander of the transport company, spread out a map and explained the advance routes hurriedly to Avi, who then returned to the company and began to issue detailed instructions. But there was already no time. The battalion began to move in buses and the officers went on with the briefing inside the buses.

The whole of the reconnaisance company attached itself to Battalion 28. They had no defined task. Their job would be clarified during the fighting.

Some "civilians" had infiltrated among the ranks: they were old soldiers, veteran members of the brigade, who had just arrived and wanted to join in the battle. Some of them had come straight to the front from the airport, after getting back from abroad. Some had been running around for days looking for us. They collected uniforms and borrowed harness and equipment, and begged humbly to be included in the assault forces.

While the companies were still busy collecting equipment, and with other preparations, the battalion commanders briefed the company commanders and summarized the final plans for the battle. The mission of Battalion 66 was the conquest of the Police School, Ammunition Hill, and the Ambassador Hotel hill. They were then either to prepare for the conquest of Old City or link up with the force of Mount Scopus. Time was ticking away. Amos, the general staff officer, went among the commanders to hurry them up: "If we want to achieve something tonight, move!"

The commanders had only just begun to issue their detailed instructions. The intelligence material was sketchy and the photographs not always clear. They pleaded for more photographs— but there weren't any. The company commanders wanted to make certain the names of the streets they should use so that they could navigate by street names and the numbers on the houses. All their previous battle experience and training had been in open areas. In Jerusalem the commanders would have to operate in densely built-up areas, through narrow winding streets, under heavy fire. It was therefore vital to have the names of the streets. Though the arrows on the photographs showed directions, it might be difficult, in the heat of a battle, to keep looking at maps and photographs. But nobody knew the street names.

At 2230, the commander of Battalion 66 finished his briefing of his company commanders and cleared additional intelligence material for the commander of Battalion 28. Yossi turned to the company commanders. Together they began to study the route they would take. Though Yossi had studied the area from the roof of the Histadrut House and had even received an evaluation of it from the intelligence officer of the Jerusalem Brigade, he wanted to familiarize himself with the smallest details.

At 2300 hours the battalion commander completed his plan and gave final orders to his officers. The period of preparations was nearly over—but knowledge of the battlefield was still very inexact. Like Uzi, he too got help from a tour of the area with the company commanders. He planned a further tour of the firing positions and breaching of the fences just before the beginning of the breakthrough.

Yod-Bet finished his briefing to the company. The platoon that was destined to be attached to Battalion 28 as a demolition team was already in position. Yod-Bet himself decided on their position in Battalion 66, which was about to set out toward the Fagi neighborhood.

The commanders of the headquarters companies, the regimental sergeant majors, and the company sergeant majors organized the transport vehicles: buses, trucks, small vehicles. The communications company stopped next to house number 85. Orni split his company into two parts, one to serve as the advance command group of the brigade commander, and the other to remain for the first stage in the rear and join in the battle later, when the brigade command took up its position in a permanent place.

The Jordanian fire had slackened, but prebattle suspense had mounted, everyone feeling "This is it!"

The too-short briefing, which worried the commanders so much, did not bother the soldiers. They had somebody on whom to rely—the officers—who knew exactly what they were doing.

Every now and then, though, a grim thought obtruded—this time it was no exercise, it was real war! The main thing was to make sure that all the weapons were in working order and to check to see if they had enough grenades, important for cleaning up the houses. They didn't like to think about dodging shells or what would happen if a shell fell on them. Soberly they fingered medical dressings and identification discs. The main thing was to get a chance to fight first, not to get hit right at the beginning.

The street was humming, city dwellers crowding around the paratroopers, causing a traffic jam. Shells dropped here and there—but still seemed far away. For the moment the feeling of war was pushed aside. Here in the street it was as though we were preparing for a parade to march past. We tightened our belts, pulled the buckles, fixed the straps of the helmets.

Someone had found more grenades and more magazines for the rifles. It was true, all this equipment was very heavy—but, later, when it was needed, it would feel very light . . . And so they filled their pockets with ammunition and pushed grenades into their rucksacks.

The demolition charges were a bit more complicated. They came in large haversacks with fuses attached to some, but not all. It was worth fixing them tight on to the charges, so they didn't come apart.

It was worth taking matches too. If someone dropped the lighter for the fuse, he couldn't use a match instead. We needed tracer shells too. The extra rods for the heavy machine gun.

The 81-millimeter people were worried: They had to find the range before zero hour, and they still had hardly any shells. The whole platoon altogether could assemble only a couple of hundred.

Zvika, commander of the support company of Battalion 71, was even more worried. Battalion 66 at least had artillery; our support was based on our mortars. And there still weren't any shells. Nor could we locate the platoon of Battalion 28.

The officer in charge of the breakthrough in Battalion 66, Giora Ashkenazi, made the final plans for the sections which were going to breach the barricades. To command the reserve section, he appointed his deputy, Micha, "to be on the safe side."

Dan, deputy commander of Battalion 71, and Eilat, the company commander, had done the same thing in their battalion. The deputy battalion commander was made responsible for the breakthrough and movement of the forces. He decided what men would take which positions. The company commander knew his men and tried to find the precise right job for each.

The doctors checked out the casualty clearing stations for the last time and also the equipment of the medics in the companies. "Have you got bandages? Tourniquets? Morphia? Plasma bags? All your instruments? ..."

The company commanders called the companies together for a short briefing. They explained to the soldiers where they would be fighting. In the dim light, they had a hard time seeing the photographs. Everyone was tense, but everyone paid attention. The main thing each man wanted to know was who would be in the section with him. The first soldiers got into the buses; to save time, explanations went on while they were walking, lining up, sitting in the buses. It was crowded in the bus. Bangalores, rifles, and machine guns knocked against each other on the seats. It was hard to find room for haversacks and charges. In the end, they managed somehow.

Suddenly gaiety predominated over tension and fear. After all, we were going to take Jerusalem! Somebody shouted a greeting in the darkness. Others answered. There were jokes and snatches of song. As the singing mounted, the tenson faded. Some still sat quietly, just thinking, or holding a picture.

* * *

When Rafi and his men arrived at the advance command group, they were returning from a tour of the area. Rafi stayed to coordinate arrangements for radio communications with Battalion 66. The battalion would come through on the internal channel of the armored company. Shmuel had gone off in a jeep to move the tanks to the deployment area. Toward midnight, the tanks reached the corner of Zephaniah Street. Rafi briefed his men on the details of the plan. Gilboa did the same at the junction of Amos and Zephaniah streets.

When Moshele and Amos finished coordinating the units they still had to collect the communications company, so they turned into the supermarket square, where they had arranged to rendezvous with Orni.

Kotik, the brigade quartermaster, and Nitzan, the ordinance officer, asked if they could go with them. The stores had already been moved forward and the available ammunition distributed, so now they wanted to go too, and Moshele agreed to take them.

After the communications company arrived, Moshele could start off with the convoy, but by this time he had lost contact with units up ahead. He didn't know where the advance command group was, so he decided to go to Schneller. But when they got there, they found a deserted yard, so they decided to return to Bet Hakerem to find out what was happening.

Just as they turned into Geulah Street, a stray shell exploded between the wheels and Nitzan's face was hit by shrapnel, damaging his right eye and covering his face with blood. They bandaged him quickly and Kotik decided to look after him.

They got out of Moshele's car so that he could go on, and cursed their fate. To be wounded, now, just before the battle was starting—alone in the darkness of the blacked-out night, without any contact with anyone at all!

Suddenly an ambulance came around the corner with darkened headlights, and they waved it to stop. The driver saw them with difficulty and braked. The medics treated Nitzan. They looked at the time and saw it was almost 0100. They were angry and they cursed.

When Moshele and Amos arrived at Bet Hakerem, they found us gone. They tried to contact the brigade.

The corner of Zephaniah Street awakened to new life. From midnight on, traffic built up. Representatives from Headquarters had again met together, and commanders of the units, on their way to the deployment areas, stopped to receive a last briefing, to make final arrangements to coordinate action, and to say their good-byes.

From out of the darkness suddenly appeared Kaposta and Mair Har-Zion. Their mission in Sinai had been canceled and they were looking for "work." But even our reconnaissance group, at the time, had no particular assignment. I promised I would find them all something to do in the morning.

The tank company had already stationed itself at the top of the street, according to plan. Rafi, the armored company commander, arrived and confirmed that everything was clear to him. The *chevra*—our "band of brothers"—had all been briefed and knew their positions and orders. Tanks, kit, and ammunition were all checked and found in order. Rafi was bespectacled, quiet, confident—a lawyer turned overnight into a tank company commander.

Amos organized the command post. Orni had just arrived. The forest of antennae got thicker and thicker.

Yablo, the radio officer, finished making arrangements with other communications officers—Jackie in Battalion 66 and Yoash in Battalion 28. The communications plan was tailored to fit the operational plan and coordinated with the tanks.

A telephone call came from Uzi Narkiss, who wanted to know

the position. The forces were already on the way. We should be able to start at about 0200.

Uzi asked me my opinion about postponing the operation till morning. I couldn't see changing plans at this stage. Everything was prepared for the breakthrough at night.

Uzi promised to give me his decision by 0045. He added that the armored brigade was already moving in the direction of Ramallah. To us this was important, because they would be able to "tickle" the Jordanians from behind.

Battalion 66 passed by. Doron, the deputy battalion commander, was taking them to the deployment area. Seeing that the tanks had blocked the road and that the buses couldn't get through, they were moving on foot to the Evacuee Houses.

Yossi, the battalion commander, and Doron, the operations officer, were already waiting for the next battalion. I had asked them to come for a last coordination talk. Though the briefings to the *chevra* had been short and hurried, it seemed that the main points were clear. I mentioned the idea of a postponement to the morning, but Yossi didn't want to hear about it at all; the advantages of the night outweighed every disadvantage.

Ziklag brought him up to date about the artillery plan. Heavy fire would be directed mainly at the Police School.

As usual, Yossi was armed from head to toe. Our talk was brief and to the point. We drew near to the column. In the darkness, everyone looked like everyone else. Only the weapons distinguished them: rifle, bungalore, Mag, heavy machine gun.

"Shalom, shalom, lehitraot, lehitraot . . ."

Doron stopped for a moment. The two of us had been together in D Company.

We shook hands . . . And "Good luck."

I put out my hand to Yossi. He removed the Uzi machine gun from his hand, leaving it hanging over his shoulder, and shakes my hand: *"Lehitraot!"* They went off to join the moving battalion.

I was reminded of a trip that Yossi and I had taken one winter's night during the battalion exercise during the last maneuvers. Men were stationed in the hills to defend one of the southern ranges. He and I went together, just the two of us, to examine the men, traveling on foot instead of by car.

"What would you do, Yossi, if you were needed in the meantime?" I asked. "After all, you're a battalion commander. If we had driven there, we would have finished it and been back in no time!"

"That's true," he replied, "but all the *chevra* go on foot . . ."

It was not for nothing that they called him Herzl!

At the advance command group, the commander of Battalion 71 was waiting for me quietly, everything in order. Only the shortage of 81-millimeter shells was worrying him: The 81-millimeter guns provided his main support, and there were practically no shells, only 220. They would soon fix the range—they had enough shells for rangefinding. Bikel, the company commander, was attending to the job himself. There was nothing to worry about, if only the shells would arrive! I explained to him that the platoon of tanks on the south would help him to crack the enemy positions. The tank men already knew the sector from reconnaissance in the area. If there were communications problems with the tanks, the battalion would contact them through the brigade. The company commander of the tanks joined us and added his comments. The battalion commander, too, didn't want to hear about postponement to morning. He smiled, transferred his helmet to his left hand and held out his right hand with a *"Lehitraot!"* Then he returned to his post, along with his deputy. Uzi and Dan—we call them the quiet pair.

Amos and Orni went out to decide on the location of the advance command group. They were assisted by Aryeh and

Alisian, from the family which had been playing host to us in their apartment. After running around, they found the telephone extension from the war room of General Command and then looked for a suitable roof, not too far from the telephone extension and yet near to the breakthrough forces. On the high building in Yoel Street they smashed open a door with an iron rod, and decided finally that that roof would do.

Then I had to fix zero hour, and tell Nehemiah so that he could set off the charges.

All the battalion commanders were in favor of starting the action at night, and did not want to postpone it till morning. Everybody was convinced that, despite one or two remaining problems, everything would be O.K. We fixed zero hour at 0215.

Amos contacted Nehemiah. "Zero hour—0215."

Nehemiah sent a runner to David: "Zero hour—0215."

The lot had been cast. All together, an hour and a half of darkness would be left—but this was enough to break through and cross the open area. If there were no special hitches it would be possible during this period to gain control of most of our first objectives.

Dr. King told me where the casualty clearing stations had been put, but I was not satisfied. Beyond Mandelbaum was too far, and the way there was exposed to enemy fire all along Samuel the Prophet Street. In Fagi too, it seemed to me that they were too far. I asked them to bring the stations forward, closer to the troops.

Dr. King ordered Dr. Zak by phone to stop everything and to come to him *immediately*, sending Ben-Zion to direct him. With the help of a citizen volunteer from the building, the medical men arrived at Zephaniah Street. From here, with a pocket torch to light up the street signs, the casualty clearing stations managed at the very last moment to reach the Dushinski Yeshiva. Dr. King then caught up the tail end of Battalion 71 and told them "This is where we are."

Then a Jordanian shell hit an ambulance, which was flung into the air and fell with a crush, spouting water from its containers into the street . . .

Dr. Kahanski explained to me on the telephone that they were located not far from the Fagi post, and had already made contact with Chaim Guri, the commander of Fagi. I instructed him to go back five hundred meters because their area was exposed to fire from Ammunition Hill, from Givat Hamivtar, and from Shufa'at, and moreover we all were going to break in to the south from there, so the site he'd selected was too vulnerable.

Dr. Kahanski and Dr. Leventhal then changed the locations of their stations and took new positions in two houses closer to the Sanhedria junction. They had no electricity, only pocket torches, the head-torches of the doctors ("owls")—and above all, tracer shells and light from the searchlights, which cast a pale clear glow.

Shells were now exploding all round. The people of the house, students of the Yeshiva, elderly Orthodox people, and children had gone to the cellar where they sang psalms, and with trembling hands served hot coffee to the soldiers. Dr. Leventhal and the old driver, "Granddad" Asher Meruchnik, moved about the streets under the shelling and completed the distribution of medical equipment among the medical sections.

0130: Uzi Narkiss gave the O.K.—start the attack at night. He himself was on his way to my advance command group in Zephaniah Street, and a few minutes later he arrived.

Orni and Amos suggested that we drive to Yoel Street. I looked around—the group was large: Uzi and his personal adjutant, all the staff officers and communications officers, as well as intelligence and operational sergeants. I felt we had better go on foot. It was pleasant to step out a little. But I agreed that Orni should go ahead by car. Amos suggested that General Narkiss go with Orni, but he preferred to walk with us, his jeep moving slowly behind. Amos went ahead to prepare the post for our arrival while Aryeh Alisian showed us the way, as he had previously shown Orni and Amos.

Round about, shells were falling and bullets whistled overhead. We just walked and talked, as if out for a stroll on a pleasant summer's night. At the corner, Orni met us and showed us the way to the roof.

The building served as a children's home and a synagogue and had three floors. The night was cool, but not cold. The roof was big and, as is usual in Jerusalem, there were water tanks. There was a one-meter-high railing around the roof, which gave a little shelter to anyone who did not have to stand up. The attic protruded a little, dividing the roof into two parts—southern and northern.

We drew near to the east railing and could see the city spread out before us as though on the palm of one's hand. To the left, near the Police School, shells dropped every once in a while. That was Ziklag, finding the range. A little to the right 81-millimeter shells were falling—that was Bikel, also rangefinding.

At times the Jordanians came to our aid, lighting up the area with tracer shells that enabled us to see the breakthrough area clearly and also made it easier for the range finders, the commanders, and the reconnaissance men to pinpoint accurately the places where they would breach the barbed-wire fences and where the pinning-down groups would take up their positions.

We heard the hum of planes from the northeast. They were ours and they were hammering the Jordanians. From time to time we saw clusters of fires as the bombs exploded, adding their light to the scene.

Brilliant bursts of bullets passed above us. Some of the shots came from the east, some from the south, some from the north. The Jordanian fire became heavier—25-pounder shells continued to fall on Jewish Jerusalem, mostly to the west of us. Few fell in our vicinity.

Orni organized the communications and placed each man where he should be. The auxiliary network was the only one that was working to serve as the rangefinder. On all the other networks there was complete silence.

The whole brigade was now on its way. From the height of the tranquil roof it was difficult to hear the growing traffic in the streets.

Battalion 66 had already reached its position near the Evacuees' Houses. The battalion commander took the commanders on a last tour of the area, the soldiers hugging the walls and stairwells, for the Jordanians at the Police School had already detected some movement and had opened small-arms and artillery fire. Shells were falling between the houses.

All the men of Battalion 66 were in their places, waiting for the order to go. They would advance under cover of an artillery barrage only, as the heavy machine guns were not yet in position. Installing them required that doors be smashed and the noise would have drawn fire.

The main forces of Battalion 71 were near Samuel the Prophet Street—close to the site chosen for the breach, the last troops coming through the streets of the Bet-Yisrael neighborhood. Now we learned that the deputy commander of Company B, Reinitz, and with him all the sections charged with pinning-down operations, had not yet arrived. In the darkness, he had attached himself by mistake to the buses of the mortar platoon. With him were the communication equipment of the battalion command.

Zero hour was approaching.

Yossi P., commander of Battalion 28, arrived. His battalion was moving on foot from Histadrut House, and he had come ahead to contact Battalion 71 and coordinate the troops during the breakthrough. Amos took him straight to Uzi's last company, where the engineering sections joined them. Eitan's section attached itself to D Company; Iran and Giora's, to A Company, and Dan's section to C Company. As they walked, the engineers finished installing the demolition fuses.

Yossi attached demolition sections to Battalion 71. These engineers would move with the battalion and remain at the breakthrough point to mark it for the battalion. The battalion took up positions in the alleys of Bet-Yisrael neighborhood, while Company A kept close to the wall of Samuel the Prophet Street, opposite the Battalion 71 forces.

More and more 81 millimeter shells fell in the area. The shortest possible time remained for the last-minute preparations: mounting the mortars, stacking the shells for the great barrages finding the range. One of the men was hit while still in the bus. The mortars had to open the left flank of Jordanian positions and the torches that showed the direction also drew fire. The men cursed and carried on. The platoon of Battalion 28 set up only four mortars. In view of the limited number of shells they had, these would be sufficient. The rest of the men took cover. The weapons were set up, ready to find the range.

We picked up on the radio:

Bikel, the artillery-company commander of Battalion 71, went on to a roof with Zviki, the platoon commander, and with Communications, near to the breakthrough area, and was beginning to find the range. His contact with the mortar post was a bit weak, so Bikel went to a higher spot where they could hear well.

From the roof of the advance command group, we followed the explosions in the field. The enemy was waking up. Apparently he suspected that something was going on. The rate of bullet bursts increased. Jordanian guns, silent until now, began to fire. This was a help to us, as they disclosed their location and enabled the tanks and pinning-down men to aim at them. The line came alive. If anyone had deluded himself into thinking that the Jordanians had fled, he was disappointed.

The Jordanian gunners were trying to hit our mortar positions, and Bikel's house had been turned into the center of a pillar of fire by the enemy 25-pounder guns. The Jordanians had apparently discovered the rangefinding group and were trying to get them.

With Zvika, the artillery-company commander of Battalion 66, matters were even more serious; Hermoni, the platoon commander, spread the platoon out quickly and began rangefinding, when a shell dropped among the men and the battalion suffered its first casualty: Corporal Moshe Balzam was killed. Next to him, two men were wounded slightly. They were evacuated immediately to the casualty clearing station.

Despite the enemy fire, the rangefinding continued.

Very soon the breakthrough would start. We were short of mortar shells, which were supposed to arrive any minute. However, zero hour could not be delayed just because they hadn't come yet.

It was 0145. Again General Headquarters asked: Wouldn't it be worthwhile, in spite of everything, to postpone the attack till morning? By daylight we could obtain maximum assistance from planes.

They pressed their argument, but I said no. The forces were already in the field, and the battle had acquired its own momentum. Night would help the breakthrough. The enemy's fortifications and the stone buildings in the city were not as vulnerable from the air as formations in exposed areas would be. Moreover, under cover of night it would be possible to achieve local tactical surprises, and the resultant confusion should undermine the Jordanians' will to resist. The value of night surprise exceeded that of help from our planes.

What was more: The war was at its height in Sinai and was likely to break out in the north also. We might wait for planes that would be needed elsewhere and not arrive, at the last moment.

Uzi accepted my view, contacted General Staff Headquarters, and received final confirmation.

He advised me: "Green light!"

On the roof it was quiet. Each man had found his place. The radios were placed next to the roof railing in a random pattern. Close to us there were only the radios essential for the ongoing conduct of the battle.

I summoned the battalion commanders on the radios for a last word before the battle. Uzi's radios still had not reached him. The minute hand on my watch ticked on toward the long-awaited moment. We turned to the right. In a few more seconds, without further orders, David's guns should thunder. At that moment, the battle would begin.

Chapter III

BREAKTHROUGH

At 0215—zero hour—our eyes were fixed on the right. Red fire streaked upward, forming a gigantic arc in the blackness of the heavens. But there was no sound. All eyes followed the arc until it fell. Then, at last, came the heavy dull thunder rumbling through the air. The first charge had hit home. Then a second fiery arc appeared in the darkness and a second shell exploded. The men smiled. As shells followed hard on each other, their arcs crisscrossed in the sky and the thunder of their explosions merged into one great roar.

At 0218 I turned to Orni, the communications officer: "Get me the tank forces." Francis, the communications man, tried to reach them. There was no answer, and then Orni tried. I butted in: "Give Rafi the order to begin!"

At 0220 Ziklag, the artillery officer, called to the firing units: "Iron!—I repeat—iron!" and the units confirmed: "Iron!"

The preparatory barrage started. Overhead were shells, bombs, whistles. To the right, the thuds of the shells. In front, the thunder of explosions.

Orni got hold of Rafi and gave the order: "Move!"

Dudu, the communications officer, called the battalions to set up contact and reached Battalion 66, Battalion 28, and the engineering company, but Battalion 71 did not answer. We kept trying and finally Orni sent Botnik on foot to find out. Meanwhile he turned to Ziklag and learned that the emergency network of Battalion 71 was in working order. We would manage through the emergency network, and Orni made arrangements accordingly.

On the left, the Police School was blanketed by fire, bombs and heavy shells falling fast. We heard the roar of tank engines very clearly and knew something had gone wrong; the tanks were supposed to coast down the slope without using their engines. It seemed that they were too heavy for this. The company commander, without waiting, had given the order to start up the engines. He reported: "The tanks are advancing down the slope of Bar-Ilan Street to take up their positions."

The commander of Battalion 71 reported that the additional 81-millimeter shells still had not arrived. The brigade deputy commander took on the problem and finally the exultant voice of Rafi, mortar commander for Battalions 71 and 28, came through on the radio: "The shells have come! One thousand shells!"

81-millimeter shells fell just in front of us. Apparently Battalion 71 was still rangefinding. They would have to hurry, for the barrage had to stop soon so the advance of the paratroopers could begin. I instructed the battalion commander to combine the ranges of both his targets, as we did in exercises, and he agreed.

There were explosions to the right, and the Jerusalem Battalion reported that their area was being shelled by the Jordanians. Colonel David was wounded in the barrage, and they evacuated him to the rear.

An officer came up to us on the roof—deputy company commander Reinitz of Battalion 71. With him were the breakthrough and communications sections of the battalion commander, and they were looking for the battalion. Amos, staff command officer, quickly guided them there, and they arrived a little late, but better late than never.

From the Notre Dame area, bright bursts erupted from time to time. Our tanks began shooting. Thanks to the reconnaissance tours, they reached their positions quickly. The detonation of their shells topped all other noise. The nonstop bursts from their machine guns filled us with confidence.

Over the command network came the encouraging voice of the Battalion 71 commander: "The breakthrough squads and the communications section have arrived. Everything O.K. Everything ready."

But the radios of the advance command group were still silent, receiving no instructions and sending no reports. Only the auxiliary network was working. The men were prepared for the breakthrough. They watched and listened intently through the artillery softening-up operation, trying to distinguish between our fire and theirs.

The area of the advance command group warmed up. Twenty-five-pounder shells began to explode, and, on the tiled roofs beyond us, new holes were torn open every minute.

We heard the sound of the dense volleys of the special pinning-down squads in action. Very soon the breakthrough assault would start. The Jordanians concentrated their artillery fire on our deployment areas, and shells began to fall in the middle of the units. The tanks were given special treatment. The shrapnel from 81-millimeter shells covered them entirely, ripping antennae and setting alight all external kit. The company commander reported his first wounded. But the tanks went on firing as strongly as ever. In the yard of the Police School, a gigantic fire broke out and roared through the building beside the school. Every now and then it blazed more brightly and the flame leapt higher and higher, illuminating the surroundings.

When the searchlights of the tanks were hit, Battalion 66 asked for assistance and Ziklag communicated with the roof of the Histadrut Building and requested that they put their search-light into operation. Giant beams of light probed the darkness, searching. Finally they came to rest on a white building—the Police School. The ray of light passed over us. Dudu, in command of the communications section, ordered his men to lower the antennae lest they protrude and cast a shadow.

Uzi Narkiss and Joel, his adjutant, stood beside us, following the battle at close quarters.

At 0230, before the advance for the breakthrough, requests came over the auxiliary network for more artillery fire. Ziklag gave the order: "Steel!—I repeat—steel!"

Shells fell all along the front. From the direction of the Police School came the thunder of heavy explosions: 160-millimeter and 155-millimeter shells. The explosions of the 25-pounder shells were swallowed up by this thunder, but their whistling overhead was nerve-racking: It was hard to know whether the shriek was from one of our shells or a Jordanian one.

Over in front—in the Sheikh Jarragh section—81-millimeter shells exploded. That sound was familiar and cheered us up. The 81-millimeter mortars were the main weapons we used in train-ing exercises, and everyone knew the sound well and relied on it.

To the right, just next to us, a 25-pounder Jordanian shell exploded on our roof. A cloud of stone and plaster rose, covering everything. But, luckily, no one was hurt. The shell had hit the railing of the roof. Two communications men—Yoram and Rafi—had been sitting with their back to the rail, but nothing had hap-pened to them. We transferred the men to the northern side of the roof.

From behind came the sound of running water. The rooftop

water tanks had been hit by shrapnel. The noise of the radios was from then on accompanied by the monotonous, unceasing music of running water.

I got the commanders of the battalions on the radios. Both of them—Uzi, commander of Battalion 71, and Yossi, commander of Battalion 66—answered quietly. Everything was O.K.

Uzi Narkiss then left us. He had more brigades to worry about and had to coordinate all of them. He and Joel, his adjutant, went down to the street, where the crowd didn't know them. They wanted the general's jeep to evacuate wounded, and his explanations were no use. In their anger the crowd ripped the cables of the communications instruments. Then a shell fell near the jeep, just as Uzi and Joel jumped in. When a bomb exploded near the back wheel, the jeep jumped forward and they were off.

A request for additional fire came through on the auxiliary network. I confirmed: "Repeat!"

Ziklag gave the order to the firing units: "Repeat!"

At 0300 I tried to contact the commander of the engineering corps to find out if they had already begun to clear the mines. "Not yet," he answered, "but very soon."

It was important that he should hurry, for it wouldn't be long before we would want to get the tanks inside.

Orni listened from time to time to the inner networks of the battalions. Everything was O.K.—no special reports about wounded. Volleys from Uzis could be heard, and at times the explosion of grenades. Hand-to-hand fighting was beginning.

The radios now picked up tempo. Ziklag received requests for fire, and passed them on to the batteries. The requests were for fire directly related to fighting for objectives.

The process was prolonged because we were compelled to use transmission gear on the roof of the Histadrut Building. But the bombs and shells landed on the enemy without a letup.

At 0305 there was some tension in the advance command

group: The breakthrough seemed to be taking too long. There was only one hour left till dawn. The artillery barrage had finished. We could clearly hear shooting from the tanks. The 81-millimeter shells of Battalion 71 raised a gigantic wall of dust and made out the fire of the heavy machine guns and the Mags. That means that the pinning-down squads were in action. Every now and then there was a particularly thunderous roar—a bangalore was exploding and another fence went flying.

Both Uzi and Yossi requested: "Repeat!" and Ziklag gave the order for uninterrupted fire, on the principle that what the commander in the field wants he should have. We were worried that they should need it, but did not want to disturb them with questions during the breakthrough. We would get our reports later.

Another five minutes passed. We stood in a huddle, noticing that volleys coming from the right had no further effect and that the shells falling round us too had become part of the picture. Our eyes tried to pierce the darkness and read what is happening in the battlefield and our ears strained to listen to the radios. At the same time we tried to figure out, from the sound of artillery, if the Jordanians were still shelling as strongly as ever. Yossi requested that fire from the tanks be stopped, but Rafi did not hear him. When Orni told me this, I ordered Rafi to deflect the tank fire to the 71 Battalion sector. Then Yossi asked, "Why are they continuing? I asked for a stop!" and Orni put the question to Rafi. "Don't ask," I shouted to Orni. "Order him!"

Breaking through barricades goes quickly in training exercises, but we realized that in actual war it would probably be different. Besides, in training exercises we could see, while here we were dependent on reports. We had to be patient.

Amos found out what was happening. It was not easy to get the battalion commanders to the radios. Both of them were occupied with the fighting at close quarters. But both gave the same reply—It's going O.K. We didn't ask about wounded. As long as the commanders in the field felt that they were advancing, that's what counted. While the medics dealt with the wounded, the others had to keep on. They must not stop, not even for a moment.

People had been wounded near our building. I recognized one, Natan Malinov, a veteran of D Company, who was now in the intelligence section of the brigade. Men near him took him into the stairwell.

Once again we questioned Yod-Bet, commander of the engineering corps, who reported: "We are already in action between the fences." Good news!

Dawn was approaching quickly, and by the time it broke we must be inside. We stood tensely, waiting for news. At 0310 Yossi, commander of Battalion 66, reported, "Breakthrough! Mission accomplished!" There were signs of relief in Brigade Headquarters. I replied to Yossi: "A kiss for you." His companies swarmed toward the Police School and Ammunition Hill.

At 0315 Uzi, the commander of Battalion 71, reported, "Breakthrough! Mission accomplished!" His forces poured out on the road to Nablus. The platoon of Sergeant Amos Wool was already in the houses that surrounded the Mosque Sheikh-Jarragh. The companies commanded by Mussa and Zamush charged down Wadi Joz Street, and Meirke began to clean up the breakthrough area.

I sent Uzi a kiss as well.

Our anxieties began to lift as the crossing of the open stretch was completed and the nightmare of the barbed-wire fences and the mines passed. In the hand-to-hand fighting, we would be on top.

Now we had to move the tanks, but Yod-Bet reported that the road was still not ready. There was yet another fence, and not all the mines had been removed.

Nevertheless, the tanks got the order to move. Organizing them would take another few minutes, and by then the road would have to be open. We urged Yod-Bet to hurry.

The enemy shelling intensified. Their forces had broken under the impact of our artillery and the momentum of the break-through by our advance units. But their guns and mortars had begun to pound our deployment areas systematically. Despite the darkness, they had perceived our men and identified our positions. Thus they trained their guns on targets determined before-hand according to a fixed plan, rather than by actual observation. In spite of this, they caused us many losses.

At the entrance of the roof, Uzi, the deputy company commander, appeared, breathing heavily. On his clothes were drops of blood. He reported that a salvo of shells had fallen in the company, causing terrible slaughter. The Battalion had continued advancing, but thirty of his comrades were lying on the slope of the road and must be evacuated.

Hagai appeared, formerly of D Company, now company commander in Battalion 28. An idealist who loved people. Almost everyone in the company had been hit, and the entire casualty station had gone too—including the doctor. I ordered the brigade medical team to deal with the wounded, and went back to listening to the command network. It was a critical moment in the battle, for fighting was beginning within the city. Moshele turned to me: "Motte—let me go down. I'll take charge of the evacuation of the wounded."

"Why should you? There is someone to deal with it."

Moshele pleaded in a whisper: "Motte—"

"Oh, O.K.—go on."

I returned to follow the advance with the communications instruments. Moshele went down below with Hagai and Uzi. On the road they found forty-five men, lying next to the walls and in the stairways. They were wounded by 81-millimeter shells, which had fallen among them as they moved toward the breach.

Dr. King, the brigade doctor, sent Dr. Zak to relieve Dr. Eliraz, the Battalion 28 doctor, who had been wounded in the face. Eliraz referred Zak to the most seriously wounded first. Dr. Zak treated them quickly and efficiently. He consulted Eliraz about his own wound as a colleague: "Raz, should I give you a transfusion?" Both of them smiled. Zak continued with his work.

We spurred on the engineering corps to complete the clearing of the minefields so that the tanks could advance.

Moshele returned to the roof. He was covered with blood.

"It's all right. We evacuated them all."

"Are there really so many?"

"Yes. Very many. Very many."

Moshele began to organize supplies and the evacuation of wounded. Longo got Kotik, the supplies officer, on the radio. Moshele ordered the advance of the ammunition vehicles. Uzi, the operations officer, was sent to Bet Hakerem to bring the ammunition trucks. When he got there, Nitzan, the ammunition officer, reported that the trucks had already left.

Reuven, the adjutant, was sent to locate squads of the brigade medical team.

Moshele contacted the Jerusalem Brigade deputy commander and asked for half-tracks to evacuate the wounded. Hagai promised to send them as quickly as possible. A few minutes later, Hagai informed us: "One half-track ready. Two more will be ready soon. We're removing the tackle. Come and get them."

The radios operated at full pitch for some minutes. This was decision-making time. The breakthrough stage had ended. Fighting among the houses and in the trenches was beginning. Artillery fire began to slacken, for with the companies and platoons split and fanning out in a broad arc, and along many axes, we could not use our support guns. No one knew exactly where everyone was. The commanders were rushing forward and sticking close to the enemy. There was no time for coordination. We had to stick to the Jordanians like leeches, and not let them breathe. Only this kind of harassment would prevent them from using their artillery and organizing in depth.

At 0330 the brigade was on the move. Battalion 66 poured from the Police School on the Ammunition Hill and toward the Ambassador Hotel. The engineering corps prepared the road for the tanks, which were getting ready for the movement eastward to help the battalions inside the city. Battalion 71 moved toward the American Colony and Wadi Joz as Battalion 28 crossed the open area and entered Nablus Road. Within an hour, the main shield of the Jordanian defenses had been smashed and the front line of forts broken. What for nineteen years had been "No-Man's Land" was in our hands. Now was the time to send in the tanks. Rafi reported that they were already in formation.

At 0345 I gave Rafi the order—"Move!" Yod-Bet reported that the path was still not clear, but there was no alternative. They had to go forward. I repeated the order: "Move!"

Rafi reported that he was approaching the fences, and Yod-Bet that the tanks were approaching him. Battalion 28 was on the Nablus Road en route to the wall of the Old City. Stage one had come to an end.

Chapter IV

BATTALION 66
BREAKS THROUGH

At 0220, ten minutes to the battalion's zero hour, the preliminary barrage on the Police School and Ammunition Hill was tailing off, but shells were still falling in the open spaces between the barbed wire entanglements and minefields that had to be overcome to reach the school. The battalion commander and his deputy commander thought that the shrapnel should tear away part of the barriers and also explode some of the minefields. Giant searchlights illuminated the Police School and the wall south of it with concentrated beams. The tanks advanced down the slope of the road and reached the battle area. In the open square of Evacuees' Houses they split up—Arzi's platoon pulling to the right and advancing between the houses. A tank was placed between every two buildings. Arzi to the left, Nissan in the middle. But Ariel made a mistake. He passed the entrance to the position fixed for him and wandered on southward along the Street of Samuel the Prophet. Fortunately he realized that he had gone wrong and came back to the right place.

Rafi, the company commander, was with Saul's platoon, spread out among the olive trees. They took up their positions. Firing on the Police School continued without ceasing. Rafi's tank was on the far left; to his right Saul, then Moshe, then Shlain.

Everyone was given his exact orders when the officers made their tour of inspection. Now the tanks were firing according to plan. Saul's platoon—to the north—shot at the tower of the Police School, at the building, and at any target disclosed by the searchlights or the tracers of the Jordanians. Arzi's platoon split open the southern part of the building and also fired on the "Hill of the Yellow Rag." The Gilboa platoon to the south hit the southern wing of the school and the building with the arches.

The area around the tanks was blanketed almost immediately by thick Jordanian fire. Mortar shells and others fell on the tanks and near them. Amios, Rafi's signaler, was hit in the head by shrapnel. He managed to jump off the back of the tank by himself and Nechama, the machine gunner, sprang into his place. The camouflage net on Saul's tank caught fire. The crew leapt out quickly, flung off the net, and went back into action at once.

The searchlights of the tanks, which lit up the Jordanian positions, were hit one after the other by shots and shrapnel. The antenna base on Rafi's tank flew off and his heavy gun was hit.

A bus and a truck of the heavy-artillery platoon came down Bar-Ilan Street. They were bringing men and equipment. When they reached the northern building, between the Evacuees' Houses, they stopped. Abe, the platoon commander, handed out orders to the sections: Gidi to the south, Mevurach to the center, and Zakkai to the north.

Even while they were still unloading the vehicles, the crews rushed their weapons to the top floors of the building. The narrow stairways made it very hard to get through with assembled parts. There were no keys to the doors, so they were forced open. It was very difficult to set up the heavy guns so that they could fire from the windows, for there was no furniture suitable to serve as platforms for the guns. Time was pressing; zero hour at hand. The enemy was firing incessantly, and the officers shouted impatient orders—they had to get the guns into action somehow at once.

The teams pushed beds and cupboards up to the windows to improvise platforms, but the windows were still too high. They had no alternative but to place the front leg of a gun on a window sill and have two gunners hold the back legs. It was not an ideal arrangement, for the guns moved from side to side as they fired, but it was too late to do anything about that. Somehow they managed to get them working at top speed.

As one crate of ammunition was emptied, a second arrived. Their target was the Police School. Extra crates were brought up from below. All the time shells were falling between the houses and the school. To the north, a Jordanian gun was shelling the windows.

Something went wrong with one of the heavy guns. The automatic sight was not working. The men had to aim by relying on their own eyes—but they went on firing without stopping for a moment.

One gun jammed. While the crew were trying to fix it, Mevurach took up a submachine gun and opened fire from the window.

Suddenly, beyond the Police School, a great yellow flame leapt toward the sky. One of the Jordanian depots had been hit by a shell.

Hermoni's mortar division arrived at its planned position; it swiftly set up its weapons. Then only a few minutes remained before zero hour. Zvika, the subcommander, made terrific efforts to work out the range fast, but the rain of shells dropping around the school made it difficult to pinpoint positions and to identify the rangefinding shells. Even phosphorus shells didn't help. Zvika knew that if he didn't find the range within a minute, he might be too late—the paratroopers acting as infantry and responsible for breaching the barricades on foot would reach them. He decided to make do with two rangefinding shells, and to go down from the roof to the battalion commander so as to get the latest information about the troop movements.

The deployment area of the companies was covered by dense enemy fire. Red bursts of bullets coming from the Jordanian lines struck the walls and streaked upward into the darkness. Shells from recoilless guns exploded on the bare walls. The buildings shuddered. Mortar shells fell in the spaces between the houses. The hard asphalt pavement was completely pulverized. The paratroopers crowded into the narrow stairways near the breakthrough area. Anyone daring to peep outside could see the relentless fire the tanks were pouring out.

The heavy guns drew the bulk of the enemy's artillery. Dudik's company, scheduled to follow the advance company into action immediately a breach in the first barrier was made, was waiting in the same house. There was an explosion that made the building tremble.

Suddenly a shell from a recoilless gun struck the wall of the room from which Mevurach's crew was firing its gun. Everyone in the crew was hit, Mevurach the worst of all. Abe, his second-in-command, ordered them to cease fire—it was clear that the Jordanian recoilless gun team had identified their position, and was aiming at it, so there was no point in continuing to operate from there. The adjoining crew helped them to carry Mevurach down the stairs. The medic, Menachem, attended to him, and the ammunition carriers took him behind the lines where they found Yehuda Laskov, still wearing sandals.

He had managed to join the battalion only at the very last minute, so he hadn't had time to put on his boots. He was helping to evacuate the wounded, thinking while he did so, "I'll get a chance to take some boots from one of the wounded, then I'll be able to join in the battle for the breach."

The doctor, Uri Freund, was in the process of moving his

casualty clearing station toward its planned position, near the front lines. But the stretcher carrying Mevurach reached him before the station had been set up, so Uri attended to Mevurach on the spot.

In the mortar post, the men waited impatiently for the order to fire. The shells were stacked, everything was cleared for action. All they needed was the order to start their mortars firing—but instead of the order "Fire!" came an unexpected: "Stop. Hold everything!"

When Zvika, the company commander of the mortars, had reported to the battalion commander, he had found out that D Company had already advanced to the barrier. These men might be endangered by our own mortars. So Zvika urgently gave the order to his men, "Stop!"

Taken aback, fuming, not knowing the reason why they could not go into action, the men put the shells down beside the mortars. They hoped they would be allowed to open fire soon. Then a Jordanian shell fell among them, scoring a direct hit.

The casualties were very heavy; everyone was hit. Moshe Balzam, the section commander, was killed. Micha Nafcha and a guide from Jerusalem were wounded and were evacuated to the casualty clearing station.

Hermoni distributed the men of his platoon in posts close to the houses. The men took cover as best they could, and waited. The seconds to zero hour crawled by as Jordanian shells kept exploding among them, hitting several men.

Not far from them, sections of the medical team also waited for zero hour. The medics heard the shells exploding nearby but didn't know what the explosions meant. But when Dr. Kahanski and little Yechezkiel, the medic, went out to see what was happening and discovered there were men wounded in the platoon, they went into action instantly, Dr. Kahanski alerting the rest of the doctors and medics and ordering an ambulance.

When the ambulance arrived, Jean, the driver, helped the doc-

tors and shielded them with his own body while they were working until a shell exploded next to him, wounding him mortally.

Meir Barak, the driver of a jeep carrying a recoilless gun, was
asked to help to drive out the wounded. He hesitated because he
might not get back to his section in time for the attack if he did
so. But the wounded had to be evacuated quickly, so he took
them in his vehicle.

The Jordanian shelling never stopped. Sixteen gunners were
hit and Abraham Binstock, Eliezer Grundland, Avinoam
Miodowski, Gideon Rosenfeld, and Zeev Shmueli were killed. The
medics, Avnor and Astrinowski, carried the wounded from the
open ground into the rooms. Sometimes the doctors went out
onto the open battlefield to tend to the wounded under fire, and to
help bring them into the rooms. Civilians, residents of the nearby
houses, offered their vehicles and helped to evacuate them.

The recoilless gun section took up its position at the intersection of Samuel the Prophet Street and the Evacuees' Houses. They
were under strict orders from the deputy commander not to enter
the firing line. There were enough tanks in the sector, and the
recoilless gunners had to avoid exposing themselves needlessly to
enemy fire. The platoon commander, Eshkoli, advanced on foot
with the battalion. Sergeant Aharoni remained with the platoon.
Jordanian shells fell in the area. They waited for the order to go
into action.

In the meantime, preparations for the assault by the paratroopers on foot were complete. Officers went through the ranks,
giving final orders, and equipment was moved wherever necessary. The officers made certain that the men understood the plan
of action clearly.

Giora called two of the commanders of the groups responsible for pinning down the enemy while the main body of troops
advanced to the barrier. They went with him into the open field
so as to observe the barricades by the light of the searchlights.

From there they could see the first barrier clearly. "When we cross this barrier," Giora explained again, but now for the last time, "you will spread out to your positions: Shlomo to the right and Simon to the left. The moment the advance begins, open fire with all your weapons—M.G.s, bazookas, the lot. Find some enemy strongpoint and blanket it with fire. Is it all clear?"

"Sure. Don't worry, Giora—it's going to be O.K."

The officers returned to their posts.

The battalion commander looked at his watch and found there were a few more seconds to zero hour. The men were keyed up and ready to go. To the north, from the olive grove, the tanks were firing. Shells were falling among the paratroopers—the Jordanians were shooting 81-millimeter guns. Our artillery fired back nonstop. The battalion commander thought for a moment that it was possible that another quarter of an hour of such heavy fire would have a great effect upon the Jordanians, and that perhaps we should wait.

But there was no quarter of an hour to spare. At 0230 the time had come for the all-out attack on the barricades. Carmi asked leave to advance and got it instantly.

"Giora—forward!" cried Yossi, the battalion commander.

Shlomo's force was in the van. Until now the boys, hidden in the houses, had seen practically nothing. They looked around in wonder to see what was going on. Banjo and Moreno fell into a trench in the ground that they hadn't seen. They tried to get out but their heavy loads hindered them, and other paratroopers had to give them a hand.

The short-range enemy fire didn't worry the men overmuch— the bullets passed over them. The heavy guns of the battalion were still firing from the windows of the upper flats, and the Jordanians were aiming mainly at them and at the tanks. Nevertheless, as the men walked they crouched, each man trying to reduce his height to a minimum.

When Shlomo reached the first barbed-wire barrier, he reported back. The battalion commander decided that they should try to break through it as quietly as possible. The Jordanians had not yet seen the main body of paratroopers advancing—it would have been a pity to reveal that they were on the move. "Wire-cutters!" Giora ordered in a whisper. The wire-cutters came to his hand almost at once—but they were not needed. Shlomo had trodden down the wire with his feet. His section followed him. Simon arrived and began to draw to the left.

Giora, the company commander, stood beside the gap and gave orders: "Look out for mines between the fences. Shoot only at targets that may stop the breakthrough."

Moving at the head of the force, Simon stopped at times to show every soldier his precise place in the operation: here the M.G. of Pas, there the M.G. of Gafni, here the bazookas. All of them lay down. Simon stretched out in front of Aaron. To his left was Tanna, with a submachine gun and some bazooka shells.

As they lay down, they realized that the grass was high, and that they would have to prepare a field of fire.

The M.G. gunners prepared the machine guns and opened the magazines, and the bazooka men loaded up shells and waited.

Shlomo's force carried out a similar action to the right.

Gilad's trousers caught on the barbed wire, but he managed to free himself at once, and took his place.

The assault forces waited under the cover of a stone wall near the corner of the building. Bloom's section was first, Buki's second, and the section of Micha, the deputy company commander—constituting the reserves—was last. Giora called to Bloom to advance. His section carried a bangalore, with which to break through the barrier and to explode the mines on both sides of it.

The line advanced in close formation and almost straight: All the men were carrying the long bangalore and were trying to prevent it coming apart into its sections. Treading as lightly as ballet dancers, they crossed the trodden-down wire. The battalion commander's group was next to them, between the barricades.

Giora and his staff joined the advance platoon and they all moved toward the next barrier.

The men responsible for pinning down the enemy opened fire. Gilad got up with his M.G. to shoot over the grass and the barrier. He had noticed that a volley of tracers passed near him, so now he was looking for the source of the tracers, his finger on the trigger. A shot from a Jordanian heavy machine gun hit him in the arm, the palm of his hand opened by reflex, and he fell. Yarkele took the M.G. and continued shooting. Shlomo realized that the position was not good enough and rushed the men forward. Zaks got up to shoot with a bazooka and Banjo, next to him, began to pull rolls of ammunition from the crate. Zaks was hit by a bullet in the head and dropped with a cry, falling on Banjo. Banjo tried to get out from under Zaks, but couldn't. Shlomo sent Moreno to see what had happened and Yitzhak helped Banjo to get free. Banjo then took up a rifle and started shooting while Yitzhak attended to Zaks. Moreno returned to his place; he also took up a rifle and shot. To the right, the M.G.s and machine gun chattered.

Simon gave his preliminary orders, and now—even in the heat of fire, with explosions and shots all around him—he calmly went on giving orders to regulate and direct the fire. Tanna fired his machine gun without stopping for a moment. He emptied magazine after magazine. Simon—while controlling the force and giving orders—pulled out reserve ammunition and filled the magazines.

Pas was looking for sources of Jordanian fire—targets for his M.G. Later he said ruefully: "I couldn't find any. So I shot at the high windows of the school. Then I aimed at the lower windows. Pity we didn't know about the Jordanians in the trenches. We only used up three boxes of ammunition."

Nissan aimed his bazooka at the buildings. He said afterward: "We fired twelve shells at the buildings and at the trench below it. Afterward, according to directions given to me by my number two man, Yehuda, I shot near the big tree to the north of the building."

Reuben, the platoon commander, sat next to the fence with a mortar section, supervising the shelling. Just as Nissan began to fire with the bazooka, Simon suspected that the Jordanians had located him and were aiming at him. "Change your position!" he called. But Reuben countermanded from behind. "Don't move, the place is mined."

Bazooka shells and other Jordanian shells passed overhead, striking the houses behind the paratroopers. Then a mortar shell fell between Simon and Tanna, and exploded right behind them. Pieces of sharpnel ricocheted and hit Simon in the face, under the eyes, while Nissan was hit in the back and leg. "I turned sideways to see how Yehuda was loading the bazooka. Suddenly a shell burst over us. I felt blows in my back and leg. For a few seconds I was stunned. But I recovered right away, and went on firing. Only when we got to the Ambassador Hotel did I notice that my blood was flowing."

A second Jordanian shell hit almost immediately, falling about a meter from Simon. "Shrapnel pierced my knee and my whole leg. I lost consciousness for a few seconds. Tanna gave me a thump and pushed across his canteen. I had a drink and revived."

Banjo noticed machine-gun fire coming from a wall to the south. "Should I fire?" he shouted. "We don't know," came the answer. So he decided: "Don't know? So I won't fire."

Aslan worked his M.G. without stopping for a moment, going from one target to another. In spite of the Israeli shelling, the Jordanians went on firing every now and then from the trenches. Aslan tried to pinpoint the men firing and to hit them.

Ariel had only just begun to fire with his bazooka when he felt a sharp blow in the leg and collapsed, streaming blood. His number two, Moshe, rushed off to call a medic. A shell burst near him and sent him flying. He rolled over and put his hand to his buttocks. Wet. Then he realized happily that it was only water—his canteen had been pierced by shrapnel. The medic raced over to Ariel.

Although wounded in the arm, Gilad crawled forward in the direction of the Police School. "They had ordered me to reach right to the target, and I did my best. I got as far as the second barricade. Then I couldn't move any more. I had a heavy pack on my back. I lay down next to the barrier."

Some of the men attended to their wounded comrades as others went on firing at the Jordanians.

Under cover of the enfilading fire, the assault forces had moved forward and had already passed the paratroopers who were firing. Every now and then, a paratrooper fell. Parts of the bangalore they were carrying separated and the men had to stop and to join the parts together again. They went on, walking slowly.

Mortar shells fell on both sides of them, enveloping them in smoke and pieces of flying shrapnel. Zachi was hit in the chest and fell. Ehud felt the bangalore break and guessed that somebody had been hit, and called, "Medic!" Gans, the company sergeant major, immediately alerted Ochion, the medic. Zachi came to and tried to make his way on his own to the rear, but the other men helped him. He was evacuated farther back.

Ehud struggled to join the severed parts of the bangalore by himself. Bloom, the platoon commander, stopped and went to help him. In a matter of moments, the bangalore was joined together again and the advance proceeded. Bloom came up against the barricade and began to push the tube in. Every man, after he shoved his section of the bangalore in, turned around and went to the back of the line to help others push.

They worked in silence, whispering the most essential orders as they pushed. At last the bangalore was through and the first part of the job finished. Most of the men went back; Bloom stayed behind, Ehud beside him. Then Bloom triggered off the bangalore and the two of them rushed back.

"Look out. Explosion!" they shouted.

The men knelt—but didn't lie down. "Get back!" roared Giora, who realized that the distance between the men and the barrier was too short. A mighty explosion shook the earth and a black cloud soared up to the sky. Bloom leapt forward to give the signal that the barricade had been breached. He handed a torch to Rami, who was on one side of him. Sergeant Zvika was on the other, also with a flashlight in his hands. They shouted and flashed the message as well: "Breakthrough! Breakthrough!"

The torches were colored green—the color generally used by the paratroopers to get the men together after a drop. It had been agreed to use this signal for a breakthrough.

A second bangalore was brought up. "Buki, forward!" came the order. Buki's platoon, holding the long tube—and having to mend it for a third time on the way—moved forward. The company commander and his staff, standing at the point of the breach, directed Buki where to go. At the head of his platoon, he reached the next barricade.

He was not surprised to find that it was very intricate, for from the photographs he had seen he knew that it was very wide and deep. He ordered Arzi to push, and the first joint of the bangalore was forced in. Arzi ran to the back to help with the pushing and, working as before, the bangalore was finally in.

Buki set the fuse. "Look out—explosion coming!" They ran back twenty or thirty meters and lay flat. A blast was heard.

"That's it!" somebody shouted and Annon got up. "Down!" roared Giora, the platoon commander. "That's not the bangalore!"

There was a terrific crush in the line. They were rather like a bunch of sprinters, waiting for the starter's signal to leap forward.

Then came the explosion. This time, no doubt about it, it was the bangalore. Buki and his men jumped up, Oded on the right, Arzi on the left. Both had green torches, "Breakthrough! Breakthrough!" Buki, beside them, was joined by Bloom.

"What are you doing here?"

"I ran . . ."

Giora, the company commander, sent back Amram, the company runner, to bring up Dudik's company, which had been waiting in reserve for the breach.

"Dudik! Dudik!" shouted Amram, as he ran back, "Come up! Go forward!"

The call to Dudik was superfluous. From the beginning of the attack to effect a breach, Dudik had followed hard on the heels of the vanguard. It was already clear to him that there was no need to wait for orders. As each barrier was breached, Dudik's men rushed forward, so that the first of them was right behind the last man in Giora's company.

They advanced. Each man tried to reduce his height. They looked around. To their right, a Jordanian machine gun fired without stopping. Fortunately he was shooting at the tracers and not at them. They could even see where he was shooting.

To the right and left of them they could already spot many wounded from Giora's company. Worry gnawed at them. They wondered who had been hit and if he was from their own village. But still they advanced. Then suddenly came a cry: "Explosion coming!" and they flung themselves on the ground.

A command from Yoav, the platoon commander. "Get up!" A 52-millimeter shell burst to the left of the platoon, only three meters away. There was a terrible blast. Bunch, Yoav's runner, was flung forward. He reached behind with his hand and realized that he had a wound in the back. Sharpnel also tore Chazzai's back. "Medic! Medic!"

Yoav continued to advance as Zvika's platoon arrived. "What's happening? Why are you stopping? Follow me!" Bunch had had time to discover that his wound was slight, so, as he put it, he "stuck to Zvika's behind." Bugin, Chazzai, and Boaz were left to get first aid. Round them, shells continued to explode. "From time to time, because of the blast of the explosion, we flew upward." A medic calmed Bugin down. It turned out that he was not seriously wounded, for he crawled to the rear under his own steam.

Boaz and Chazzai remained on the battlefield, waiting to be evacuated.

From the left and right, our guns were firing.

Ilan, section commander in Dudik's company, was tense. He stole a look ahead to see what was happening there. All around was the thunder of shellfire. He wondered if he would be able to distinguish the blast of the bangalore from the exploding shells.

The answer lay in the thunder of the bangalore, which was always greater than that of the shells.

"Lie down!" Ilan said to himself. "There's still another barrier to blow up!"

Sure enough, they heard shouts: "Buki, come up! Come up!"

From behind, Dudik, the company commander, hurried forward. "Come on! Advance! Get going fast."

Ilan got up and ran forward, stooping. He looked back. Everyone was moving.

Then came a sudden stop and a shout: "Down! Lie wherever you are!"

Ilan knelt, aware that something unexpected had happened.

Nir, the deputy company commander, sprang over to him. "What's happened? Why have you stopped all of a sudden?"

The abrupt halt had caused a sort of concertina movement behind. One man falling on top of another in a dangerous crush.

"Get back!" Dudik ordered. "Keep your distance!"

Without comprehending what was happening, but without asking any questions, they moved back, cursing. In spite of the tension, somebody laughed. "The army's always like this—contradictory orders—forward, back; forward, back . . ."

Giora explained to those who could hear him that the first bangalore had only exploded partially, and that they had to wait for the rest of it to go off.

From the front came a cry: "Explosion coming!" followed this time by an even louder noise.

"B Company, advance!"

Up front, a green torch flashed, and there was a shout: "Breakthrough! Breakthrough!" Ilan's section rushed straight forward in the direction of the explosion, going at great speed. Suddenly, the ground seemed to heave up in front of them. They had reached a sort of embankment. To the left of them a Jordanian post opened fire on them. They had to act, fast.

Ilan jumped forward. "What the hell? Another barrier!" Nir, the deputy company commander, joined him; they inspected a barbed-wire barricade. While Ilan called for another bangalore, Nir disposed of the strongpoint on the left with a burst from his Uzi. Gans, Giora's company sergeant major, who had maintained contact with him all the time, shouted to the platoon sergeant with the reserves: "Micha, come up with a bangalore!"

After completing the administrative preparations of the company, Micha, Giora's deputy, had served as commander of the reserves with the bangalores. He hadn't been happy with the job, for he really wanted a well-defined and unambiguous post in the command. But it was better than nothing.

Now had come this sudden call to go forward, so unexpectedly and swiftly that he did not have time to find all the men under his command, for some had been cut off from the others while the troops had been on the move. Now he simply did not have time to get them all together again. He dashed forward.

Near the barrier, a group of top-level officers had gathered. When Bloom, the platoon commander, heard that they had struck another barricade, he hurried forward to see if he could identify it and if he could help. He pulled a torch from his pocket to tell Micha what direction the reserves should take. All Micha's scattered men saw the signal and each one began to make his way separately in the direction of Bloom's flashlight. The section commanders, Nissim and Eliezer, rushed up, so did David Fuchs. Eliezer and Fuchs brought parts of the bangalore to Micha, who was already busy trying to improvise one.

Bloom's bangalore did not detonate. Buki, the platoon commander, ran up to the middle of the barrier and tried to pull out a piece from the parts that had not exploded.

"Play safe—put in another one."

Sergeant Ami of A Company came up from the right to see what was happening. Micha was having trouble fitting the detonator to the bangalore. Bloom wanted to help. The connection of the detonator had to be improvised in such a way that it would not break off when it was pulled.

From the nearest corner of the Police School, and from two windows to the left of the door, the Jordanians were pouring volley after volley of well-aimed fire on them.

The tanks behind them fired at the top floor of the school with both shells and machine-gun bullets. The ground shook from the impact of the shells on the concrete walls. By the light of the tracers, which ricocheted on into the sky, Ilan and Ami made out the figures of four Jordanians coming toward them from the depths of the yard. "Where do they think they're going, the fools?" the two Israelis wondered, looking at each other. Looking backward, Ami saw a dense crowd of paratroopers between the barriers, and whispered: "There'll be murder here! Murder!"

Close to them, the men were still struggling with the banga- lore. Bloom got furious with Micha. In the tension, he forgot the difference in rank and post, and called out angrily, "Oh, give it here!"

But he never managed to take it. A Jordanian hand grenade exploded near him, covering him with shrapnel. He was wounded near his mouth, his eye streamed blood, and shrapnel in his back and chest stabbed like sharp needles.

Bloom went to the rear as Micha set off the bangalore. "Mind—explosion!" he roared, and ran back. Ami and Ilan were busy keeping track of the four Jordanians, who were coming nearer. From the other side of the bangalore, Nir and Gans were also watching the approaching Jordanians. Every paratrooper present secretly counted the passing seconds. Ami counts aloud, "Twenty-one . . ." Ilan decided that there wouldn't be any explo- sion, and that they would have to kill the four Jordanians or endanger the breakthrough. He got up to fire at them—but then he was flung back on his friends by the force of a mighty blast. The bangalore had gone off, after all.

Between them and it there were only a few meters. But the embankment had sheltered them. A cloud of black dust and smoke covered them.

Gans was the first to move forward after the explosion. Even before it went off, he heard whispers in Arabic from an adjacent position. Now he hurled in a hand grenade. The thunder of its burst and a cloud of dust mingled with the noise and dust from the greater explosion of the bangalore.

Ilan and his group leapt forward and scaled the embankment at top speed. When they reached the top, Ilan suddenly saw a Jor- danian post at his feet. From a trench, two Arabs appeared and entered the post. Every second of delay would cost many lives, as the paratroopers came behind him, massed together. Ilan began to fire and did not take his finger off the trigger. His burst hit the two Jordanians, and when he got down to the post, the two were stretched at the bottom of it. Ilan leapt across their bodies to the trench.

Suddenly he discovered that his magazine was empty. He glued himself to the wall on the left. "Magazine!" he called desperately. Just as if they were out on maneuvers and not dealing with a real enemy, Joshua ran forward, his submachine gun in his hand, and calmly and systematically set about mopping up the trench.

Behind them, Gans was shouting, "Breakthrough! Breakthrough!" He was holding a pocket-torch covered with green and guiding the forces into the gap.

When Yair Goldberger, Zvika's sergeant, heard the shout, "Breakthrough! Breakthrough!" he raced forward to join the men who were held up. In the momentum of his dash, he streaked over the embankment into the trench and was killed by the explosion of an antitank grenade.

The platoon drew near to the barrier.

Suddenly Ninio felt a severe blow in the buttocks and was thrown to the ground. Even though he managed to dress his own wound, Zvika sent a medic to him.

While B Company was forging ahead, Bloom made his way to the rear, one hand holding his wounded eye, the other his mouth. He couldn't get to the wounds on his back and chest as well . . . Near the big breach, he found Zvika, his sergeant, and handed him his radio transmitter, saying, "Good luck, Zvika!"

Bloom stopped for a second next to Giora, the company commander. "I handed the radio to Zvika. I'll get out by myself. Good luck, Giora!"

Giora turned to Rami. "Go with him to the casualty clearing station." But after a few minutes Rami returned. "Bloom insisted that he was O.K., and that there was no need for me to go with him. So I came back."

Behind them, from a corner of the Evacuees' Houses, the light mortar section fired continuously. The air was full of smoke and bullets and shells.

The tanks continued to pour out fire and made it difficult to see what was happening. But the lights of the great searchlights set up on the Histadrut Building helped. It was still hard to make out small targets. Furthermore, the powerful rays of light shone between the tanks and the companies; as a result, all the time during the breaching of the barricades, the men in the tanks could not make out what the assault troops were doing. Only when the first paratroopers reached the vicinity of the Police School could they be seen against the background of the wall. Now their progress could be followed. The artillery and machine gunners were firing like men possessed, kept busy by the still-active Jordanian posts.

Meir, Shalyan's driver, put his head out and made out paratrooper sappers clearing a path through the minefields. He pulled his head in again to warn his machine gunner that his own men were there, but it was impossible to talk because internal communications were cut. Instinctively, he hit the machine gunner on the hand to warn him not to shoot.

Forces, cleaning up, entered the trenches. The battalion commander ordered the tanks company commander to shift his fire to the left, northward. Rafi instructed Arzi's platoon to change its position and to cross over to the area to the north of it—between them and the Fagi neighborhood. From there it would be possible to control Ammunition Hill properly, and, to a certain degree, Givat Hamivtar and Shufa'at.

The movement was carried out rapidly and the platoon took up its new position.

Rafi set target on Ammunition Hill and Shufa'at. They opened fire.

Giora, commander of the company that effected the breakthrough, began to gather the company. "We've done our part," he said to his staff with manifest pride. "Now we must move onwards. Call the men pinning down the Jordanians till now to join in. They're no longer needed where they are."

Aram ran to the rear. "Shlomo, we're through. Your men are to join us in the next advance."

Shlomo instructed his men. "Follow me." The men got up. He called to Simon, leading the other group pinning down the enemy. "Simon, Simon—join in behind me."

But Simon never heard this order, for at that very second, a mortar shell fell next to him. He was hit by a piece of shrapnel and lost consciousness. His men stayed where they were. Shlomo's group reached Giora—but without Simon's.

"Simon hasn't come yet!"

"There's no time to wait for them!" cried Giora, "Let's go!"

The companies advanced, one after the other. By the light of the great fire from the burning Jordanian depot and of the tracers, they saw soldiers moving along the communications trench and beyond it. Through the upper windows of the Police School, they saw the figures of groups of men passing along its entire length, mopping up.

From all sides shouts were heard: "Onward! Forward!" Everyone moved except Simon who, meanwhile, had recovered but was waiting for orders from Shlomo. He did not know that Shlomo had gone forward with Giora.

The battalion commander and his group were near the trenches. Immediately after the breakthrough, he had come to the spot where he stood now and directed the advance of the paratroopers. When A Company had crossed, he ordered the tanks to stop firing—the speed of the advance should not be slowed by his own tank and artillery fire. The men were in high fettle, moving forward. In the trench they saw the Jordanian casualties. Between the barriers were our own dead and wounded, waiting to be evacuated.

Uri Freund, the battalion doctor, worked like an automaton. Even before he managed to set up his station at the selected site, the wounded started to reach him. He dealt with them on the spot although the site was not appropriate, as shells were falling all around him and every now then volleys of bullets filled the air. But he had no alternative. So he placed his casualty clearing station "temporarily" at the spot. Mevurah died. Three wounded were treated and Uri wanted to send them further to the rear, but when a salvo of shells fell in the open space behind him, he realized the danger involved in transferring them was greater than the danger of keeping them on the spot.

An order came from Doron, the deputy battalion commander, to move closer to the breach. Ginger came to help with the transportation. The casualty clearing station moved and one of the men was hit. They were still bandaging him when a wave of wounded reached them. The doctor was worried—he was not sure that all the men knew where his station was not situated.

He sent runners forward to the houses in front to evacuate the wounded and to bring them to him. Doron sent Bloom, and others wounded in the breakthrough, to the rear. The medics received them and put them in the passage in the house. Doron himself briefed the wounded and the medics where to go to reach Uri, and how to get there.

The doctor asked if he could go on the battalion communications network to announce his position. Unfortunately they didn't manage to make contact. The doctor organized stretchers to hasten the process of evacuation to the rear. Men ran ahead between the breached barriers to take the wounded directly into the shelter of the buildings and into the hands of the medics and doctor.

Shriki, the medic of the recoilless-guns platoon, worked on and on, at top speed. Aharoni arranged that the jeeps of the recoilless guns should be used to transport the wounded. As soon as Shriki completed his first aid, Danny and Uziel took them to the station. On each jeep they placed a man on a stretcher and a less serious case unable to walk, Others, who could walk, were evacuated on foot.

As the number of wounded grew, the men removed a recoilless gun from one of the jeeps, so that it became more serviceable for carrying wounded. Among those evacuated were several Jordanian prisoners, who were treated on the spot. They supported each other until they reached the doctor.

Jordanian fire was still not stopped. In the area of the Sanhedria crossroads, 81-millimeter, 52-millimeter, and mortar shells fell from time to time. Bullets from heavy machine guns from Jordanian posts sprayed sand around the recoilless gunners.

The battalion commander decided to move forward. Dudik's company was still fighting in the trench. Gaby's company was already mopping up in the Police School. Dedi's company was pouring in, while the deputy battalion commander moved with it and directed it on its way. The battalion commander went all along the trench, between it and the wall of the Police School. At the corner of the building, he stopped. From here one could see Dudik's battle area very well; it was the best place from which to direct the forces.

Dedi's company arrived. The battalion commander transferred it toward Ammunition Hill.

There were dense crowds in the area. The Police School was already almost cleared of the enemy. Covering forces of A Company were stationed in the south wing.

Yossi decided to change the direction of the attack by Shamrar's forces on the Hill of the Yellow Rag. Instead of bypassing the Police School on the east and attacking from the rear, he would order Shamrar to attack from the direction of the breach, without outflanking. By this maneuver, the overcrowding of the forces would be reduced, and Shamrar would not be exposed to fire from Ammunition Hill.

From the incline of Dudik's trench, and from the houses at the bottom of Amunition Hill, shots were fired. Dudik's M.G. men were ordered to cover the advance of the troops.

Shamrar arrived. The battalion commander explained his change of plan. Shamrar listened, nodding his understanding, and went on his way.

B Company was supposed to clean up the trenches, but Dudik, the company commander, thought that they were going too slowly. He never stopped roaring orders and trying to hustle his men forward, so as not to lose momentum or allow the Jordanians to recover from the sock of the night attack.

But getting through the maze of trenches became more and more difficult. When Joshua tried to relieve Ilan at the head of the column, he found that the trench was so narrow that two men could not pass each other. So Ilan had to crouch while Joshua clambered clumsily over him. Joshua then ran forward, firing. Very soon he found that his magazine was empty. As he shouted for more ammunition, Yair, armed with an antitank rifle, caught up with him. He couldn't pass so, without thinking twice, he simply grabbed Joshua and threw him out of the trench to the right.

Joshua found himself suddenly out in the open, next to a barbed-wire fence, only two meters away from the high wall of the Police School. Above him he heard the howl of the shells from the tanks, and the crash as they pounded the upper storeys. The earth shook. Joshua tightened his helmet.

Yair went rushing forward in the trench, firing his antitank rifle from his hip. Behind him he heard Ilan, urging the men on; in front of him he heard shots and couldn't tell who was firing at whom. He pressed on until his magazine was finished. When Ilan came up and couldn't get past him, Ilan gave him the same heave-ho that Yair had given Joshua a few minutes before.

An enemy grenade exploded close by, the blast flinging Yair onto the fence to his right. He felt a sharp pain in the thigh, and called to Ilan as he pulled out his personal dressing. In the dark, it was difficult to locate the exact spot of the wound and even more difficult to bandage it himself with shaking hands. But somehow Yair did it.

Mike, the platoon commander, was pressing forward, and the frequent holdups exasperated him. He tapped on the helmet of the man in front of him and yelled, "Move!" The soldier answered evenly: "Mike, we can't. The trench is so narrow that our knapsacks keep getting stuck."

Ilan was again at the head of the column, his Uzi machine gun spraying every meter ahead. In the trench it was pitch dark except for the flashes from the bullets. Beyond the Police School, a huge flame reared up, lighting the whole surface area. But the trench was so deep that those inside could see nothing.

As Ilan's eyes searched for enemies, his feet became entangled in wires and he struck his head against a wooden beam running across the width of the trench. Mike's patience gave out and he leapt out of the trench. "Trench blocked," roared Ilan. Behind him, he heard the instinctive order of Nir, the company sergeant: "Climb up! Pass on the right." The squad clambered up. A grenade exploded next to them. Yair saw in horror that the spearhead force had been cut down to almost nothing. Every member of the group had been wounded, although Ilan, with a piece of shrapnel in his neck, ran on. Menderer was hit in the hand; Totah, in the elbow; Benny, in the leg; Itzik, in the head. Totah's wound was the worst. The bone of the elbow jutted out, filling him with panic.

"Medic! Medic! My bone's sticking out!"

Yair, who had finished bandaging himself, called to Totah and whispered a few soothing words to calm him down. In the trench, the men continued to make their way forward. Itzik managed to say to Magril, the section commander, "I've been wounded!" Magril answered, "Sit at the side and wait," and went off. When a medic, Zohar, arrived, he attended the wounded, but didn't help to take them back—instead he apologized to them and said, "I think I must go on. They'll need me more up front."

The wounded didn't make it hard for him. "Sure. Go on. We'll manage."

From close by came the sound of shots and the explosions of grenades. One of the *chevra* suggested to the wounded that they should wait in the trench to be evacuated.

Zohar did not get very far. A Jordanian grenade hit him and Ivan, the quartermaster, and both were thrown into the trench. Dudik urged the company on. The narrowness of the trench, now filled with wounded, made movement difficult. The shots and grenades exploding in front and behind confused the soldiers. In the darkness it was impossible to distinguish between ours and theirs. From the bottom of the trench, cries could be heard every so often: "Be careful! Don't tread on me! I'm wounded!"

Dudik thought of only one thing: "Forward . . . Forward . . ." He roared, pushed, spurred the men on.

The platoon commanders were doing the same: Svika and Yoav rushed among their men urging them forward. But Yoav stopped for a second beside Yair, his great friend.

"What happened to you?"

"Wound in the thigh."

"Let me see," said Yoav. When he realized that the bandage was loose, he tightened it. "See you, Yair," he said.

Ilan saw from above that Dudik and the *chevra* were passing below him, and he got back in the trench. There he saw Eli, commander of the Mags, and was pleased. "Things were moving," he said to himself. Running along, he saw three bodies, close together. Since they were Jordanians, he thought: "Must have been from Yair's antitank guns. Must tell him about this later. He'll be thrilled." He went on his way. Now the trench was free and the *chevra* in front were racing ahead.

Dudik stopped beside the three bodies to make sure the Jordanians were dead. He had had a frightening experience. When he jumped into the trench from the embankment, he had seen two Jordanian corpses stretched out, and everyone else had been sure the men were dead. But Dudik noticed that one of them moved, and he carried a radio on his back. Dudik finished the Jordanian off—he didn't want any of his men killed through carelessness. Nir was shouting up front, "Don't stop! Don't waste a second. The fellows behind us will clean up. Come on!"

On the left side of the trench, black gaps appeared at intervals. These were the openings to machine-gun posts and bunkers. The cleanup required a great deal of ammunition. As a result, there was a constant change in the leadership of the squad, as ammunition was finished: Nir—Kendel—Shoka—Monk.

Every post required a grenade and a volley of shots from a Uzi. When the magazines were finished, the first man shouted "Magazine finished!" and sprawled on the ground, and the man behind stepped over him and advanced, firing. The others followed, and then the first man got up. Fresh magazines and grenades were sent forward from the rear. Passing them from hand to hand took less time than would have been needed to bring them up in the narrow trenches. Suddenly they came upon a larger bunker than the others. Avraham Katan—with a bazooka in his hand—ran swiftly forward. Urieli bumped into Shoka and stopped for a moment. When he started off again, he suddenly saw a figure in the trench and, not knowing that Katan was ahead of him, and before Katan could call out, "It's me, Katan," Urieli fired. Fortunately, only a ricochet hit Katan in the leg.

Urieli, appalled to think that he had nearly killed his comrade, sighed with relief. Dudik reached Katan and told him to go back and get medical attention.

Katan wouldn't go. He put on a bandage himself, tested his leg, and rushed after the *chevra*.

A whole group, cut off from the company during the breakthrough, now ran through the trench. But at the sight of the wounded they stopped. They felt that they could not leave the wounded there. They passed their ammunition forward and helped to evacuate their comrades to the rear.

This was the group led by Itzik Yifat and Zvika. When they had reached the breach in the fence, Zvika's platoon had cut into Cabi's A Company, which had advanced after B Company. When they had emerged to Zvika's left, they had separated him from Yoav's forces in front. In spite of the shouts, "Company A, to the right," "Company B, to the left," the result was a real mess.

In the communication trench, Yoav and Chaim organized a small private war at the rear of the advancing forces. From a post on the left they heard a suspicious rustle. Yoav threw a grenade. While it was still in the air, Chaim pushed the barrel of his rifle into the opening of the post and sprayed the interior with fire. The explosion of the grenade covered them with dust. Then they ran forward again.

Now the company was scattered all along the trench. The company commanders went ahead, while behind them other men waged "private wars" with the Jordanians in posts which the spearhead squad had bypassed.

The battalion commander with his staff had also got ahead of the soldiers fighting below in the trenches. In his desire to set up a suitable command position on the battlefield as soon as possible, Yossi had advanced over the open area between the trench and the wall of the Police School. The wounded, seeing the staff, felt an added sense of security; the men fighting in the trench, hearing the movement and voices speaking Hebrew, decided that they had to move even faster in the trench to catch up with the command above them.

A dazed Jordanian, looking for a way to escape, entered the line without realizing it, until suddenly Yossi Leibowitz noticed him, disarmed him and took him prisoner before he could do any damage.

Tzuriel, the redhead, holding a Mag, and swarthy Naphtali, with a machine gun, rushed forward to catch up with those in front of them. Tzuriel's legs got entangled in the mesh of wires, and, just as Naphtali tried to free him, a Jordanian soldier jumped into the trench. He saw Naphtali, ran backwards, and disappeared into a bunker. Naphtali had not managed to distinguish who he was. "Ours, or not?" he asked himself. "Hey, you, in there—who are you?" he and Tzuriel roared. When nobody answered, Naphtali threw a grenade into the post and waited for the explosion. When the smoke and dust settled, not a sound was heard. Puffing and panting, Tzuriel succeeded in freeing his legs from the tangle and, in their excitement, both men leapt out of the trench to get around the obstacle.

From behind, another section was pushing forward. Dumbinsky and Merchavi—Tzuriel's number two—tried to catch up with their number one, in vain. The narrow trench maddened them. Suddenly a gigantic figure seemed to loom above them. Eytan Naveh had got tired of running in the trench, and he had climbed up "to get a breath of fresh air."

At the corner of a house Yossi and his staff waited. When he arrived there, Eli, the Mag company commander, decided to bring up a weapon to protect them from any fire from the open square between the building and Givat Hamivtar. Rocky was exactly in front of him. He shouted, "Rocky—get above me to cover me."

Rocky jumped up and tried to shoot, but the Mag wouldn't work. Rocky told Eli that Menderer, his number two, had been wounded on the way. Shwartz turned to Eli: "Should I go up to replace Menderer?" Eli said, "Yes!" Shwartz leapt up and stretched out beside Rocky.

The rest of the men went on moving in the trench. They were in a weird sort of line as if waiting for a movie rather than searching for enemies to kill in bunkers and strongpoints.

Gordon joined Shwartz and Rocky jumped back into the trench.

To his right, Shwartz saw Doron. He was standing at the corner of the house and directing the fire. "Be careful of the *chevra* who are crossing the fence," Doron called to him. The crowd of signalers was close to the wall. In the intervals between the volleys, Shwartz noticed that it had suddenly become quiet, almost too quiet. The tanks had stopped shooting. The Jordanians were hardly firing.

The two slipped back into the trench.

"Stay here and cover the evacuation of the wounded," Doron ordered, and turned with his signalers to join Yossi, who was already going forward with Dadi.

Rocky, Shwartz, and Gordon moved to the gap in the fence and set up their machine guns. Not far from them, on the left wall of the trench, was a small strongpoint. "Yoram, go and see if there's somebody there," Shwartz whispered. Yoram peeped in, came back and said, "It's O.K." The three scoured the area with trained eyes. To their right, a figure appeared—Zohar, the medical orderly. Another figure came from the left. This time it was a Legionnaire, grenade in hand. Gordon cut him down with a burst. The Jordanian fell, but the open hand grenade rolled out of his hand. Before the *chevra* could jump backward or lie down, the grenade exploded. All four were wounded: Zohar and Shwartz lightly, Rocky and Gordon seriously. Yisraeli, Amit, and

Ninio, himself wounded but able to move about, bandaged Shwartz and Zohar. Amit ran back to alert medics to evacuate Rocky and Gordon.

Yisraeli and Ninio took Shwartz outside the trench. Suddenly, about a step away from them, an armed Jordanian appeared. Ninio fired, a rapid burst. The Jordanian fell.

Perspiration streamed down their faces.

Shwartz went to the rear by himself while Yisraeli and Ninio remained to guard the badly wounded until they were evacuated. The medic, Uri Ben-Zeev, soon arrived, and, after further treatment, Rocky and Gordon were evacuated to the rear.

The battle in the trench was still raging. Now Buki, a platoon commander in D Company, came in with his platoon. He had been told to wait for orders from Giora, the company commander, but hadn't received any, so decided to move without them. Ganz, the company sergeant major, tried to stop him, but in vain.

In the trench and above it were the walking wounded, while medics carried the more seriously wounded. Motke and Ochna stepped out of the trench at the head of the line of men. Suddenly a shot was fired at Motke from a nearby post. The bullet passed close to his head and hit Ochna, who fell and did not get up. Ganz leapt at the post and threw a grenade inside it, and the post was silenced. Buki and his platoon continued to the corner of the building, where they joined Yossi with the advance command group, as did Ganz.

Later, a letter came from Ochna from his father, who lived abroad; it had been mailed before Ochna was killed. Ochna had been alone in Israel for twelve years. "My dear son, at last the time has come to join you. I am coming to settle in Israel . . ."

Ilan and Eli, who had stopped next to the Mags at the corner of the building, came back for reinforcements. In front of them, Debach was running with his rifle when suddenly the three saw volleys of tracer bullets from an enemy strongpoint aimed at the spot where the company was concentrated. The three stopped and pulled the safety catches on their grenades and threw them in one joint salvo. They followed the grenades with machine-gun bursts and rifle shots. Three explosions were heard, one after the other, and the tracer bullets stopped.

Kendel went to the head of the line, Uzi in hand, and behind him came Binyamini with a rifle. At this point the trench continued straight for some distance, and Kendel could see no sign of the enemy. Suddenly, from the left, two Jordanians sprang as though out of the ground. They gaped for a moment, not knowing where to turn. Then they rushed straight at Kendel. "I shot at them," Kendel said afterward, "but they continued to run toward me. I stopped where I was and went on with a long nonstop burst. In the momentum of their rush, they reached one meter from me—and then they fell."

From the corner of his eye, Kendel saw another figure fleeing to the left. While still changing the magazine, he passed Binyamini and gave chase to the fugitive Jordanian.

They came to another long trench. Binyamini ran into it, spraying it with quick shots. The trench curved and then forked, each fork leading to a post. Binyamini swiftly hurled his grenades into the two posts and followed them with rifle fire. After the explosions, there was complete silence. Binyamini believed that the enemy were destroyed. Sweating and excited, he turned back and took his place again behind Kendel, still in the lead. All of a sudden, Kendel heard a single shot behind him— and a cry.

"I turned around—Binyamini was stretched out on his back. I threw a grenade into the post and knelt down to see what had happened to him. Binyamini was dead. I went back to the main trench to inform the *chevra*."

Later Kendel returned to take his place in the line.

* * *

When Dudik arrived at the junction of the trenches, he ordered the group forming the spearhead to move along the main trench and not to turn left. Some meters on, they came to a second fork. This was the objective originally set for the company. So Dudik took the microphone and told Yossi: "We are at the fork. Mission accomplished."

Yossi was standing next to Dadi, commander of C Company, at the position chosen for the breakthrough to Ammunition Hill. He did not want to lose the momentum of the attack, so he asked Dudik: "Do you think you can carry on to reach Ammunition Hill?"

"It seems to me yes," answered Dudik. "I'll check immediately."

Dudik looked around. To the right, there were three double-storey buildings next to each other. In front of him towered Ammunition Hill. A little to the rear stretched a long wall and next to it, in the open area, a car and a recoilless gun jeep were on fire. "By the time the *chevra* finish, we'd better organize perimeter defense," Dudik decided. He placed a squad on the right to cover the open space.

The platoon commanders Yoav and Zvika arrived, each with only a handful of soldiers. Only now did it become clear to Dudik how hard the company had been hit. Only with difficulty could he muster a platoon fit for action. From the stories of the men, he gathered that the reorganization of the company would take much longer than he had thought at first. Once again, he called Yossi: "I'm sorry, but I find we've had heavy losses, and that the company is scattered. I'm afraid we'll have to stick to the first plan. Use Dadi's company to tackle Ammunition Hill."

"Right," Yossi decided. "We'll start at once. You reorganize and get ready to move in support."

Dudik turned to his men. First of all he warned them not to fire to the right, because Dadi's company would be crossing there very shortly. This order disturbed Naphtali. By the light of the burning jeep, he had discerned the figure of a soldier. With his finger about to press the trigger, he stopped because of Dudik's order and shouted out, "Password!" But he didn't wait for an answer, because he made out a Jordanian helmet, and fired a short burst. The Jordanian fell.

Dudik reorganized the men left in his company. He put a platoon under Mike in reserve. They had been in the van until now, and had earned a short rest. The platoons of Yoav and Zvika—or what remained of them—were sent forward. It was difficult to organize them into battle squads, so few were left. First came Omri's squad; then Zvika's depleted platoon, then a squad led by Yoav.

Nir, the deputy company commander, moved ahead of the company to wait for its advance on the battlefield. Now he returned, his hand to his eye. He had been hit by a piece of shrapnel from a grenade, and his eye was full of blood. Dudik sent him to the rear for medical attention.

Men used the lull in the fighting to rebuild their stock of ammunition and to work out what had happened to their missing comrades. Now there was time to translate casualties into personal pain. The men who were dead and wounded were not just gaps in the platoons but bosom friends of long standing, closer than brothers through the intense comradeship of war.

While reloading the magazines, the *chevra* swapped experiences and impressions: how they killed, how they were wounded, how they had had to go over corpses—ours, theirs. The hands and clothes of many of them were defiled with blood. The officers held a hasty conference. They too exchanged impressions. They were hoarse from shouting endless orders to the men.

Thus there were mixed feelings—deep sorrow about the dead and wounded, great satisfaction because of the perfect execution of their assignment. The officers summed up the position so far.

The casualties had been far worse than they realized during the fighting.

During the time that Giora's B Company was engaged in cutting through the barricades, the men of A Company remained sitting under the shelter of the wall of the Evacuees' House. They felt shut in, isolated, almost claustrophobic. From all sides they heard the sounds of shots and explosions—but they were not participating in the action. The curious who dared to raise their heads saw tanks maneuvering backward and forward amid mortar fire from the Jordanians, who now realized that the tanks were firing on the Police School.

Shells exploded in the open square in front of the school and they watched these anxiously, concerned lest some of our men might be there. Sometimes they looked up into the sky, where tracer bullets shed brilliant light above the blacked-out city. Some Jordanian shells crashed into the walls of the nearby houses, and shrapnel and rock splinters flew in all directions. Then even the most inquisitive lowered their heads.

Suddenly they got the order to go into action. The company advanced toward the fences. Danny, the sergeant of C Platoon, was wounded, and had to return to the stairwell. Later that afternoon, after treatment, he rejoined the company.

Crossing the open area went slowly. There was dense crowding at the front—no one asked why. From the northern end of the trench next to the Police School, the Jordanians were shooting high, at random. They heard shouts from the front, and orders: "Bangalore—explosion!" "Lie down!" "Get up!" "Advance!" "Sit!" "Back!" "Enough!" "Kneel!" "Bangalore!"

Ami, the deputy company commander, rushed forward to find out what was going on, why there was such confusion.

Gabi studied the Police School. Earlier, when the officers had toured the area, an armored car of the Border Patrol had passed through the Evacuees' Houses and the Jordanians had shot at it constantly from the second floor of the Police School, and from the Hill of the Yellow Rag to the south. Now there was almost no shooting from these points. The smoke of the exploding banga-lores made observation very difficult.

Gabi went forward, wondering if the tanks had driven the enemy out.

The company reached an area just in front of the last fence, where the men sat and waited for orders. In front of them were the wounded from B Company. Calls for medics mingled with the shouts of the officers. Finally came the order for which they were waiting—"A Company! Advance!"

In front they saw torch signals and heard shouts: "Breach! Breach!"

Gabi and Ami were in the lead. They climbed on the embank-ment, passed the signalers, and turned half-right in the direction of the main door of the Police School. A cattle fence stopped them. Somebody pulled out a wire-cutter and cut a gap. They went through on the double, avoided the entrance hall on the right, and reached the main door.

They went inside. The darkness inside the building seemed to be as absolute as was the silence.

During the advance at the double the platoons of Companies B and D were mixed with those of Company A. This caused great confusion. Pinia took his platoon, which had arrived first, into the building and up to the right wing. When Gadi went in with his platoon, Gabi appeared on the stairs, and directed them to the left wing. Ofer and his platoon arrived and went up the stairs, according to the original plan, without knowing that two other platoons were already operating in the building.

Fortunately, Gabi came to the stairs again, and shouted to Ofer: "Go back! You're not needed inside. Clean up down below on the left side of the building."

The *chevra* smiled knowingly to each other. The usual mixup. They hadn't gone up yet, and already they had to go back.

Ami placed the Mag section under the command of Uri Dan, the platoon commander, in a position to fire on The Hill of the Yellow Rag. Because of the fire from the hill in the afternoon, and the plan that Shamrar would only reach there to clean up later on, he decided that he had to safeguard the flank.

The whole company was now in action in the school. Two platoons were in the top storeys, a divided platoon was operating below, and the Mag force was covering the flank. The crates of the Mags were piled outside the main door, so that they wouldn't interfere in the mopping-up operations in the rooms.

According to Gabi's orders at the time of the briefing, the men were organized in two-man squads to clean up the rooms. When one couple entered a room, the second couple went on to the next room.

The long passages were completely dark. Only here and there did glimmers of light come through the windows from the burning store and the bursting shells. After each flash, the returning darkness seemed even blacker. The men tripped and fell. Outstretched hands groped like those of a blind man. The officers decided that it was impossible to operate in such a way, and flashed on their pocket torches, despite the risk of attracting fire.

When the order of the platoons had been changed, Pinia's platoon had been the first to enter the building. The stairs were dark. From outside, they heard shots. Inside it was quiet. They ran quickly up the stairs. A passage went off to the right. The quiet continued. The platoon went past doors and windows. Along the passage to the left they glimpsed Gabi's platoon. Pinia reached the end of the corridor. All was clear and the right wing was secure. Pinia signaled this to Gabi by flashing his torch.

When Gadi reached the main door of the Police School, he

found no one there but a single sentry, who knew nothing about what was going on inside. Gadi stopped for a second, fearing that in the darkness inside the building his platoon and Pinia's might clash. Suddenly Gabi came down from the top of the stairs and directed them to the left wing, the one from which the Jordanian soldiers had fired in the afternoon. Yonaton's section went into action, Eytan, the platoon sergeant, at its head.

The *chevra*, bending down instinctively, advanced, stooping. Eytan opened a door with a kick and threw a grenade inside. When it exploded, he rushed in to the left wall, and Yonatan rushed to the right. They fired short burst to both sides.

Outside, Yonatan S. and Arik were waiting for their turn to clean up the next room. During the briefing, they had been instructed to wait until somebody came out of the first room to announce it was cleaned up. Now they waited for a few moments, and then decided to go on. In the next room, they did not throw a grenade—but only shot bursts with their machine guns.

Gadi realized that there were no enemy soldiers in the room and ordered the men to stop firing. Then he took a torch and flashed a beam around and saw no one.

They decided that the cleaning up could be done just by checking the rooms, so Eytan and Yonatan placed themselves at each side of the door and Gadi lighted up the inside through the top windows. For most rooms, this light was sufficient, but there were some rooms so large that the beam of light did not reach far enough. Here Gadi smashed the window with the butt of his Uzi and they went in. All were empty.

From the end of the corridor, Gadi signaled to Pinia. They turned to clean up the corridor connecting them jointly.

Eytan and Yonatan broke into locked rooms. Uzi bullets smashed the locks easily. The mopping-up was completed without their encountering any resistance.

At the conclusion of the operation, Gadi instructed his platoon to take up positions along the outside wall on the west side of the building. From the school windows, they saw blacked-out Jerusalem below them. The buildings of the Fagi neighborhood and the Evacuees' Houses were opposite. Right underneath them, the evacuation of wounded was still taking place.

They realized how strong the Jordanian position was, and how exposed the assault forces. Yet they had made it. The *chevra* took out boxes of ammunition and loaded magazines for the next phase of the battle.

Ofer divided his platoon into two. He sent Gadi's section to the right wing where Ami joined them. Ammon's section was allocated to the left wing, where they were joined by Ofer himself. To cover their advance, he instructed Ammon to fire a few bursts into the corridor. Uzi volleys and dense rifle shots raised a great echo.

Taking advantage of this cover, Alon and Yehuda ran into the first room, together breaking in the door and jumping inside—each in a different direction—firing their rifles as they did so. No enemy. Ammon rushed into the second room while Issachar stayed on guard. Ammon entered, close to the left wall, and fired a burst with his Uzi. Still no enemy.

Ofer decided to stop the shooting. As there was no resistance, there was no reason to waste ammunition. "Stop firing, everybody!" The order reached every corner. Zeev and Rafi examined the third room. The door was shut. They kicked it open and combed the place, but no one was there. Ofer went forward with the torch. The cleanup proceeded quickly. They went back to the entrance and met the second half of the platoon.

On being sent to the right wing, Ami ran ahead. To the right were the toilets, to the left, in the wall, a locked door made of colored glass. This roused his suspicion and he broke the upper windowpane and threw in a grenade. It didn't explode. A second grenade made the door fly in his face. It was enough to glance in—no need to shoot. The section continued to clean up the rest of the rooms. Ami opened each door and fired a short blast. No fire was returned.

While the cleanup action was still proceeding in the building, the company commander sent forces onto the roof to make sure that there were no Jordanians there. Ami, the deputy company commander, led the men. He found that the roof was empty. The only movement was caused by water running from the tank that was hit. Gabi and his staff went up to the roof. From there they saw five Jordanians running from the building in the direction of Givat Hamivtar. The Police School was clean and Gabi returned to the men.

Ami commanded Pinia to send two men up on the roof to secure it, and then joined Gabi. Gabi reported to the battalion commander: "The school is in our hands. All cleaned up."

After they had rested for a short while, an order came from the battalion commander: "Prepare to move in the direction of the Ambassador Hotel. I'm waiting for you at the roadblock at the exit from the Police School. Leave a platoon to guard the school. Shmerer's force will relieve them later—then they can join you."

Gabi organized his company accordingly.

In the afternoon, when the officers were inspecting the battle-field, they had seen enemy movements on a hill south of Police School. From this hill the enemy were able to shell the area of the breach, so it had to be neutralized as soon as possible. In the center of the hill somebody had hung a yellow blanket or cloth, so they called it the "Hill of the Yellow Rag." Yossi ordered an artillery bombardment of the site, and also allocated a special force under Shmerer to take it.

This force was composed of platoons of shock troops and reconnaissance men. While Shmerer examined the photograph that Yossi held, Yossi told him, "I want you to attack from behind the hill. The enemy trenches, guns, and forces are all deployed in the direction of the breakthrough area. So I don't want a frontal attack. If you move behind Dadi's company, you can storm the hill from the rear."

It seemed to Shmerer that the hill was small, and that he didn't need two platoons to take it. "Take them," said Yossi. "If you don't need them, all the better."

Shmerer went down to brief his men about the mission. He appointed Rafi's platoon to lead the advance. The reconnaissance platoon would follow. There was no time to study the movement axis or any complicated maneuvers. So Shmerer said: "I'll lead as far as the trench. You mop up."

It was just before they got into the buses that Zami, the reconnaissance platoon commander, arrived. Shmerer brought him up to date as to the nature of the assignment in a few words. "And the rest, we'll explain and carry out in the field," he concluded in haste, and the two jumped into the bus.

In the deployment area, under cover of the Evacuees' Houses and the stone walls between them, the force assembled behind Dadi's company. Jordanian bombs fell close by, and shells and machine-gun bullets whistled among the houses. While moving toward the fences and passing through them, Shmerer took a look at the scene of action. From the photograph he identified the front wall, the grove, the house he had to reach, and the recoilless gun post next to it.

When he reached the last fence, Shmerer turned left and began to move along the wall of the Police School, according to plan. At the corner, he found Yossi and his staff.

"Shmerer, stop. It's too crowded here. I've decided to change the plan. Instead of bypassing the building, and getting mixed up with Dadi's and Gabi's companies, take your force back and storm the trench and the wall, from north to south."

With shouts, Shmerer turned the force round and ran. In the

trenches and next to them there were already many killed and wounded.

When he reached the southern corner of the building, Shmerer found the trench assigned to him. But when he looked back he saw that, besides Rafi, there were only four other men with him.

"Rafi, men are missing. We'll have to slow down a bit until they all collect."

Shmerer stopped at the entrance to the trench. Rafi slowed down too, but continued forward and entered the trench. Shmerer called out: "Here, to me!" Various groups of soldiers, lost and looking for their units, collected there. He sorted out his men and hurried on after Rafi. Movement in the narrow, deep trench was difficult. The walls were upright, made of a mixture of cement and stones, some of which stuck out. On the right were strong-points and bunkers, and on the left the slope of the hill and a maze of trenches.

Rafi and two soldiers functioned as a spearhead squad. Shooting Uzis and throwing grenades, they moved forward, mopping up the trench in front of them.

Shmerer overtook them. Behind him he posted a radio technician. Running in the narrow trench with a heavy radio was very tiring. Every now and then Shmerer was compelled to stop so as to help the radio man pass the sharp protruding stones.

They suddenly saw a large object looming ahead in the darkness. "Recoilless gun!" somebody shouted.

"Look out! I'm throwing a grenade!" Splinters of phosphorus lighted up the area a little. No enemy was seen. The recoilless gun, on a jeep, began to burn. As the fire grew stronger, shells of the gun, which because of holes in their cases had not exploded, caught fire. Then they exploded like fireworks on Independence Day, but nobody was amused, because shrapnel flew in all directions.

The only way to advance was to jump out of the trench and go around the burning gun. Shmerer leapt out, went round the gun, and returned to the trench on the other side of it. "Follow me!" he ordered. The cleanup of the trench continued.

Dawn broke. Instead of the gloom lit by burning flashes there was the early morning light. Now Shmerer could see a communication trench on his left, running down the hill slope. All along its length were strongpoints. The nearest force to it was Rafi's platoon.

"Rafi, take the trench on the left and mop it up. But take care—Gabi's platoon is round about there somewhere!"

As he turned back in the trench, Shmerer called Zami's platoon to him: "Zami, forward! Come up to me!" he roared. Rafi went to the communication trench while Shmerer waited. Further back, Zami and the reconnaissance men skirted the exploding recoilless gun and ran up to Shmerer. He told Zami, who was still puffing and panting, "Move along this trench to its end. Clean up the house too. I am going on with Rafi. Send one squad to examine the second house as well."

Rafi's men went one after the other to the left, from the main trench into the communication trench.

A machine gun was stationed near one of the bunkers to provide cover. Suddenly a Jordanian leapt out of the bunker. "Shoot him!" Rafi roared. But the machine gun did not fire—the machine was empty. "The hell—ammunition finished!" The Jordanian, no doubt thanking Allah for his miraculous survival, disappeared.

In the growing light they could see that no enemy were left in the trenches. Rafi ordered them to advance without firing. The movement was carried out quickly, as was the cleanup of the house. A section went up to the roof, but found no one there.

The men were disappointed. "Call this war? Not even one Jordanian here to make it worth all the trouble!"

Yossi tried to reach Shmerer on the command radio but

failed. He was concerned about the platoon's fate, so Zvika decided to go ahead and to discover what had happened. He found Shmerer and Rafi, exultant at the ease with which they had accomplished the first mission.

"Get your force together," Zvika commanded Shmerer, "and move to the school building. There you'll receive new orders." Zvika returned to Yossi.

Shmerer sent for Zami's force to come back from the end of the trench to the south of the fortification. But Zami had not yet completed his mission. He had decided to comb the two-storey house which dominated the trenches. Zami, keeping close to the wall, shouted to the people to come out but heard no reply. "I kicked the door. It did not open. I called for an antitank gunner. We went down into the trench and I told him to shoot at the door. He shot. It opened."

Zami entered and sprayed the first room with bullets and grenade. Opposite him there were stairs going up. He took up a position on the side, and shouted for more *chevra*. Sergeant Toledano stayed with a covering force below, while Zami with two squads went above. They threw a grenade into a room, fired bullets. No reaction. Opposite them stretched a long corridor with many rooms. "After the grenade, we entered the room. We saw that it was empty. It looked like a command post: books and kitchen. I judged that the whole house must be empty. We went from room to room. Any door which was closed we forced open. But in fact the whole house was empty."

From below, they heard shots. A Jordanian soldier had tried to escape, but this one was unlucky. Shaul Karo said laconically, "This time there were bullets in the magazine."

The reconnaissance men continued mopping-up operations without having to fire. Beside the house to the south they found a jeep and recoilless gun, intact and in good condition. Nobody answered their shouts when they moved to the next house, and they decided to break in by force. At the noise of breaking glass, an old Arab appeared and assured them there was no one in the house. Zami decided to search for himself—he suspected that the recoilless gun team must be in the vicinity. In one room, there was a large cupboard, which Zami pulled open, revealing an old woman and a young couple. After a short conversation, Zami let them be. At that moment the order came from Shmerer to leave and Zami turned and went outside, gathering his men to return.

While waiting for Zami, Shmerer had toured the battlefield. The results of the artillery barrage were apparent everywhere. There were deep holes in the ground and trees had been cut down. Suddenly someone yelled: "Gideon, stop. There's an Arab soldier here."

Gideon aimed his gun into a broken eucalyptus tree lying on the ground. A Jordanian sniper came out from behind it, his hands up, and they took him captive.

"There's another Jordanian soldier in the post," they called to Shmerer from the trench.

"Bring him out."

"He won't come."

Gideon sent his captive inside to persuade the other man to surrender. He succeeded. When they came out of the entrance to the bunker, they jumped over the dead bodies of their comrades—one in the trench, one in the entrance to the post, one, an officer, inside it. The *chevra* returned to the Police School with their two prisoners. There they helped in the evacuation of the wounded, who had begun to arrive from all the companies. Yossi sent an order to Shmerer: "Take up positions in the Police School and free Pinia's platoon, so that they can join the company on their way to the Ambassador Hotel."

Yossi decided to go on toward the battalion's final objectives, which, for this stage of the battle for Jerusalem, were two hospitals at the crossroads and the Ambassador Hotel. He ordered Giora and Gabi to bring their companies to him at the roadblock near the Police School. Shmerer's force relieved Gabi's company at the Police School. He instructed the tanks to come to him quickly and sent Tiger, the operations sergeant, to bring forward the casualty clearing station.

While these orders were being given, Yossi and his staff arrived near the roadblock, only to be suddenly subjected to a salvo of fire from a hut near the roadblock. Micha, the operations officer, and Jackie, the communications officer, raced toward it to mop it up. Jackie went to the left, Micha to the wall, where he got out a grenade. A bullet hit Jackie. Micha threw the grenade, but the window was barred by a grid and the grenade fell outside. He broke the grid and threw in another grenade, which exploded.

At that moment, Giora's company arrived. They evacuated Jackie for treatment and went into battle.

Giora's company was almost at full strength. It moved in the following order: Buki's platoon, Zvika's platoon, Aharon's Mags, and Reuven's platoon. To the left of the company and in front of it the thunder of explosions and shots continued. Every now and then support troops were called on to perform local mopping-up operations. The company did not wait for these to end, but hurried on, and very soon met Yossi at the road leading to the Ambassador Hotel.

Yossi explained the plan to Giora: Advance the full length of the road and take control of the Ambassador Hotel area. Behind them, Gabi's company would capture the hospital area.

Buki and Arzi approached the gate of the roadblock. It was locked and reinforced by an intricate chain. Micha came up to help them to open it. Angel's section carried Jackie to the casualty clearing station.

The gate was opened. Giora instructed Buki how and where to advance, and Buki began to move. Behind him, explosions and shots were still audible. To his right, in a row, stood a few houses, white and beautiful, surrounded by flowering gardens and fenced with chiseled Jerusalem stone. To the left stood a very large building with many rooms. It was a girls' school. South of it there was an open area, which stretched up to Givat Hamivtar. Opposite were the hospitals, high, dominating the road.

The flag of the Spanish Consulate flew on one of the buildings to the right. Giora, moving close to Buki, instructed him to check the building, and Buki sent a force to do so. The company stopped and a number of men with Mags and machine gunners took up firing positions facing the open area; they were helped by a roadblock of stones and earth.

Suddenly the company was fired on from the houses on the slope of Givat Hamivtar and from the environs of the girls' school. One bullet hit Avraham's smoke "candle"; another struck the spade with which Dov was digging and ricocheted onto a crate of Mags, where it remained stuck between the chains.

Reuven, the platoon commander, and Wagnets, the company sergeant major, rushed left to the fence and swept the yard of the girls' school with grenades. Shneider shot off a long burst. The Mags and machine-guns joined in the firing to prevent any possible enemy attack.

Buki's section reached the roof of the Spanish Consulate and found the house was empty. Three Jordanians were seen crossing the open area from the direction of Ammunition Hill toward the hospitals, and everyone opened fire on them.

They were hit and fell. Tanks could be heard approaching from the direction of the Police School. They were coming to help gain control of the area. The *chevra* continued along the southern line of houses while the tanks provided cover for their advance.

The machine-gun fire and the appearance of the tanks obviously deterred the Jordanians and their fire ceased, so the advance on the Ambassador Hotel proceeded without further hindrance.

Men from Giora's D Company entered the hotel, where they found everything quiet and serene. Giora instructed them to comb all floors immediately, and to place security and fire-fighting forces everywhere. "On no account is anyone to touch anything valuable, and lying on the beds is not permitted," he ordered sternly.

Arzi sent security sections into the garden that was in the back courtyard. The group of company commanders went to the roof to plan the continuation of the action, and came down again immediately.

The platoon of tanks stopped for a few minutes. They were waiting for Gilboa's platoon, which had been delayed by a minefield.

Yossi ordered D Company to remain in the hotel and to clean up the surroundings.

Giora rested for a moment. The picture of his family kept coming into his mind. Ami Gilboa stood beside him, and Giora turned to him: "Wait a minute, Ami. I want to send a postcard home." Giora pulled out a pen and began to write in square letters.

"Why are you writing like that?" Ami asked.

"It's for the children. So that they can read it . . ."

As soon as Gabi received Yossi's order to come to the roadblock, he moved forward with two platoons, Gadi's and Ofer's. Pinia and his platoon had to remain at the Police School to defend it until Shmerer's men arrived.

While he was on the move, Yossi instructed Gabi to send a platoon to look for Shmerer's men, because it was impossible to make contact with him on the radio. Gabi selected Ofer's platoon for this job. Ami joined them. Gabi continued on his way toward the roadblock with Gadi's platoon.

Near the UN roadblock, hard by Battalion Command, a volley of shots came from the pine wood on Ammunition Hill. Nehemiah, the platoon medical orderly, was hit in the leg. The stream of blood gushing strongly upward indicated that an artery had been struck. Nehemiah called for help and Gabi applied a tourniquet and a bandage. The shooting continued.

Then came the order to move. Dehan remained with Nehemiah while the rest of the company advanced. Nehemiah heard a rustling noise in the bushes and, by a great effort, he raised and fired his weapon. Dehan too shot into the bushes. Through the branches, a Jordanian soldier came out with his hands up. Dehan disarmed him and stood him up against the wall. But the Jordanian, apparently convinced that they were going to shoot him, tried to run away. Dehan shot and wounded him. Then the Jordanian stopped, came back, and sat down next to his captors.

The two Dorons, the deputy battalion commander and the company medic, came along the road. Doron the medic bandaged Nehemiah anew, and also attended to the wounded Jordanian. Later, in the hospital, Nehemiah and the Jordanian lay in beds next to each other. Dehan rejoined the company.

From the direction of the Police School, Ofer's platoon arrived. They had made contact with Shmerer. Everything was in order. Gabi went to Yossi to get orders. According to the previous plan, he should advance along the road toward the Ambassador Hotel. Yossi said that there was no change in the plan, and Gabi gave orders accordingly.

In the meanwhile, reports came in from Ammunition Hill: all the medics had been wounded. Yossi instructed Gabi to send his medics there.

From Giora's company, en route to the Ambassador, came a report that they were being fired upon from the group of houses on the rise to Givat Hamivtar. This fire might endanger forces in their rear, especially the supply and evacuation vehicles, so Yossi ordered Gabi to send a platoon to mop up the houses. Gabi gave Ofer the assignment, and Ami joined him. Gabi went on toward the Ambassador with two platoons.

The company had only just begun to move when the tanks appeared on their way to the Old City. This was Gilboa's platoon, which had finally gotten through the minefields. Yossi ordered Gabi to allocate a covering force to the tanks for the first time that they had to move among houses. The mission was given to the section led by Eyten and Chaim. Yonatan was stationed with a machine gun to guard against snipers, and the combined force then went on its way.

The rest of the company followed behind. To the left, from Givat Hamivtar, there was continuous fire, more or less accurate. To the right, from within the buildings, the Jordanians, who at first had taken fright when D Company suddenly appeared, were once again sniping. The *chevra* returned fire at every fluttering curtain, and went forward. The tanks seemed to fire in every direction.

At the hospital intersection, the forces split up, the tanks continuing along the Nablus Road to join the two platoons waiting for them there, while Gabi's A Company turned to take control of its objectives: the hospitals and hotel, at the crossroads.

Because of its central position, giving it complete command of the road to Givat Hamivtar, the Eye Hospital was selected as the first objective.

Gadi and his platoon sealed it off from the north; Eytan, with Chaim's section, did the same from the south.

Shots from the tower of the hospital endangered the movement of the squads, so Arik fired a machine gun at the tower and the shooting stopped. The narrow road looked quiet and still. The houses on the left protected the men from fire from Givat Hamivtar. The northern entrance to the hospital was through an inner courtyard, a glorious sanctum of fountains, flowers, and greenery. The relative quiet permitted the *chevra* to enjoy the beauty of the spot.

But in the corridors of the hospital they were reminded that they were at war. As they entered, a Jordanian policeman in uniform appeared, a rifle in one hand, a cartridge belt in the other. From the left, another armed figure emerged. A quick shot chased him back again. The policeman's equipment was removed and he was taken prisoner. A doctor came down the corridor. He said aggressively, as if there were no war, that he had to leave the hospital. Gadi explained politely that outside there was shooting, and that therefore the doctor could not leave. Very angry, the doctor accepted the verdict and stayed. He showed the *chevra* the way to the stairs.

Gadi went with Shalom Levi's section up to the roof, and there they took up positions. In Gadi's knapsack was a flag, originally intended to be hoisted on the El Arish police station. Avner Gilad now hoisted this flag on the flagpole of the hospital. In the first glimmer of morning light, the Legionnaires on Givat Hamivtar saw it and immediately made the hospital a target for concentrated, deliberate artillery fire. Nevertheless Gadi also took the company commanders' staff up and they fixed this roof as the command post for the next stage of the fighting. Next to him was a Mag squad.

On the other side, Eytan and Chaim went through the other wing of the hospital. Eytan and Arik broke in the door with the butt of the machine gun. At the very beginning of the corridor, they came across a great concentration of patients and nurses, trembling and frightened. Eytan calmed them down and placed Zadok there to guard them, before going on. A doctor came out in a white gown and asked something in Arabic, and Chaim translated. It seemed that the doctor was asking for permission to proceed with an important operation. The permission granted, the doctor returned to the operating theater.

They searched the hutments and nearby buildings. The surroundings were clear of the enemy. When Gabi saw that everything was under control in the Eye Hospital, he took a squad in to the French Hospital. The French workers displayed open hostility. When Uri translated what they were saying in French, Gabi took a Mag team onto the roof. The sisters argued that there were no soldiers in the hospital. Their behavior was suspicious, and after a search, eight Jordanian soldiers were discovered lying in bed like patients, their uniforms, cartridge belts, and weapons hidden under the bed. Two more soldiers were found disguised in white gowns, posing as workers in the hospital. All ten of them were taken down to the cellar as prisoners, and Gabi went onto the roof.

Pinia's section now arrived at the intersection. Shmerer's force had come to relieve them and they were now available for further action. The sniping from Givat Hamivtar increased and Yeshayahu was hit.

Gabi instructed them to jump over the fence and take up positions facing Givat Hamivtar. Over the radio Gabi reported to Yossi: "The intersection is mine!"

Yossi ordered him to organize in the intersection and its surroundings, with most of the force facing Givat Hamivtar. Control of this intersection was of the greatest importance to enable the troops to advance into the Old City and up to Mount Scopus. The intersection would safeguard the flank of the whole brigade fighting inside the city. Yossi instructed the company commander of the tanks to station two tanks opposite Givat Hamivtar, so as to safeguard movement on the road and to prevent counterattacks.

Gabi organized the platoons for the two parallel missions. One with automatic weapons faced Givat Hamivtar, its purpose being to pulverize the sources of fire from there, and to prevent any enemy movement. The infantry section was sent into the nearby houses to clear them of snipers' nests.

Ofer's platoon had still not returned, for while their company was still completing the conquest of the hospital intersection, they were also engaged in fighting for Ammunition Hill.

While the companies of Giora and Gabi were advancing toward the taking of the Ambassador Hotel and the hospital intersection, the companies of Dadi and Dudik went on with the fight for Ammunition Hill and its environs.

After crossing through the fence torn apart in the initial artillery bombardment, Yoram's men ran towards the long house. Through the doors and windows, they shot bursts of fire and tossed hand grenades into the dark rooms. The squad then turned to clean up an elevated position, but found it empty.

From Ammunition Hill came the thunder of the shelling. In crossing the wall, Yoram saw a burning van to his right. Next to it was a Jordanian soldier. While running forward, Yoram ordered Heyman, who was alone, to inspect the van and see if it wasn't a booby trap. Heyman, who had just joined the platoon and did not know all the men well, passed the order on to Yochai. Close up against the wall stood Zeev with a bazooka.

At Yochai's command, Zeev turned the weapon on the van and pressed the trigger. The shell struck the van and the Jordanian standing beside the van fell wounded. But the shell also hit the adjacent wall; splinters and shrapnel struck Zeev in the face and Yochai in the legs. The burns on the face were serious and Zeev groaned with pain. On hearing his cries, Shmaya came up and bandaged him. Very soon four medics arrived and Zeev was taken to the rear.

Now the *chevra* began to feel that they were really in a war: the first wounded, Zeev's cries, the burning van, and the shots around them. Tension rose all at once. The flames from the van were accompanied every so often by the explosions of the shells and 0.5-inch bullets that had been inside it.

To the right stood a Jordanian recoilless-gun jeep without a team. In front 25-pound shells were exploding and flaming cones from the pine trees flew in all directions.

Yochai turned aside to inspect his leg. Leibowitz, the orderly from Miller's platoon, bandaged him. His own platoon had been swallowed up in the darkness, so he had attached himself to Miller.

Running past the burning tender, Yoram found himself in the houses of some Jordanian officers. "Send a bazooka ahead!" he roared. Yaacovson ran, lifted Zeev's bazooka from the ground, and passed it up to the front.

They fired a few bursts at the walls of the houses and Yoram rushed between the houses. It was still dark and difficult to make out details. He found that there were communication trenches running between the houses. Yoram jumped into one that turned right, and called: "Yochai's section—to me!" The *chevra* went to him, but explained that Yochai had been wounded. Yoram called to Milmudi: "You lead the section. Spread out to the left and storm the hill."

The command was self-explanatory. They had done this time and again in exercises. The idea was to fight both in the trenches and outside them, especially at night, to get quick results. The fire from Givat Hamivtar continued. The group spread out in formation and advanced. When they had gone a few steps they were blinded by a strong flash accompanied by a mighty explosion. When the smoke cleared, not one man was left standing, and everyone was wounded. Shaul had been flung high up and had fallen to the ground on his back with a tremendous thud. He felt his back and found that he was able to move a little. To the right, Kaplansky was groaning: "Mother! Mother!"

On the left, Milmudi managed to cry: "Shaulik, take command!" and no more. Then Shaulik called to Kaplansky: "Come here. Near me." Kaplansky answered in a stifled voice. "I can't move. I can't!" Uri Feivel did not answer, nor did Yaacovson.

Shaulik crawled over to Kaplansky. "Where are you hurt?" Kaplansky lay on his side, muttering and mumbling. In the dark Shaulik turned Kaplansky on his back and found huge wounds, which he bandaged, and soothed his friend: "Be quiet. Be quiet. Very soon they'll evacuate you."

When the medic arrived with a stretcher, Kaplansky was dead. But Shaulik found that he himself was not badly hurt.

He remained alone. The platoon was already far away. Dawn was breaking and he had to move forward. In the dim early light he saw the communication trench and went back to it carefully. He crawled down and turned left, and began to work his way along. Suddenly confident, he walked erect, clearing the trench of the enemy with bursts, short and measured, from his Uzi. Some of the *chevra* saw what was happening. They ran up to the barracks. Enemy fire was now confused and inaccurate. The dark and the swift advance prevented the Jordanians from ascertaining exactly where the Israelis were.

When the trench reached the road, it continued eastward alongside. On the left, close to the trench, there was a high stone wall. On the right, across the road, was an open stretch, with a wood and a few small scattered buildings. At the side of the road, a truck had broken down. In the murky light everything was blurred. Yoram ran into the trench as Eshkol went by on the road above. He caught up with Yoram and told him that on the right in the wood and next to the stone wall outside it, Miller's platoon was advancing. "So you must only fire ahead of you."

Yoram had not realized that he was not in the west trench, but in the middle one, and that he had taken the trench planned for Miller. Now it was clear to him. "All right—we'll shoot only in front."

Yecki, who had taken Zeev's bazooka, ran along the line looking for some shells for it. As he passed Gadi, the mortar man, Gadi asked him, "Have you pulled out the safety catch?" Yecki stopped and looked. The catch was inside. They pulled it out.

Yecki and Gadi advanced to the front of the line. Gadi had a Uzi machine gun, Yecki a bazooka. Suddenly Gadi heard Yoram call out ahead: "Look out! Jordanians!" Yoram was close to the wall. With a quick step forward, Gadi sent a burst into the trench. A Jordanian fell. Eshkol, who had come up behind them, asked, "Is there someone there?" While changing his magazine, Yoram answered simply: "There was . . ."

From ahead and from the left shots were heard. Yoram drew near to the edge of the stone wall. Opposite was a small building. Between the wall and the building was an open stretch. Yoram wanted cover to enable him to cross this area, so he called, "Machine gunner—here!" Eilon sent Aryeh forward. He had been lying on the road, ready to fire his submachine gun. The submachine gun spat fire. Yoram got up and, with a leap, rushed to the building. While hugging the wall, he searched for a window or door through which to throw a grenade. At the same time, he ordered: "Heiman—forward!"

Heiman and Oved Yichyeh, Yoram's signaler, got up to join him and both ran to the square in front of the house. Two explosions were heard. The square was lit up with a blinding flash of light. Yoram had managed to throw his grenade into the house, but Heiman and Oved did not join him. A shell had fallen between them. Oved screamed, "I've been hit in the groin!" With difficulty he moved back and sat in the trench, waiting for treatment. He gave his radio to Shalom. Heiman seemed to have disappeared after the explosion.

Yoram jumped back into the trench, took out another grenade, and threw it into the house. There was an explosion, then silence. On the left, the stone wall continued along the road. Yoram stopped for a few seconds to decide how best to advance.

He called to Eilon to take the fence to the right of the road and to cover the advance from there. Eilon took Gadi and Aryeh with him and ran to the right. They found, sticking out through a hole in the wall, a large gun, and jumped across to the other side of the wall and took up firing positions. It was still not light and they could see very little. Left and right, the noise of battle was heard. The squad moved forward and took up new firing positions.

The advance of the platoon continued. Yoram, first, erect, rushed ahead. Opposite him appeared two Jordanians. There was a burst and both fell. Jumping over them, they went on. Zidkoni noticed that one of the "dead" Jordanians was reaching for a rifle, so he pulled out a knife and stabbed him.

Realizing that the resistance was strengthening and that the fire was intensifying from the side trenches, Yoram slowed down and checked every step. Opposite were two long buildings, presumably barracks. Yoram stopped, working out a plan to mop them up. But his thinking was interrupted by a call on the radio.

Dadi wanted to know where they were and what was happening. Miller's platoon, in the trench to the right, had run into fire from the center of the target area and Dadi was afraid that it was from Yoram's group. So Dadi called for Yoram; before Yoram could answer, Oved, his signaler, was wounded. A few seconds passed before Yoram's relief signaler, Shalom, took over. Shalom called to Yoram: "Dadi is asking where we are!" Yoram looked round him, shrugged, and answered: "Tell him we're on target."

Again Dadi asked, "Where are you in relation to Television House?" Yoram once more looked around. It was hard to explain. "Tell him, in a straight line drawn from the moon through the antennae."

Dadi was pleased and surprised that Yoram had advanced so far, and asked, "What are you doing there?"

Yoram burst out laughing. "What do you think we're doing? We're fighting—and advancing."

Meanwhile, he realized that Dani Yizchaki's platoon was following him. Advancing anew, Yoram asked Dani for a machine gunner, because his, Aryeh, had gone to the right with Eilon. Dani sent Crispal, and shouted to Yoram that he was going left with his platoon to clear up the middle of the target.

Three platoons were now operating on separate axes: Miller was near Television House, Yoram near the dwelling houses, and Dani cleaning up the center trenches. Behind him was a Mag section under the command of Zvika Magen.

When Dadi got their reports he was delighted. The advance was proceeding without any problems and it seemed that within a few minutes their whole mission would be accomplished.

On the other hand, the area was full of wounded, and the Jordanians were still firing from all directions. It was difficult to pinpoint their position. Fortunately, in the darkness, the Jordanians fired indiscriminately, without aiming at specific targets.

Eshkol went to Yecki and fixed the position of the bazooka. Yoram placed Yecki with the bazooka and Crispal with the machine gun on the road to cover the advance. Crispal shot a long burst at the door of the barracks and Yoram threw in a grenade.

Yoram's grenade exploded. The cleanup squad rushed into the building. Yoram and Zidkoni were close to the wall beside the door. The rest of the *chevra* hugged the long wall. The door was closed. Yoram jumped to the other side of it and shouted to Zidkoni, "Throw another grenade!"

Vida standing next to an open window, beat Zidkoni to it. When his grenade burst, Yoram and Zidkoni kicked the door and then broke it open with a salvo of fire. Along the walls were military beds, showing signs of having been slept in only a short time before. Blankets, equipment, and clothing were scattered about everywhere. By the first light of day, the two saw that there was nobody in the barracks, and they turned to leave.

Beside the stairs they stopped for a second and Dardashti, who was standing next to them, cried out suddenly, "I've been hit!" and fell. Instinctively Yoram turned right and fired at the entrance of the building opposite. Zidkoni automatically cast a glance behind him, as did Chaim Shalem. They both saw a Jordanian soldier marching on the road, his rifle cocked. Zidkoni even saw eyeglasses on the tired face of the Jordanian, who continued moving toward them. They fired. The first burst did not hit him, but a joint blast from Zidkoni and Chaim knocked the soldier off his feet and he fell onto the road. At that moment Nir was wounded, right next to Dardashti. No one saw where the bullet came from.

The squad under Yoram went on to the second barracks. They kicked open the door and found beds and belongings, but no soldiers. Yoram looked outside. Now there was more light and he could make out what was a small building surrounded by a high stone fence, left, and next to it ran a parallel trench. Behind them, the hill came down a steep incline. On the left there was a small building surrounded by a high stone fence, apparently a munitions bunker.

Yoram called for cover. Zidkoni sent Vida to the end of the barracks. Yoram's squad gathered at the corner of the trench. Suddenly a soldier appeared from behind them. At first they thought he was one of them, but the helmet gave him away. Yecki shouted, "Jordanian," put down his bazooka, and fired his rifle. So did Elimelech. The Jordanian fell wounded beside Dardashti and Nir.

Over the road, two helmets appeared. Yecki and Vardi opened

fire. One Jordanian was killed, but the other one escaped. From the wood came shots. Yosef Elimelech was wounded and fell.

Yoram looked around him. Up till now, in the fervor of the advance, he had not realized that a number of his men were missing.

"Where are Nir and Dardashti?"

There was no answer. Everyone seemed to be too busy. Nobody wanted to be the bearer of unpleasant news. Yoram understood. Only a very small group was left with him. There was nothing to be done about it. They went on.

Hugging the wall of the house, Yoram and his men advanced to the munitions bunker. They heard shots and shouts in Hebrew from the other side of the fence.

"Who is there?" Yoram called.

"It's me—Zvika Magen."

"Good. Don't shoot in our direction. We are going on."

Yoram turned to the *chevra*: "I am going to throw a grenade into the bunker."

"Not worthwhile," answered Yecki. "The store may blow up."

But the grenade was already in the air and Yoram followed it with a burst from his Uzi. The bunker was empty.

"Nothing here," called Yoram and jumped into the communication trench that ran down the slope, his Uzi at his hip. He led his dwindling group on its way.

An enemy bullet from inside the trench hit him in the chest and he dropped, calling out, "I'm hit." Crispal shot above him into the trench. Dangoorie dragged Yoram to a nearby post at the side. Breathing with difficulty, Yoram pointed to his chest and told the boys how to deal with him. "Do it for me and I'll get up again," he said in a whisper, even showing them how. The *chevra* at the back were stunned. They wondered what they would do without their leader.

It was quiet in the trench. He was sitting at the side, and they didn't know where the shot had come from. Nor did they know where to go.

Somebody remembered that a few minutes before Yoram had spoken to Zvika Magen. "Let's call him."

They began to shout "Zvika! Zvika!" There was no answer. "Let's shout together," Vida suggested. They knelt in the trench in confusion and shouted "Zvika! Zvika!"

From across the trench came an Arab voice and the sound of shots. Vida put his head out to look and a bullet hit him through his helmet. "Keep your heads down!" Zidkoni shouted.

Tension grew. To raise their spirits and to discourage the enemy they fired some shots. Yecki said to Zidkoni: "There is no alternative. You have to take over the command."

He himself began to move forward. Dani came behind. Chaim got up and threw a grenade at the enemy voices. From across the wall, Zvika Magen arrived. "What's the matter? What are you doing? Where's Yoram?"

They explained. "Yoram is wounded. He's inside." At the back, Shapira arrived with a Mag and joined the group. Hearing shots ahead, he tried to pass, but when he reached a turn in the trench was stopped by enemy fire.

Zvika went to Yoram. Weakened, almost not breathing, Yoram explained to Zvika: "There are only Arabs in front. Go on down the trench."

Zvika said a few comforting words and ran outside. "*Nu—* come on! Let's go! Who is the front squad here?"

Yecki and Gadi answered: "We are."

"O.K. Get going!"

Gradually, under great tension, the two advanced into the winding trench. Outside it was almost light, but in the trench it was still pitch dark.

Yecki went first. He remembered Yoram's briefing. With a pocket torch directed at an aerial picture on the notice board, he had said: "Be careful of trenches covered with roofs." And he had also said there were three trenches. "At the end we'll meet up with Miller's *chevra*." Opposite there was a black opening. Yecki thought it was a roofed trench, and decided not to go in there. He shot a bullet into it. There was no response. He turned left and stole a look backward. Next to him was Gadi. The trench was very tortuous, with lots of crossings to the right and left. Yecki spotted a helmet with a gun and wondered if it was Miller. He stopped and turned to Zvika: "I see a soldier and can kill him, but he may be one of ours." Zvika replied, "Make sure before you fire!" Then, from the right below them, somebody fired at them— and a grenade came through the air. They threw themselves down. The grenade exploded but nobody was hit. Zvika quickly threw a grenade back and called, "Pass me some more grenades— fast!" Gadi fired at the same time, shouting to Vida above the trench, "Hey, Vida! Shoot down inside!"

Grenades were sent forward from behind and Zvika threw another one in the general direction of the attacking Jordanians. There was an explosion. "Good! I think I got them!"

From a nearby post came a shot. Yecki fired at the flash and Zvika threw a phosphorus grenade. There was quiet, and Yecki was left holding a grenade from which he had released the pin.

"What should I do?" he turned to Zvika. "I don't want to waste it."

"Go on holding it."

"With my gun in my hand as well?"

"Then throw it." Yecki suddenly saw a Jordanian close to him in the trench. Before he could move, the Jordanian had fired three bullets at him, but they missed.

Quickly he hurled his grenade at the Jordanian and the soldier fell. To make certain, he fired a couple of bullets into him, then commented, "I didn't waste the grenade." They jumped over the dead man and went on.

Another fork in the trench, another black opening from which came flashes of fire. A strongpoint. Yecki was glued to the wall. He shot from the side and shouted, "Grenade!" But Zvika saw what was happening and called to Galili to fire an antitank shot into the strongpoint. Galili came up, stood close to the right wall, and waited. The moment the shots from the strongpoint stopped, he exposed his left shoulder (he being left-handed) and pressed the trigger. From the blast, he was flung back, but there were no more shots from the strongpoint.

Zvika lifted his head to look around and saw a Jordanian soldier running right, on the ground above the trench. He also saw a recoilless gun there. "Shoot him!" Zvika shouted. "He's running to the gun." The *chevra* fired, even though from where they were they could not see the Arab.

Zvika decided to go for the gun. "Bazooka here!" he shouted as he ran. At once Yecki's bazooka passed from hand to hand. Zvika picked it up to shoot. "Wait," shouted the *chevra*, "the blast will kill us all."

"All lie down," Zvika ordered. He put a shell in the bazooka. All lay, while he stood erect, aimed, fired.

They were stunned for a moment by the explosion. When they recovered they saw that the recoilless gun was ablaze. They went on, Yecki now taking the lead. Then Zvika joined him.

Yecki came to a new post. He pressed the trigger of his Uzi, but he found that he had only one bullet left.

"Magazine!" he shouted, glued to the wall. Zvika and Vida passed him.

The group advanced in single file. Suddenly they saw a grenade flying high up in the air. Galili and Zidkoni ran back. The grenade exploded in the trench. No one was hurt.

Zvika ran forward. There were strongpoints to the right. Zvika shot into them as he ran, and went on in the main trench. There was a sharp turn left. From up on the hill, in the communication trench, Fink and Gertner, from Dani's platoon, joined them.

While reorganizing his company, Dudik got a call from Dadi for support. Yossi also ordered Dudik to give it. Without any delay, Dudik shouted: "Zvika, forward! Yoav, forward!"

"Platoons not yet organized," answered the platoon commanders.

"Not important. Push ahead—move!"

To their right, close up against the trench, was a building, one of three. From beyond the corner, on the slope of the hill, Jordanian fire was pouring down over the area. Dawn had broken and the Jordanians saw now what had happened and where the Israelis were. The *chevra* cursed the sun.

Omri had just begun to move with his squad when accurate fire was directed at them. Dudik gave instructions to mop up only the outside of the building. He said they should not look for unnecessary trouble by entering the rooms. Omri jumped out of the trench, to the building. A bullet hit him in his leg as he came out of the trench. "I'm hit!" he called, and fell inside the trench. With a little help he was taken out of it again. He hopped by himself to the corner of the house. Benny Shiffer, the medic, was already beside him.

Benny shouted to Michael, "Bandage!" Michael threw it, and Benny bandaged the leg.

Omri's place at the head of the line was taken by Zvika. Then he was hit by a ricochet. Zvika rocked forward and backward. Merhavi, standing in front of him, took the radio from him. Zvika fell down in the trench.

Merhavi shouted: "Medic! Medic!" Yigal, the medic, came from the front. The *chevra* spread out in the trench. Yigal couldn't help treading on them as he hurried quickly to Zvika.

The next squad lifted Zvika out. They laid him down next to Omri. Eytan Naava was stationed to guard them with his machine gun, while Yoav went ahead and the advance continued. When the Mag people entered the trench, Zuriel was at their head. Behind him was Eli. From the left wing, the enemy continued shooting at the trench. Zuriel picked up the Mag and shot while on the move. Suddenly the Mag jammed. Zuriel stopped to repair it, so Eli broke forward in front of him. Naphtali ran behind him, close in his track.

Suddenly a Jordanian emerged from a hidden post and, as he ran, fired a burst at them. Eli was hit in the chest. On his lips were drops of blood. He tried to go back but crashed against Naphtali because the trench was so narrow.

Naphtali lay down on the ground and Eli stepped over him to go back. Zuriel saw him as he passed and was startled. At that moment a grenade exploded beside the trench and smothered them all in a cloud of smoke. Eli continued to the rear. Yigal, the medic, tended his wound and left him to be evacuated.

Zuriel finished fixing his Mag and went on. Naphtali, in front of him, shot nonstop. "Magazine!" Zuriel heard, and was pushed forward. Again the trench was narrow. Again Naphtali lay on the ground and Zuriel jumped over him and went forward. Naphtali changed magazines and joined him.

At the end, the row, now very short, Michael joined them with his platoon. In front, Yoav and his men were busy. Dudik, crowded back among his men, pushed forward.

From inside the trench, a Jordanian leapt up and ran toward the corner of the house where Zvika and Omri were lying. All at once, Eytan dropped him with a machine-gun burst. Zvika and Omri dealt with other wounded, carrying them from the trench to a safer place where they could receive attention.

While running, Dudik saw that murderous fire was coming from the left. Opposite was a junction of trenches. Precisely here, the trenches were shallow and exposed to fire from the slope of the hill. One particular Jordanian bunker on the left was causing a lot of trouble.

"Yoav, take the left!" he roared. Yoav did so swiftly. A mixed group followed him.

"Mike, go forward!" called Dudik, and watched the force split up. Mike and his men were standing up in the trench. Mike saw figures in front of him, but when he shouted the password, "Spearhead," heard no answer. Then he realized that they were Jordanians and at the same time that he was being attacked from above.

In a second, Dudik saw that his men were caught in a very dangerous situation. The trenches were shallow and the enemy was in the stronger position, firing calmly by daylight.

The trench had become a trap. The first man hit was Didiyah, the medic, whose arm was hanging by the skin while blood gushed from it. Dudik ordered his men to open fire with all weapons, but when Magril stood up to shoot, he was killed almost at once. When Mike also stood up, he felt a great blow in his left arm, which then hung limp, blood gushing from the veins. As he looked in wonder at it, a great stream of blood shot out of his throat.

While Chaim Saba, the machine gunner, fired at the Jordanians up on the hill, Michael whispered: "Medic! Medic!", his head fell to the side and he caught at his throat, trying to find air to breathe. The he took off his equipment and loosened his chin strap. "Air . . . air . . ."

Didiya lay on his side and called: "My arm! My arm!" Yigal, another medic, was with them and, though shaken by what he saw, attended the wounded skilfully and efficiently. Dudik realized that any further delay in the trench would cost extra lives, and ordered Slutzki, the company sergeant major: "Take six or seven men with you and storm the position above. If the fire is too strong for you, take shelter and give cover to the platoon." He called to Harlam: "Jump to that rock."

"And what'll I do when I get there?"

"Give us cover." Dudik talked fast. It was now almost completely light. The *chevra* could make out Jordanian helmets as the enemy soldiers ran back and forth in the upper trench, firing at them with all weapons in their possession.

Slutzki called to his men to join with him in an attack on the Jordanians above the trench. Benny, Ilan, Harlam, Merhavi and Urieli, got up immediately, firing from the hip and then they started running. Slutzki saw that bullets were hitting the ground next to them as they ran. Before him was a large rock, so he commanded, "Lie down!" and the squad ran behind the rock.

Slutzki looked around. Beside him was Harlam, with a Uzi, and behind him Urieli, with a rifle. No one had been hurt. Shooting the Jordanians in the trench, as they fired back, was hard for both sides. To aim down, the Jordanians had to stand up above the trench. To shoot at the Jordanians, the Israelis were forced to stick their heads out above the rock. But the Jordanians had the advantage of a communication trench which gave good cover and allowed them to move from side to side. Nevertheless, most of the Jordanian bullets passed over their heads, although a few struck the rock, causing a lot of sparks. When Harlam's magazine was empty, Zilpah took bullets out of his haversack to refill it, and the rest did the same.

There was a pause. Slutzki lifted his head to watch the enemy and started to ask Harlam a question, but was cut off when a bullet sliced into his shoulder, knocking him backward. Then he realized that his arm was paralyzed, and ran back to the trench where Yigal, the medic, looked after him. Slutzki saw that Michael was bandaged and that Gilead was helping to take him to the rear,

Michael walking almost on his own. Yigal now got up and started to shoot. "Lie down, Yigal," Slutzki called. "It would be a pity if you were to get hurt."

But Yigal kept firing his weapon. The gory sights in the trench had upset him and he was no longer prepared to sit quietly and wait for more wounded. Didiyah's arm and Michael's throat and Magril's death had been too much for him.

He was amazed at Didiyah's calm as Didiyah quietly showed the *chevra* how to help him—when Yigal came to him, Didiyah sent him off to attend to Michael first. "I'll be all right." With his one hand he helped to tie a tourniquet round his shattered arm. "Not so terrible. In work like mine, I can manage very well with one arm." Ilan, whose weapon had been damaged, wanted to take Slutzki's Uzi. Slutzki refused. "But you're wounded!" Slutzki still wouldn't give up his Uzi—it had become a part of him.

Dudik decided that there was no sense in continuing the frontal assault. He shouted to Yoav to go on, and he himself turned to the men near him: "Whoever wants to live, get moving!"

When Slutzki had jumped into the open area, Yair, Michael's sergeant, had leapt over Michael, Didiyah, and Magril, so he was now in the lead, with Kendel close behind. At Dudik's call, the two got up and, shooting from the hip, advanced to the corner of the trench, at the junction with the stone wall. At the corner they found a Jordanian bunker and Yair fired a burst into it, and would have liked to stop and mop it up, but Dudik roared from the back "Go on! Go on!"

Yair looked back. Of the whole force, only a few men had come with them, headed by Dudik and Saban. Yair waited for the others to join them and then began to run along the trench, which continued on the other side of the wall. To the left was a high wall, to the right the street, and beyond a wood and open area.

In the trench itself, soldiers were lying, some wounded, some killed, some stunned. They were part of the Mag platoon of Zvika

Magen, cut off from their commander. The platoon had been virtually wiped out.

In his rush forward, Dudik lost contact with that part of his company which remained behind, and, because he paid little attention to those who were not there with him, it never occurred to him that he had so few men left.

The sight of the wounded Mag men in the trench infuriated him. He yelled at them to get up and get going, and passed them with a leap as he continued up the rise of the road. With his squad he cleaned up a small bunker. At the corner of the stone wall he found Dadi.

This was the first time that the two company commanders had met since the battle began, although they had been in constant touch by radio. Dadi told him gloomily that his company had suffered heavy casualties, the Mag platoon being practically wiped out, and the others all split up and scattered.

They separated, Dudik going left to the trench that led to the center of the target area, without knowing that Dani's platoon had already gone through there.

So he met no resistance until he came to the great bunker and heard from Sergeant Fink, who was wounded in the arm, that the enemy were in the bunker in great strength.

When Dudik's cry of "Get moving!" reached Yoav, it was clear to him that any advance in this trench would only mean losing men for no reason. From his position, he could see the trenches of the Jordanians and knew the Israelis would be going into a trap.

He shouted to Dudik to warn him of the danger, but Dudik did not hear, so Yoav had no alternative but to obey orders and to go on.

As the trench went deeper, shots were fired from inside it at anyone who advanced. The paratroopers fired back and threw grenades, but nothing helped. The Jordanians were protected by the curve in the trench, and by an inside wall. From above and to the right, other Jordanians were in a position to shoot down at the Israelis in the trench. Still others fired from the trench and from bunkers to the west.

Ziklag set up his Mag on the edge of the trench and fired nonstop. But every time he lifted his head the Jordanians shot at him with everything they had.

On the steep slope of the west trench, leading from the hill above, three Jordanians were running and two more came in. A salvo of fire and bullets forced them to take shelter. It looked as if the Jordanians were preparing a counterattack, but it never came.

Yoav realized that there was no sense remaining in such an exposed position. He had lost contact with Dudik, and also couldn't figure out what was happening. With only four men left, he decided to try to operate from another direction.

At that moment Nir arrived. The wound above his eye had been bandaged, and he had been looking everywhere for Dudik who, he was sure, needed him desperately. But instead he found Yoav, obviously in trouble.

Without knowing exactly what was happening, he ordered, "Nobody must retreat." Yoav shouted to him that it was impossible to advance, adding that they would have to get more men if they were to mount a fresh attack.

"You wait here. I'll send somebody with more men," Nir said.

Yoav explained the difficulties of the position, and Nir realized quickly that it was impossible to go on. The Jordanian position was far too strong. The movements of the Jordanians also made him fear that they might be planning a counterattack. His lack of contact with Dudik worried him. "I'm pinned down here," he thought, "and Dudik must be going mad without me."

To ward off any counterattack, he posted Naphtali to guard the flank while he himself tried to make contact with Dudik.

Alex, an armor bearer who was bringing three crates of Mags, began to offload the crates in order to be free for action. On the left he saw Zuriel shooting with a Mag and gave him ammunition. In front of him he spotted a Jordanian helmet and, behind a rock, he saw the remains of Slutzki's group. Alex crawled back a little to change position.

Yoav stood and directed Dov Amaslas with the bazooka. The target was the western trench.

Yoav felt this point, the junction with the cross trench, was important. Two shells missed, but the third scored a bull's eye. Next to Yoav stood Meir Shnur, a marksman, who quietly fired his rifle. Dumbinski supplied him with ammunition. Yoav indicated to Meir what targets should be hit, and Meir zeroed in on them. A little to the right, Alex lay with a bazooka, and next to him was Zilpah, his number two man. On seeing the bunker in the wing of the trench, Alex raised the bazooka to fire, but a Jordanian shell sliced the barrel of his weapon, showering shrapnel on Alex's head and putting the bazooka out of action. Yoav pointed out other targets to Dov, who shouted to the *chevra* to pass him more bazooka shells.

Yoav looked for a Mag, but there was none, so he shouted, "I need a machine gun here!" and Joshua produced one. Yoav pointed to the bunker on the left and ordered him to shoot at it. In this way, gradually, Yoav had managed to mount sufficient firepower to cover both the cross trench and the difficult points in the west trench.

By 0400 Yossi, Gabi, and Giora had reached the Ambassador Hotel. The reports from Ammunition Hill indicated that the momentum of the Israeli onslaught was dying down, but the battle raged on. The company commanders still painted optimistic pictures over the radio, but Yossi wanted to hurry things on so as to move on to fresh objectives.

He sent Doron to Ammunition Hill to find out what was happening. When Doron got there, he realized that the fighting in the trenches was not going at all well, and that something had to be done urgently, so he contacted Yossi and asked for tanks. There was no doubt that tanks and half-tracks would help to end the Jordanian resistance in the trenches.

Yossi agreed and Rafi ordered the two last tanks in the row to go to Doron, and within minutes they arrived at Ammunition Hill.

When the paratroopers heard the sound of the tank tracks coming suddenly from behind, the paratroopers were frightened for a moment, thinking that Jordanian tanks might be coming against them.

But Yoav recognized them at once and shouted, "They're ours!" and rushed toward them. "That's just what we need. Tanks!"

The first tank, with Doron on it, had already begun to climb the road to the top of the hill. The tank commander was Gigi.

On the second tank sat Yoash, operations sergeant in the battalion. Ariel was the tank commander. Yoav ran to the tank and managed to stop it between the pine wood and the communication trenches. He dashed to Yoash and explained the plan to him. "You cover us in the direction of the top trench and we'll storm it." Yoash briefed Ariel and Yoav jumped back into the trench and called out: "Come on, boys! Get up! Follow me!"

Yoav's enthusiasm and the presence of the tank rejuvenated the tired men. They jumped up from the trench and from their hiding place behind the rock, and began running slowly forward, shooting from the hip. Then they surged up the hill. It was their third assault on the position that morning; they had been beaten back with heavy losses the first two times. But this time they could not be stopped. The tank opened machine-gun fire; within seconds the men raced forward, Yoav and Meir at their head, and took the cross trench that had caused them so much trouble, so many casualties. Elisha, the tank gunner, shot as they moved along the road.

On crossing the trench, Alex, who was on Yoav's right, came up against a stone wall, turned left toward Yoav, and together they went on toward the west trench. In the meantime Harlam reached the water reservoir and Meir and Amsalam ran up on Yoav's left, Ehud following behind. As he ran, Alex noticed a Jordanian head coming up from one of the trenches. The Jordanian fired at Yoav and Meir. Yoav gripped his stomach and chest, crying: "Ay! I'm hit!" and fell. Meir, also wounded, managed to go back to the other side of the trench.

Alex pulled out a grenade and threw it into the trench from which the Jordanian had fired. As it exploded, a Jordanian helmet flew up into the air.

"Good," Nir cried. "We hit him."

Alex had seen a building made of blocks and cement in the middle of the area and a head poking out of one of the openings. Alex realized it was an Israeli helmet, and waved to it not to shoot. From the building somebody waved back. It was Dudik.

Alex took out a hand grenade and threw it into the same trench into which he had thrown his first grenade, and Amsalam did the same. Then they ran into the deep trench. A Jordanian was lying close to them. Alex couldn't maneuver his gun to fire, because it was too long, so he shouted to Amsalam, "Shoot him," and dropped down. He heard the burst of an Uzi above him and the Jordanian was killed.

But it was not enough. A burst of fire came from in front of them and Alex was hit in the arm and leg. As he fell he heard Amsalam's cries—he too had been wounded.

They moved back to get medical attention and then they met Nir, who sent them to Yigal, the medic, who had already collected a few wounded and was treating them at the junction of the trenches.

The left half of Yoav's assault squad stayed beside the trench. Dumbinski saw Meir come back wounded and at once went to him. During the time that they had been in action together, the unique bond of brotherhood which is developed in soldiers who have been through fire together had grown very strong.

Dumbinski was supposed to serve as Mag number three to Uri Shwartz, but he had lost his squad in the trench. Without knowing that Shwartz had been wounded, he went on until he reached the junction in the shallow trenches where, next to him, he found Meir, standing up straight and shooting with his rifle. Beyond was Yoav, who was pointing out the sources of fire to Meir. Dumbinski freed himself of the heavy crate-carrier and supplied Meir with ammunition.

Then Meir fell and lay in front of him with a great open wound in the left side of his chest. "He's badly wounded!" Dumbinski shouted, and Harlam came across to see. "Are we allowed to give him water?"

"Let's see first where the exit hole is." Carefully they turned Meir over, telling him what they were doing so that he would cooperate. While Dumbinski supported him, Ilan bandaged him with two firm bandages and lay him again on his back.

From the left came Nir's call: "Anyone up above, join me in the trench. Leave the wounded to Yigal. Everybody, come here! To me!" So they left Meir and took their place with Nir and went on with the battle.

Sitting in the pillbox, Dudik heard the sound of an approaching tank and saw Yoash sitting on it. So he went up to him and asked Yoash to bring the tank directly down on to the lower trench. Yoash disagreed. He thought it was wrong to take his tank into the stronghold as antitank weapons were firing at them from all sides. He thought they could achieve better results by shooting from where they were.

He opened fire from beyond the stone wall, but the slope was steep, and part of the hill was hidden from the tank. The tankmen used their machine guns because they were afraid that if they used their cannon, they would hit their own forces in the trench on both sides of the great bunker. Facing Dudik's post, the bunker could not be seen; it was hidden by the slope of the hill.

Meanwhile Nir felt that time was running through his fingers. His attempts to contact Dudik had been fruitless, nor had Yoav returned. He realized that there was no sense in staying where he was—they had to advance. The fear of a Jordanian counterattack had passed. The movements of Jordanian squads in the trenches had almost ceased, and at no time had there been any major aggressive action.

Nir collected his men and prepared to move. Meanwhile, on the right, in the open stretch, Yoav's assault had begun. To a large extent the tank had silenced the Jordanians, and now Yoav's assault provided excellent cover for Nir.

Nir's squad began to move along the west communication trench. Very soon Nir learned that he could see nothing inside the trench. It was very deep, its walls rising two feet above him, so he knew one of his men would have to get out of the trench to provide cover, to act as a lookout and maintain contact with the other squads, to keep them from harming each other.

Zuriel, who had already used his M.G. on the cross trench, was the first to act as lookout; as the squad moved in the trench, he moved along above it, to the right. Every few meters, a secondary trench branched off from the main one, leading to a pillbox or a bunker. Nir decided not to bother about mopping up these strongpoints. His main purpose was to reach the center of the target area as soon as possible, and to take it. So the squad made do with throwing a grenade and shooting a burst into each side communication trench before going on.

They went through the trench until they came near to where two trenches joined. At this point Zuriel's ammunition had given out and Nir turned to Naphtali, the machine gunner. "Naphtali, go and relieve Zuriel." Zuriel slipped down and Naphtali put the machine gun on the edge of the trench and climbed up after it. Bullets whistled overhead, some of them hitting the branches of the pines, so that branches and pine needles dropped down. Naphtali lifted the machine gun waist-high and advanced.

The squad reached the junction. On the right, Naphtali saw Yoav's force in action, going across the main trench, and beginning to advance toward the west trench. Naphtali moved in their direction. There were sudden shots from the trench and Naphtali felt a sharp pain in the waist. He climbed down into the trench and said to Nir, "See what I've got there." Nir saw an open wound, flowing with blood.

While still holding the Uzi in his left hand, Nir pressed with the thumb of his right hand on the wound to stop the blood. "It's nothing. It'll be all right."

Yigal came up from behind. He had gone on sortie to collect more bandages and dressings.

"Nir, I'm taking him. It's all right. You can go."

"O.K.," said Nir, and returned to his men. Few men were left in the squad—Eli Tamir, Eli Sias, Zuriel, Bunch and Eytan Naveh. Seeing Yoav's men in the cross trench nearby, Nir decided to join forces with them. "Yoav's squad to me! Men with Uzis and grenades, come here!"

Yigal finished treating Naphtali and sent him to the rear. Naphtali hopped along by himself, his arm on his hip. On the way he turned to see if the Jordanian near the burning car, who fired before the assault began, was really dead. When he was sure of this, he went on to the casualty station.

Yigal now turned to Meir, who was still lying near the cross trench. The place was comfortable, especially for a man with a chest wound, and so he was left there. Any attempt to move him without a stretcher would have increased the danger of suffocation. Meir contended that his wound was not that bad and chatted with Yigal all the time Yigal attended to him.

In the meanwhile, Dumbinski, Ehud, Alex, Harlam, Shifer and Kochavi had joined Nir.

"Uzi men, forward!" Nir ordered. "At the back, *chevra* with rifles and machine guns. Ehud, forward! You lead."

But their magazines were empty—they had to fill them first. Close to the walls of the trench, the *chevra* pulled out cardboard boxes from their haversacks and hastily filled their magazines. It was also a good moment to exchange ideas and experiences, while heads were bent over fingers inserting 9-mm bullets into the narrow openings of the magazines. Nir tried to identify other forces working in other sections of the hill. He tried in particular to spot Dudik. Among the long barracks he saw a tank, looking for a convenient position. This was the tank that worked with Yoav, and was now beside Dudik.

The magazines were refilled.

"Ehud, forward!"

Ehud led. At every bend he stopped, keeping close to the wall and spraying the trench with a burst. Then he went forward, walking, sometimes fast, sometimes slow, until he came to the next turn. Bullets flew about in the air and he heard shouts. Suddenly he saw Eytan above him with a machine gun, spraying the trench in front.

Behind Ehud came Alex, after him, Harlam, and then Nir. It seemed to Nir that the advance in the trench was going too slowly. Because the trench was so deep, it was impossible to see anything of what was happening outside. He knew that if somebody did not help them from above, they would be cut off inside the trench, and would not be able to advance. He decided to place somebody outside the trench to run on the ground parallel with them, as Naphtali and Zuriel had done before.

"Go on top, Eytan," he ordered. "Run parallel with Ehud and spray the trench in front of him. Hit anyone you see." This was the kind of thing Eytan liked. He jumped up the high wall of the trench, lifted his machine gun and "began to play like a pianist," as he put it.

In the trench, Ehud could now go faster. The presence of Eytan up above made all the difference. He saw Eytan changing magazines at astonishing speed. Eytan fired and fired, moving from right to left, even getting a little ahead of Ehud.

The trench twisted. Eytan followed it from above, firing, Ehud moving down below, also shooting ahead. Suddenly it seemed that the trench had come to an unexpected end. Up above Eytan was on concrete; down below Ehud faced an even deeper blackness. He made out somthing thick, concrete. A bunker? He feared the unknown in the darkness.

Ehud pressed the trigger and sprayed the gloom with a long burst. No fire was returned. Eytan fired from above. From his vantage point, Eytan could see that the trench continued beyond the concrete, so he turned his gun that way. Ehud went forward cautiously in the trench. There was a sharp bend left, another to the right, then light. Ehud understood that the concrete was a sort of roof running the whole length of that part of the trench. The light drew them on. Ehud was already through, beyond the cover of the roof, and Eytan was above him. Both of them sent bursts ahead and the nearby bend was mopped up. At the end, a trench went off to the left to a bunker.

Eytan had no grenades, so Ehud took one out and Eytan bent down and took it from him. Ehud took out another grenade for himself. Eytan held his gun for a moment in one hand; with the other he drew the safety catch of the grenade and threw it into the bunker. The gun was again on his hip and a burst followed the grenade. Ehud was close to the wall, the grenade in his hand ready to throw. He put out his head to look into the bunker and saw the slit through which the occupants were firing.

Then everything went suddenly black, for a bullet had hit the bunker and splinters of stone pierced his eyes. His face was covered with blood. Yet his fingers pressed strongly on the grenade lest the safety catch come up, and he turned around. Eytan bent a little so as to aim into the bunker. Again there was a burst, and Eytan fell. From behind came the order, "Go further in," but Eytan did not move. Ehud, although his face was full of blood, could see again; he threw the grenade through the slit and added a burst.

Harlam had a magazine ready in his hand. He heard a cry in front, "I've been hit!" and shouted for more bullets. The *chevra* in front of him also shouted: "We haven't any bullets." He yelled, "Either take magazines or get out of my way!" Alex said, "Pass." He was pushed forward, but was pressed against the wall, the trench being so narrow that it was almost impossible to move. They crushed up against each other. Somehow Harlam got through. He got to Ehud, whose face was streaming with blood. Once again Harlam squeezed past with difficulty, taking care not to expose himself to the slit of the bunker.

Harlam studied the trench in front of him. It was empty, with smoke rising in it. He looked left into the bunker, and suddenly two bullets were fired at him from inside the trench. He saw two Jordanians close together and shot in their direction. Suddenly he felt that he was standing on air, with no support from his left leg. He fell backward, and the end of his burst went up into the air. He shouted: "They're coming!" In his hand he was holding an open grenade, ready to throw. Now he concentrated all his strength on not letting it open.

Harlam's fall took everyone by surprise behind him, for they were so close to each other that his fall caused a chain reaction, rather as if they were toy soldiers, not real soldiers in battle. Nir found himself lying on his back, with men on top of him. He made out the bloodied face of Ehud.

"Get up at once!" he roared, pushing angrily at the whole group with all his strength.

They disentangled themselves and got up—everyone except Harlam. He remained lying down, too badly wounded to move. Ehud went to the rear. Nir and Shifer started to go forward.

"For God's sake don't step on me," Harlam begged. Shifer tried not to do so, but could not get past. He had to put one foot on Harlam, but did so as lightly as possible. Then he went on. Nir came behind him.

Shifer realized that he had no grenades left, and very little ammunition. He shouted to Nir to give him some. Nir did so. Shifer threw a grenade into the bunker and followed it up with a burst. From the bunker came cries of dread in Arabic.

When Nir passed Harlam, he bent over him and carefully took the open grenade from him, holding it in his hand and advancing. On hearing Shifer's cries for grenades, he passed the order back: "Grenade to me! Magazine to me!"

The two, Nir and Shifer, now worked together as they moved at the head of the line, exchanging places with each other when necessary. On the left were the openings of side trenches leading to bunkers. No Jordanians could be seen in the trench, nor was there firing heard. But the moment anyone tried to pass a bunker, there was shooting from inside, so that movement was slowed down. There was no alternative but to mop up each bunker before going on.

Nir remembered that he had to coordinate his movements with those of other forces. He saw the tank to his right up above, and even heard the *chevra* talking opposite. But he still could not see them. Now and then he went up above the trench to make sure the tank knew where they were.

From the back, the *chevra* were passing grenades and magazines. As soon as Shifer and Nir received them, they used them at once. They didn't go into the bunkers, but they made do with throwing in grenades and firing bursts before going on.

Four bunkers were mopped up on the left. Benny was now at

the head of the line. When he got near a trench fork, the one he was in and one coming from the center of the hill, he heard cries from inside the trench and saw helmets—ours! Somebody shouted to him not to advance further, because they were preparing to blow up something. So he should take care. He entered the trench on the right.

Nir spotted Ofer standing in the trench opposite and Ofer signed to him to stop, pointing up above. He gave Nir to understand that they were preparing something, and that Nir's squad should stop shooting. Nir turned to his squad and said happily, "We've met up. Don't shoot. Take care!"

On his way to the Ambassador Hotel, Doron collected all men in the area and brought them up on the inner road, as far as the long barracks on the hill. They heard shots all about them and entered the trenches.

Pass heard shouts, "Grenades! Pass up grenades!" The men reached Meir, wounded, and found, next to him in the trench, a dead Jordanian. Several *chevra* refused to step on him, and went to a bypass trench. Pass went on by himself in the straight trench. He talked to Meir. Meir said he was all right, and that the medics were dealing with him. Above, shots were fired. Inside the trench Pass could see nothing. He climbed up to look for the rest of the *chevra* and ran across the open area. Shots passed him as he ran to the cross trench and drew near to the bunker. From his right, they shot at him, and from the same direction the *chevra* shouted to him for grenades, which he gave them.

At 0500, without knowing about the existence of the great bunker, all forces on Ammunition Hill were making their way toward it. The first to reach the area was Dani's platoon. Later, they were joined by Dudik and his men. In the lower trench, two platoons were moving forward, one behind the other: Yoram's, now under the command of Zvika Magen, and Ofer of A Company.

From the side of the Police School, in the west trench, Nir's force was advancing. At the top of the hill were the two tanks, one facing the trench sector and the other Givat Hamivtar.

Zvika Magen, Michael Gertner, and Sergeant Fink formed a mopping-up squad and began to advance in the lower trench, shooting continuously from the hip. As they emptied their magazines the three kept changing the lead. Vida ran close to them and immediately behind, Galili, Shalem, and Yecki.

This group had just completed mopping up a large post and had been left almost entirely without ammunition. While running, Vida suddenly detected a strange noise from the haversack on his back. He was afraid that the 52-mm shells would explode on him and he turned aside, took off the haversack, and pushed it into a side bunker. So Zvika Magen, Gertner, and Fink went forward without him.

Now Fink was first. He saw the opening to the bunker on his right, and pressed close to the wall as he shot into it. A bullet from inside hit his left arm. Zvika changed positions with him. Fink went back a little to find out what had happened to him. There was an opening to a trench, which he entered.

Zvika and Gertner moved forward and a grenade was thrown. Fink heard an explosion and shots. Both Zvika and Gertner were wounded. Zvika fell at a distance of a meter from the bunker, Gertner two meters from him. The Jordanian grenade raised a cloud of dust.

Next to Fink stood Avraham Katan. They decided that when the cloud of dust settled, they would go in and mop up in the bunker. But just as Katan moved, another grenade was thrown by the Jordanians, and he was wounded. This was his second wound. Katan went into a side trench to dress it.

Vida joined Fink. "Vida," Fink said, "something must be done. All the fellows are being killed."

Behind Vida came more men. Fink led them toward the bunker.

Fink's magazine was empty and Vida passed him, pressed close to the wall. He found he had no grenades. He shouted: "Grenade!" Nobody seemed to have any left. Then one was found and passed to Vida. He threw it into the bunker. Suddenly he heard behind him: "Vida—look out—grenade!"

A grenade was rolling next to his foot. He rushed back and the grenade exploded. He was not hurt, but Crispan, next to him, was wounded and went back to the rear.

Weakness overcame Crispan on the way, and he went to one of the posts to sit and to rest a little. Yecki was in there. Hearing cries for grenades up front, he had had an inspiration—he had gone into the post to look for abandoned Jordanian grenades. Sure enough, there were boxes of grenades lying there—new, unopened boxes. Yecki took out a few grenades and stuffed them into his pockets. He also saw a Jordanian 0.3-inch machine gun standing there. "Worth using," he thought. But it was not working. Suddenly Crispan came in. Yecki took out a canteen and gave him a little water. "I can get back to the casualty clearing station mysef," Crispan whispered. "You go on."

Yecki went out and returned to the trench. He saw Vida and Fink, and as he passed them Fink shouted, "They're shooting in front!" He found two of our men killed. On his right, there was an opening to a trench. He went in. It continued to a round post, made for a bazooka. Inside was a Jordanian lying with a bazooka, wounded. Yecki shot him. Yigal joined him and called: "They're throwing grenades and shooting all the time!"

From the great bunker the Jordanians poured out bullets and grenades without ceasing. The trench was full of smoke and dust, and as bullets struck the left wall, sparks flew up with a scream. Fink's wound needed dressing, so he went up above. The shots

and explosions drew Dani. From his position above, he could not
see what was happening in the trench, for the slope was steep, the
trench deep. He decided to go down to see for himself what was
going on. At that moment Dudik arrived. Dani went down into
the communication trench on the right and slipped and fell. He
saw two dead men in the trench and somebody called to him
from the left that they were throwing grenades there.

Dani went forward and joined Yecki and Yigal. Yecki showed
him the position from which the fire was coming. He was worried
that the grenades might be "our grenades." They were still discussing this possibility when one flew at them.

Dani was standing in front. He jumped back and lay down
next to the dead Israelis as the grenade exploded. Nothing happened. He ran to the bunker and threw in a grenade. When it
exploded, he rushed forward, firing his Uzi until he reached the
slit. Something exploded inside and he was thrust back, with
blood on his face. But he went forward again.

Suddenly he realized that he had dropped his Uzi, so he went
back to look for it and the men gave him another. He got out of
the trench to get his wounds dressed.

In the trench Yecki and Yigal went on throwing grenades.
Every attempt to advance on the bunker met with well-aimed
fire. Then the grenades gave out and Yecki shouted, "Grenades!"

Pass passed them the one grenade which he had left and the
chevra collected more and passed them forward. When Dudik
realized that the fighting down below was still going on, he sent
in a squad formed of Dan Arzi, David Shalom, and Shaul. Arzi
came across the wounded Dani and helped him until Ephraim
hurried up and bandaged Dani.

Shaul turned right. David Shalom reached Yecki. A few seconds later, Kendel came, from a parallel trench, shallow and full
of gray dust. Yecki explained the position to them both. Kendel

tried to advance, but stopped when a grenade was thrown from the bunker, so he jumped back and lay down.

The alternative was to get out of the trench, crawl on top of the bunker, and from above poke a grenade through a slit. And that is what Kendel did. From the trench with the bazooka post, he climbed on the bunker, crawled quickly to the slit, put his hand in, and tossed the grenade inside. As it exploded he ran to the trench on the other side of the bunker. Yecki and David Shalom did the same thing, and all managed to pass the slit of the bunker. In the trench David Shalom suddenly saw Jordanians. Instinctively he fired at them and they disappeared. The three men stood side by side—on the other side of the bunker, it was true, but by no means sure that the bunker had been mopped up and was clear.

Yecki and Kendel decided to return to the near side of the bunker, approaching the slit slowly. There was no fire so, with a leap, they passed the opening, accompanied by a salvo of shots which missed them.

There was a lull. Yecki and Kendel stood at one side of the opening, David Shalom on the other. Kendel collected ammunition from Zvika and Gertner and turned back to find more grenades. At that moment the men of Ofer's platoon arrived. Ofer came up to see what was going on. Yecki explained the structure of the bunker and told him what had been happening to them. Ofer decided to tackle the bunker with a bazooka and called Yossi.

Yossi came and met Yecki, who showed him the bunker. Zvika and Gertner were lying in the trench. Yossi went to the left wall of the trench and fired a shell from there. It hit the wall of the bunker. After the smoke had dissolved, Yossi looked for results but found nothing. He had a phosphorus bomb and he put it into the bazooka. He didn't have his number two man with him, so he shot from another angle, but with no results. They began to despair.

Ofer suggested that he got out on top of the bunker and throw a grenade from above. Yecki explained that Kendel had already tried that without success. Then, to the left of the trench, a tank appeared.

Next to the barracks, Dani met Dadi and told him what was happening. Dadi instructed Dani to fetch the tank. He did so, and guided it to the stone wall. Yoash was on the tank. Dani showed him the Jordanian post from which the bazooka was fired. "Why have you brought me opposite a bazooka?" called Ariel, the tank commander, angrily. A bazooka at short range was a tankist's nightmare. Dani explained about the bunker.

The tank aimed its cannon at the bunker, but from its position it was difficult to identify the bunker, as its roof was completely camouflaged by earth. But the main problem was that the bunker was too near and too low for the use of the cannon, while shells might endanger the men in the trenches.

Yoash shot a burst from a Uzi to guide the tank. The machine gun on the tank opened fire, the bullets passing overhead. "Sorry. I can't get it," said Ariel.

Dani went back into the trench where some of the *chevra* were kneeling, some sitting, as they watched the tank wide-eyed.

The tank was still maneuvering above, while the *chevra* in the trench discussed what to do. Yecki suddenly spotted a haversack of explosive material on Ofer's back, and he had an inspiration. David Shalom was on the other side of the bunker. "We'll throw him the bag with explosives, with detonators. David Shalom will place them on the wall of the bunker and set them off. An explosion like that will certainly destroy the bunker and the people in it."

Ofer took off his bag and ran to the rear to bring other explosives. The Jordanians could only hit the left wall of the trench up to a certain range. Yecki drew near along the right wall while David Shalom pressed hard against the solid wall on the other side. Yecki threw him the first bag and David caught it and put the explosives against the apparently impenetrable wall. Meanwhile the Jordanians fired terrific bursts as they gathered some new threat was coming.

Three more bags were placed on the first. David set the connecting fuses and pulled the detonator. "Explosion!" The shout echoed along the whole length of the trench. David was the last to run. He went into a side trench, where he found the first of Nir's men. In great suspense they waited for the detonation. There were several blasts, the second much greater than the first.

The wall was breached and in the opening lay a Jordanian. They shot him. Opposite, Nir and his force came up and they asked him for a grenade. Nardi threw it in through the breach. From inside the bunker they heard shots and cries in Arabic. Nardi threw in another grenade, and he fired two magazines from his Uzi. Quiet reigned. Then Yecki went in, firing from the hip.

The battle for the great bunker was over. Ammunition Hill had been conquered. The time was 0515.

With the end of the battle for the great bunker, the forces on Ammunition Hill organized to evacuate the wounded.

Doron and Dudik directed the work. Squads were set up which combed the trenches and gathered the wounded together. During this operation, they found Jordanian soldiers who had pretended to be dead during the battle, and were now trying to escape or fight for their lives.

Nir stayed with Dadi and helped to organize the perimeter defense and complete any mopping up in the trenches. Shots, salvos from Uzis, and explosions of hand grenades were still heard from time to time. In pairs and in squads the cleaning-up operations went on.

In the Police School yard, Doron and Bunch took over the station and then went up Ammunition Hill to speed the evacuation of the wounded.

Tenne found a path through the minefield; as a result, the seriously wounded could be taken straight to the casualty clearing stations, and then to the hospital.

From Givat Hamivtar there was still sniping. Ofer got up to shoot at a nearby group of Jordanians. A bullet hit him in the chest and he was taken quickly to an ambulance. The doctor at the casualty clearing station said he would have to be rushed to the hospital, but he died before he could be moved.

Yoram was lying in the yard of the Police School. Shmaya turned to him: "Yoram, how are you feeling?" Yoram opened his eyes; Shmaya thought, "I'll never forget his eyes—blue, beautiful." But Yoram closed his eyes and never opened them again.

Meir Shnur was not holding his own; his breathing had stopped. A shell fell on the casualty clearing station. Eli Kahane was hit by shrapnel in the armpit. He laughed. "It's nothing." But he was sent to the hospital, where he died. A piece of shrapnel had touched his heart.

On Ammunition Hill, the forces were reorganizing to advance on the Old City and the hills around it.

Chapter V

BATTALION 71 –
MISSION ACCOMPLISHED

By 0030, when Uzi, the battalion commander, returned to the battalion from the meeting with me at the corner of Zephaniah Street, he found that the situation was not at all satisfactory: The selected breakthrough squads, and all the battalion's radiomen, had not arrived. This force, under Reinitz, the deputy commander of the breakthrough company, was in a bus that had gotten lost in the narrow Jerusalem streets.

Zero hour was approaching. Uzi gave instructions that new breakthrough squads should be organized immediately.

Eilat, commander of the breakthrough company, began to put together new squads from among the forces intended to pin down the enemy, and from the reserves. He sent Zvika, the platoon commander, and Shaul, the company sergeant major, to the reserve companies for bangalores. Shells were exploding nearby, and the paratroopers pressed themselves against the walls as they watched Zvika and Shaul pass along the length of the lines, exposed to fire. The two reached Marico, the company commander, explained to him what was needed, and the collection of the bangalores began.

In the Bet-Ysrael neighborhood, Bash, the company commander, chose an open area between two streets leading to the breakthrough zone, and instructed the doctor, Dr. Yigal, to spread out the unit there.

The regimental sergeant major, Chekel, organized transport and ammunition. Bash and his staff went down below to the men to explain where they would be and how to reach them.

The shells falling in the vicinity served as a warning of what could be expected, so the men were spread out a little more and the vehicles moved some distance.

Bash took a truck to the Schneller Compound. There he found another truck loaded with shells and took it straight back to the battlefield.

Uzi and Dan, his deputy commander, visited the men in the companies. Now and then they stopped to check an item of equipment. Some of the men leaned on the wall of the houses to the west of the road. The officers instructed them to join their friends on the east side of the road, because there the concrete wall would protect them from flat-trajectory fire.

Raviv, the platoon commander of the mortars, a Jerusalemite, knew his city well and had based his selection of a position for his mortars on this knowledge. He remembered where there was a small crater with heaps of stones to provide cover. This crater was near the Sanhedria crossroads, so Raviv went there.

Just as his column, consisting of two buses carrying two platoons, a weapons carrier for communications, and a civilian truck loaded with ammunition, reached the site, Raviv heard the whistle of a shell. He told his men to jump off the vehicles quickly and to spread out before the shell exploded.

Itzik, still in the bus, was wounded in the groin but jumped out of the bus by himself and lay down beside it. Other shells hit the area. The men rushed to Itzik, and Raviv ordered his immediate evacuation to the rear, as he was losing a lot of blood. The precious time before zero hour was passing quickly, so Raviv decided not to change his choice of site, and to place the mortars in position at once. Shells kept falling amid shouts and yells as he hurried the men to their posts. The radiomen took their instruments off the weapons carrier. The crews placed the mortars in position. The officers took care to put the guns between the heaps of stone and earth, for protection against shrapnel.

Raviv reported that he was ready to start range-finding.

Bikel, commander of the support company, went with his personal runner and Zvili, commander of the mortar platoon, to a three-storey building close to the border to try to get the range. The house was exposed to Jordanian fire. This fire was of course very troublesome, but Bikel was worrying more about the lack of sufficient shells for his mortars. The large truck, loaded with shells, that had been promised by the Jerusalem Brigade, had not come.

He had very little time available for rangefinding—only fifteen minutes. In the north he heard the thunder of the preparatory barrage around the Police School. From the south he also heard heavy shelling, and shells were exploding behind him and behind the house, in the middle of Jewish Jerusalem.

Ignoring the Jordanian fire, Bikel calmly measured the range. The distance from here to the target was very small—not more than two hundred meters. It was dangerous—a small mistake and the shells could hit our own men. Asaf also worked out the range to hit the Jordanian mortars.

Bikel advised Raviv on the radio of his calculations. Raviv answered, but could not be heard. Bikel went up to the top floor. From there, contact was good. Bikel advised Raviv of the range to the breakthrough area, and Asaf did the same in regard to the Jordanian mortars in Wadi Joz.

Raviv gave orders: "Fire." Bikel and Asaf counted the seconds. The noise round about made it hard to hear the shriek of the shells. Would they be able to pinpoint the explosions in the darkness? They spotted one, then another, and Bikel gave the data to correct the fire. The rangefinding continued.

Only ten shells were fired. The stock of bombs was small—about a hundred for each platoon. Bikel decided to save time and bombs. If necessary he would give the gunners further data during the action.

Next to them, in a narrow lane leading into Samuel the Prophet Street, the recoilless gun platoon took up its position. Since the battalion had been given only one platoon of tanks for support, it was essential to make use of recoilless guns. Dan took Goren, commander of the recoilless gun platoon, near to the area chosen for the breach and explained the plan of action to him, indicating the sector allocated to the recoilless guns. Goren went back to his platoon. Shells and bullets were falling there, but no one had been hit. Goren ordered the gunners to take up their positions. The jeeps carrying the guns were placed in Samuel the Prophet Street, south of the site chosen for the breach.

Goren explained the assignment to his men: "We have to smash the Jordanian positions, which may endanger the men breaking through." He went from jeep to jeep to fix the position of each accurately.

Uzi and Eilat had just finished improvising new plans for the breakthrough, because of the lost busload of the original groups, when from the north along the road came the sound of soldiers in a hurry. It was Reinitz bringing the lost busload of signalers and breakthrough squads. Reinitz, breathless, told what happened:

"Because of the shells and the darkness, the bus was cut off from the one in front of it; instead we followed behind the mortar-platoon buses. When a shell fell near the buses, we looked and saw that we had reached the wrong place. I decided to go back to Schneller, thinking that from there we'd get directions. After rambling around the dark streets, we came to the advance command group of the brigade. They showed me where to go."

There were only a few minutes left to zero hour.

Reinitz's appearance was like a shot in the arm for the battalion.

Uzi gave orders that the men who had just arrived should go to the front, and Reinitz helped Eilat organize the breakthrough company. The Jordanian shelling was steadily increasing in strength and shells were falling nearer to the advance command group. Three dropped at the entrance to the house, and Malinov, the intelligence sergeant, was hit. The breakthrough squads and the signalers pressed up against the walls and took cover. Malinov groaned and a squad ran out and brought him into the stairwell.

Gadi, the platoon commander who would lead the spearhead of the breakthrough force, called the men to form up behind him.

Because of the noise of explosions and the search for cover from the exploding shells, Zichri, the officer appointed to command the pinning-down forces on the right, did not hear Gadi's order and remained behind. Gadi did not look back, but went on to lead the men Reinitz had brought with him to their destination. All along the path shells were bursting, and there was considerable confusion as these men hurried to take up their position ahead of the others.

They reached the company just as it was beginning to move. "Where the hell have you been? They've already put men in your place for the breakthrough," snapped a voice. The men entered the ranks, and sighed with relief. "We made it!"

The men from the signalers' platoon joined Uzi's advance command group.

Puchi, the communications officer, reported to Uzi that the signalers had arrived from Yechezkel Street and were joining up with Gilboa's tanks, which were taking up their positions on the edge of the road; the streets were so narrow that the caterpillar on one side of the tank had to travel on the sidewalk. At the Samuel the Prophet Street crossroads, the tanks turned south and moved to the opening in the concrete wall. With a creaking of caterpillars, the tanks entered the opening.

Puchi checked his contacts with the companies—all networks were functioning efficiently.

At one minute to zero hour, enemy fire aimed at the house from which Bikel was doing his rangefinding became dense. Bikel said a few words to Raviv, the rangefinding ended, and the group left the house on the double. As they turned left to go to Battalion Headquarters, they heard a crash behind them and stopped for a moment to look back. The balcony on which they were working had vanished—only the knobs of the iron railing were left. "Missed us," Bikel said laconically. He went on to report to Uzi, "Rangefinding more or less in order. But what about the shells?"

Uzi had good news for him. A truck with seven hundred shells had just arrived. Bash had brought it from Schneller.

The mortarmen fell upon the shells like hungry lions on their prey. Within minutes the mortars were ready, amply supplied. Enemy fire did not stop for a moment. There were no salvos, and the guns weren't carefully aimed; nevertheless a shell fell every minute. Asaf's north section was too near the middle of the position for comfort, so he moved it south. All the men, who had finished getting their mortars ready for firing, dug in close to their guns.

Raviv reported to Bikel, "Mortars all set."

Uzi and his staff breathed sighs of relief. Now the mortars had some presents for King Hussein's Legionnaires, the battalion was set for the breakthrough. The time was 0225.

Gilboa's tanks took up their position: Gilboa himself on the left facing the Police School; Ben Gigi in the center; Albez facing south, close to the breakthrough area. They opened fire.

Dan came from the direction of the fences, together with the commanders of the squads responsible for pinning down the enemy, Nimrod and Shpitzer. The latter ran to their men, while Dan asked Uzi for another minute, because he had to explain something to a tank crew.

Albez, the commander of the tank, a cap on his head and stripped to the waist, was in charge of the tank's gun. Since they had opened fire, he had been taking a crack at every Jordanian post that revealed itself by shooting. By the light of the large searchlights that lit up the Police School area, he also spotted Jordanian bunkers that were keeping discreetly quiet, and went for them as well.

Dan stood beside the tank and called to Albez as loudly as he could, but Albez didn't hear. Dan picked up a small stone and threw it to attract his attention, but Albez thought it was shrapnel and ducked inside the tank for a second. Dan gave up and returned to the battalion command, saying to Uzi, "For my part, we can begin!"

Uzi looked at the watch. 0230.

"Bikel—begin firing. Dan, take a position with the pinning-down squads. I'll tell you when to begin to move."

Bikel contacted Raviv and Asaf.

The mortars launched three minutes of fire to paralyze the enemy. Eilat, leader of the breakthrough squad, gave Barnes a bangalore. "You put it on the fence." Barnes was excited that he would be the one to place the first bangalore.

It was the moment the mortarmen had been waiting for. They worked fast, putting shells into the barrels and taking cases out with a swing. They fired rapidly, fourteen shells a minute. Every now and then they stopped to check the balance and direction, then they continued firing.

The recoilless guns on the jeeps also opened fire. The blast made the walls of the houses shudder, and the thunder echoed in the alleys.

Eilat called Nimrod, the commander of the pinning-down

squad, on the left, to follow Dan, who brought them into position. They went into the trenches, which had been built back in 1948 during the days of the War of Liberation. On their right a tank was firing continuously. In the trenches were pieces of equipment and haversacks left by members of the Jerusalem Brigade, who had occupied the trenches all day. The heavy machine guns took up their positions, Nimrod showing where to direct their fire. Nadav, the section commander, instructed his men to open fire, and one heavy machine gun began, followed by the Mags and light machine guns.

Shpitzer, who was moving to the right, struck a barbed wire fence and turned to identify it with the help of Perach and Eytan. They had to hurry—soon the breakthrough force would arrive. A tracer shell added light. In the command group, field glasses were being used to observe the enemy and every suspicious movement was examined. The three minutes of the mortar barrage was nearly over.

The roof of one Jordanian building began to burn. From now on it would be called "the house with the burned roof" by the *chevra*.

"We've finished," Bikel reported.

"Go!" cried Uzi.

The men got up and began the advance. Our artillery shells were still falling on the barricades, while enemy shells fell around the tanks and the pinning-down squads. The tanks drew the heaviest fire.

When Eilat and his men got near the first barricade, he realized that Shpitzer's pinning-down man was not yet in place. He shouted an angry question and Shpitzer explained that he had struck barbed wire. Eilat contacted Uzi and asked for "repeat" for a few minutes to enable Shpitzer to complete his assignment. Uzi agreed, and the order was passed on to the mortars. They responded with another three minutes of heavy fire.

Eilat explained the problem to Dan. But Dan had noticed that the enemy was not shooting. Apparently they had not realized that a breach in the barricades was imminent. So it was better for Shpitzer to keep quiet.

Dan and Eilat headed the breakthrough squads toward their own barbed wire entanglements, opposite the enemy's. A number of enemy posts were firing, but now that the squads had got down to the bottom of the valley, the bullets passed over their heads. Dan, Eilat, and Gadi reached their wire and Eilat cut it quickly.

The light crack of the snapping wire sounded to the three men like explosions, but in the general roar of battle the noise was completely swallowed up. Very soon a wide breach was made. Rafallo and his squad stood next to it and called "Breach! Breach!" But since they suspected there were mines between the two barbed-wire positions, Dan whispered: "Put in a bangalore to explode the mines."

"Bangalore here," Eilat ordered, and Barnes rushed forward and put the bangalore on the ground. The distance between the Israeli and Jordanian fences was not more than two meters.

"Explosion!" called Barnes, and he ran back only to have the seconds pass with no explosion.

Dan ordered, "Bring another bangalore!" This time Gadi took the bangalore and ran ahead. Forgetting the danger of mines, he went through the area between the fences. No mines exploded. He put the bangalore on the Jordanian fence and pulled the detonator. "Explosion!" he roared, and ran back. "Lie down!" At the rear the men were crouching on top of each other. A mighty blast rent the air. Gadi ran back to the place of the explosion, took out a pocket torch and called: "Breach! Breach!"

"The way is open!" Dan signaled Marico's company.

Marico got up and the whole line started to move ahead. Eilat, with Zvika's breakthrough force, was still in the front line when suddenly Eilat came up against another altogether unexpected barbed-wire fence.

From the tank, Karni the gunner noted the forward movement of the paratroopers and redirected his fire accordingly, so as not to hit his own men.

"Dan," called Eilat, "the fence is very complicated. I am putting a bangalore on it."

"Right," Dan answered.

"Three more minutes of mortar fire," he called back to Uzi.

The crowding became worse. "Stop. Go back," called Dan. "Back, back!" The men passed the order back. Eilat showed Zvika where to place the bangalore. Zvika and the pinning-down man attached to him looked for a suitable place to put the explosive. "If we put it there, it could go off without making a breach." They found a good spot, and went back, but only a few meters. "Explosion!" they called. "Are you crazy? Put your heads down!" the soldiers at the back shouted at them.

The explosion was followed by a wave of smoke and stones which covered the *chevra*. Eilat ran forward, convinced that that was the last fence, but his leg caught in more barbed wire. "To the devil," he hissed. "Another bangalore here! Everyone back!" "Forward, back? Forward, back? What's going on here?" the men in line grumbled.

Another bangalore was sent forward as officers at the back tried to control the crush caused by the unexpected delays at the fences.

Uzi was worried by the slow progress at the breach. "What's happening? What's the delay?" He urged them to hurry. Eilat put down the bangalore on the deep tangle of wire and detonated it. "Explosion! Move away! Lie down!" But the men couldn't move away because of the crush from behind. "Lie down, then; close to the ground!" All lay down—curiously there was almost no fire from the enemy. Shells and shots from the tanks and the mortars passed overhead toward the Jordanian line.

A great blast cut through the air. "Forward!" came the familiar cry. The men could hardly believe that they were going through at last. Eilat and Zvika raced ahead at the front. The breach was there, and no more fences. Zvika's boys took out flashlights and again yelled the news they all had waited for, "Breach! Breach!"

Now they did believe it. "Follow me!" shouted Marico, the company commander. He was already inside. "Follow me!" shouted the officers all along the line. "Hey! You're blinding us with your flashlights!" men complained. The officers pointed their flashlights down and covered the glass with their fingers. "Breach! Breach!" came the repeated cry.

Some soldiers made a mistake and took the wrong direction in the darkness. "Hey, you there! This way! Breach here! Here!"

Dan stopped for a moment next to Zvika: "When the *chevra* are through, widen the breach for the recoilless guns."

Marico's company poured through.

Uzi came to the breach and took up his position there.

Bikel ordered Raviv, "Add one hundred meters!" Raviv ordered Bigun's section, "Add one hundred! Aim at the wall and the Wadi Joz crossroads. Fire!"

The breakthrough had been achieved. The conquest of the Sheikh Jarragh suburb and the American Colony area had begun.

In passing through the fences, Marico's company had joined Eilat's. Their assignment was to clean up the Jordanian forces in the breakthrough area, so that the other companies behind them could advance to their more distant targets in the area of the American Colony. Fire from the Jordanians during the breach of the barricades enabled them to identify the Jordanian positions.

In the aerial photograph, according to which the company

action was planned, there was a communication trench, with pill-boxes all along its length. Only a small number of these pillboxes were now active, but it was not clear whether they had been destroyed by the artillery and the tanks, or were just waiting to ambush the attackers as they came closer.

Yossi, commander of the first platoon, was attached to Marico. His platoon had to clean up the houses between the breach and the great wall running along the side of Nablus Road. The photograph showed that in this wall there was a narrow opening, but only one. They had to find it quickly, because they had to secure the Wadi Joz crossroads. The companies of Mussa and Zamush depended on their doing so.

Gideon and Brown, commanders of the other platoons in Marico's company, looked to the left. There was the lower Sheik Jarragh suburb, which they had to mop up. They too were per-plexed by the silence. No shooting from there.

Marico and his men pushed forward. Dan showed him the way through the breach. Marico turned back to help his men pin-point it. After passing through, the men gathered on the left, near the ruins of a house, and waited. Others went right and found shelter behind a concrete wall. From here, Eilat's company made contact with Jordanian positions, firing from the building blocks, which were endangering the forces passing through.

Yossi collected platoon number one and began to move. He intended to reach the opening in the wall as quickly as possible despite the darkness and smoke. Unexpectedly a wall of stone and concrete cut across the open area before him, and behind it was a low house sunk in quiet shadow. The platoon went along this wall. Beyond it they saw another house, this one two-storeyed.

It stood in the middle of the area, and was vital from all points of view. Marico ordered Yossi to clean it up, and to make sure that no enemy was inside.

Yossi placed Oded with his machine gun in a position to cover them and, with Pedico, went up to the window. As he took out a grenade, he noticed that it was a phosphorus grenade, but it was too late to change it. Yossi shot a burst at the window, smashing the glass, and prepared to throw the grenade. Then he saw that the window was barred. He pushed his hand inside through the broken panes and dropped the grenade. Before they had time to get away the grenade exploded, shooting splinters of phosphorus at them.

Yossi began to burn and ordered Amos, the sergeant, to take charge of his platoon. His burns were very painful. Pedico's were slight and he went on with Amos. Ilan the medic helped Yossi— they flooded his burning clothes with water from a tap in the yard and Ilan bandaged the larger wounds, while Yossi wet the bandage to soothe the burns a little. Marico came up and sent Yossi back to the casualty clearing station.

Amos went on with the platoon, around the house, until he reached its main door. Pedico threw in a grenade and emptied a magazine into the house.

Now they could proceed to the Nablus Road wall. Amos found the opening. It was narrow, but they pressed through and stood on the road to Nablus. They had to cross to the hill opposite them. As they did so, they heard the whistle of bullets, but these were high and ineffective.

The platoon ran south along the Nablus Road. On their right was a petrol station; to their left, the Sheikh Jarragh mosque. Oded pinned down a machine gun while Dori mopped up the position with a burst and a grenade. The platoon continued until they reached a huge building. They looked for an entrance but there was no entrance on Nablus Road, only a stone fence with sharp-pointed iron railings. They went on. The road turned to the left. A few meters farther, beyond the corner of the street, was the gate to the yard. They entered and took up positions to cover the road as some members of the platoon spread out near the gate and others kept close to the fence along the Nablus Road.

The southern flank of the battalion's breakthrough area was secure!

The companies of Mussa and Zamush passed along to the east. At the crossroads of Wadi Joz, to the south in the direction of the Old City, no Jordanian forces could be seen. Except for a few distant shots, all that could be heard now was the crackling of flames on a burning roof. The *chevra* felt secure.

Suddenly bullets began to strike around them. True, these were isolated shots, but accurate. A quick look identified the source of fire as from across the road, some meters to the south, from a house with a large yard, its windows and verandas fortified. At the entrance to the yard stood a Jordanian recoilless gun on a jeep, with two Jordanians next to it. Everyone who spotted them opened fire, and the two disappeared into the house.

Amos sent Alex to the corner of the house opposite, instructing him to pin down any Jordanians in the yard.

From the opening in the wall, between the burning roof and the house, a Legionnaire appeared. "Amos! A Legionnaire!" Pedico cried. "Wait. Don't shoot yet," Amos replied. "Let him come closer." But the Jordanian vanished. Pedico watched the place with riveted eyes. The Legionnaire reappeared. This time Pedico didn't wait. He fired. The Legionnaire sank beside the wall, then tried to get away. A burst pinned him down.

Suddenly a hand grenade exploded right in the middle of the *chevra*, injuring four. Dudi, the nearest to the blast, was hit in the back and shoulders. Oded was wounded in the arms and back, but was saved from a more serious injury by the radio he was carrying. Amos was hit in the foot, Ami in the hand.

Dudi had to be evacuated immediately. Amos spread the men out to cover the house with the walled yard. Then Alex saw two

Legionnaires coming down the Nablus road toward the house. To shoot at them he would have had to expose part of his body. One of the Jordanians rushed into the entrance of the yard, and the second entered the house opposite and disappeared inside. In the street there was a tense silence, with occasional shots. It was dangerous to move.

Mussa was waiting for the breach behind Marico, who in turn was behind Eilat's breakthrough company. Mussa was anxious to get across the open area between the fences as soon as possible so as to reach the Wadi Joz road, the area assigned to his company.

The targets for his platoons were clear and he had organized them accordingly Izmirli's number one platoon would serve as the spearhead, and would secure the platoon's movements along the Nablus Road to the Wadi Joz road. Then they would take up positions on the hill, behind rocks above the crossroads.

From there Nudelman's platoon would take over the vanguard and move to clean up houses along the Wadi Joz road. The platoon of "Kushi" (Aryeh Dvir) would move off to the left and clean up the Jordanian mortar positions in the wadi.

A squad under Reuven, the deputy company commander, would turn right at the first crossroads and mop up the upper road, which ran across the American Colony area. In preparation for the advance the company commander placed himself behind the spearhead. Marico's company had begun to move toward the fences. Izmirli was attached to the rear of this force, moving behind it.

From the front came a blast—explosive bullets from medium machine guns that hit the walls of the houses across the road and burst in a blinding halo of light. Nudelman, curious, approached the corner of the wall to see what was happening and a burst of bullets sprayed shrapnel at him, one piece hitting his knee. "Curiosity doesn't pay," Nudelman decided, and tumbled hurriedly backward. The first men of the company began to go toward the beach.

A burst passed over the company command and the spearhead, which was at that moment in the depression at the bottom of the slope. Everyone lay on the ground. "Stay where you are," roared Mussa to Nudelman. "You there, lie down and don't move. And don't crowd together so."

Movement stopped and they waited.

"Get to Mussa and ask what's up," Nudelman told Gabi, his runner, who rushed out to the open area. It was hard to run, for he was treading on people. "Mussa," Gabi asked, "what's up?"

"Get back there. I'll let them know what to do. Get going! Run!"

Suddenly from the Jordanian positions yellow rockets shot up, and the area was flooded with light, blinding, disturbing. The tanks and recoilless guns turned their muzzles toward the sources of fire. A few tracer bursts marked the path. The shells exploded on the Jordanian bunkers and blessed darkness reigned again in the crowded line.

The whole company was now already on the slope going down to the breach. Suddenly at the top of the line came the cry: "Explosion. Back! Bangalore! Back fifty meters!" A push backward began with shouts and commands. Reuven, the deputy company commander, left his force and rushed forward to get some order into the company. "Mussa," he shouted, "what's going on?"

"Move the men back," answered Mussa. "I'll stay here."

"Follow me!" Reuven called to the troops, and turned around. The line, winding like a snake, moved back. Then they began to straighten it, but before they could do so, the order came, "Forward! The whole company, forward."

The line wound in the opposite direction and went back to the breach. There Marico was helping to pinpoint the crossing through the fence.

In the gloom, the dust, and the smoke, several paratroopers lost their direction. "D Company, here!" the officers roared, running after those who went wrong, catching them by the arms and directing them to the breach.

"Breach, breach!" came the familiar cry, and the forward rush continued. Suddenly there was the shriek of a shell and on the slope at the back a mighty explosion, followed by the cry, "Medic!" "A recoilless gun shell, for sure," whispered Baruch to himself. "Some poor devil caught it."

On the right of the crossing was a house, and Izmirli suspected that the shot had come from near it. At the head of his platoon, he approached the house and cleaned it up with a burst and a grenade. On the left was a heap of ruins. While waiting for new orders the *chevra* took cover there. Across the fence Dan waited for them, and the company advanced toward him.

"Who is it? Mussa? Carry on straight. Behind the building, turn left. From there, you will come to the opening in the wall. On Nablus Road. Marico's crowd are already there."

"D Company, follow me!" Mussa shouted again. "Dani, here! Dani, here!"

When they crossed the Nablus Road, Mussa summoned the platoon commanders to make sure that they knew where they were in the field.

"Nudelman," called Mussa, "can you identify the area?"

It was dark all round them. Nudelman stared right and left.

"Sure," he grinned. "It's all right. Everything clear."

"Good. Then forward. And remember—keep close to the fences. Another thing—don't get busy with houses that don't start with you. And move fast. When you reach the crossroad report."

Nudelman called his platoon sergeant. "You go left and I'll go right." Running, the platoon divided into two forces and began to move.

"Kushi, here!" called Mussa. "From here you divide and go down into the wadi."

"No problem," answered Kushi. Everything was clear to him. He had to attack the Jordanian mortar positions and destroy them: nothing could be simpler. "Platoon, follow me!" He crossed the street and rushed down the steep slope of the wadi.

Mussa looked round him. Until now everything had gone according to plan. Izmirli was providing cover. Kushi had already gone. Nudelman was cleaning up. Reuven and the Mags were following.

The company command caught up with the last of Nudelman's men. It seemed to Mussa that the platoon was going too slowly, and indeed, Nudelman now and then cast an inquisitive eye into the yards. It was dark, of course, so he couldn't see much, but still, "It's better than nothing."

Mussa urged: "Don't stop. Pity to waste time."

Nudelman identified the place where the road forked. Mussa had shown him this on the photograph, at the time of the first briefing. "When you get to the fork, report and take the house on the corner to the right."

"I've come to the fork," Nudelman called back.

"Take the house and wait," Mussa answered.

"Arnon, here!" Arnon, the commander of the Mag platoon, went to Mussa. At the briefing, Mussa had said he would direct him in the field. Now he showed him a flat concrete roof at the level of the street and directed him to it. "Set up the Mags here, facing the wadi, and help Kushi to clean up the mortars."

Arnon and his men climbed on to the roof. On the west side they set up the Mags under Yisrael's command. With him were Kuniak and Yair. On the east were Yoeli, with Zemach, Giora, and Kimchi.

The first light of day was just beginning to show. To their

tired eyes, this half-light offered neither light nor darkness. They threw off the carriers and began to set up the weapons.

Across the road, Nudelman was turning right to enter the house and take up his position there.

Stairs with a half turn led into the house. Nudelman was at the head with Rami, his runner. The bazooka men Paldinger and Neuberg were still at the entrance.

On the road to the left was a spearhead squad under Yisrael's command. In the middle was Brisler with the antitank rifle, and on his right, Motti.

Nudelman and Rami tried to open the door, but it wouldn't open. Both fired Uzi shots at the lock but, they still couldn't open the door. Suddenly there was a cry from the street: "A Jordanian truck is coming!"

From the top of the Wadi Joz road a truck without lights came hurtling down. "Hit it, quick!" Mussa roared from behind, and ran forward. Paldinger aimed the bazooka.

"Antitank gunner," shouted Yisrael. The truck reached the crossroads. Breisler shot the antitank gun, the shell hitting the fuel container. The truck skidded to the left, struck a wall, and began to burn. Solo, roused by Mussa's roar, pressed the trigger of the Uzi and sprayed the cab with bullets.

Reuven, who had rushed up with the rear, detected a flash of fire from the Mags on the flat roof. When Arnon heard the shout, "Jordanian truck!" he called to the men: "Finish it off!"

Shooting instinctively from the hip, with Uzis and Mags, the spearhead squad stormed the truck and its ammunition began to explode.

Suddenly bursts of fire emerged from above the Sheikh Jarragh neighborhood. Kimchi fell and cried, "Medic!" Beside him, the whole Mag squad lay bleeding. A bullet hit Arnon's Uzi. He turned his head.

When he saw that many of his men had been hit, Arnon thought at first that some terrible mistake had been made, and he began to run to his men with hands spread out, shouting, "Stop! Stop!" as if he wanted to stop the bullets with his own body and protect his friends.

"Idiot, lie down!" Kuniak called to him from behind. Then Arnon saw that the bursts were coming from a more distant area. Under cover of the wall the *chevra* were already dealing with the wounded men.

"Mussa, we have many wounded. Send a medic," Arnon called. But Efal, the company medic, was already there.

"Send another medic," he called, and went to Yoeli, who was streaming with blood. Harpaz, another medic, arrived and went to Zemach. Zemach said to him: "Leave me. Go to Giora first!"

Micha, Nudelman's medic, also arrived, but was told he was not necessary. "Go back to the platoon."

The medics moved the wounded to the wall of the roof for cover against sniping. Arnon stayed to help his men. He sent Yisrael and Yair with the Mag to the top of the road to provide cover. Kuniak took a stand and shot in turn at each of the windows containing potential snipers.

"Nudelman, go on," Mussa ordered. "When you reach the next crossroads, take up your position in the house on the right and report."

In two files, the platoon continued to clean up the Wadi Joz road. Now Mussa called Reuven. At this crossing he had to turn right and begin his independent mission—to clean up the main road of the American Colony area, which ran parallel to the Wadi Joz road.

"From there, you turn up the road. Don't forget that we are down below you."

Reuven drew to the right, bypassing the burning truck and taking the path that cut through the bend. On the left, in the

Wadi, Mussa heard shots where Kushi's platoon was fighting. Mussa went on toward Nudelman's platoon and the company split up according to plan, each commander moving on a separate axis.

"I have reached the crossroads," Nudelman reported.

"Take the house, secure it, and wait for orders."

Men of Zamuch's company, A Company, who until now had moved behind Mussa's, began to pass them going up the road in the direction of the Rockefeller Museum. Mussa looked back and tried to follow what was happening to Kushi and Reuven.

The contact with Kushi was poor because he was deep in the wadi. He had divided his platoon into two. At the head of the spearhead force was Penso, with Natanson on his left with a submachine gun, and Nachum on the right with an antitank gun. He himself led the rest of the squad.

When the spearhead squad reached the building, they went in to examine it while the rest waited. But over the radio Mussa urged them to go on, insisting that every second was precious.

Suddenly the spearhead squad came across two camouflaged Jordanian trucks under a tree, and Penso saw a number of Jordanians fleeing into the wadi. He prepared to shoot them down.

"No! No!" called Kushi, mindful of Mussa's orders, "Don't worry about them. Go on!"

In front of them they saw some burial caves, and somebody noticed the barrels of mortars sticking out of them. They threw grenades in and opened fire with Uzis, and after some return of fire there was silence. It seemed that their assignment to identify and destroy the mortar position had been completed, so they organized perimeter defense.

Suddenly they saw a Jordanian soldier running in the direction of the mortar position, and Ze'ev brought him down with a shot. A second Jordanian appeared, heading toward Rafi. There was a quick burst and the Jordanian fell.

Things seemed to be going very well when all of a sudden Yotam was hit in the leg, the shot coming from out of the darkness, and Ze'ev was also hit. He shouted to bring Yaron, the medic, who assured Ze'ev that it was only a slight wound.

Rafi heaved Yotam on to his back and carried him to the street, as Penso and the squad combed the tunnels and the approaches of the burial caves. Penso put Natanson with the submachine gun opposite the entrance.

Suddenly they heard muttering from inside the caves, and Natanson spied a Jordanian helmet and fired a burst. As Penso listened intently, he heard a woman screaming, and children and fowls. He told Kushi, who sent Edmund to go to the other side of the cave and call to the civilians to get out. Kushi and Penso stayed on the west side as the civilians began to emerge.

Kushi got a bullet in the neck, so Penso caught him by his equipment and dragged him to a tunnel. The bullet had gone straight into his neck, and his body was ominously still.

Now the platoons changed positions. It was clear that there were still Jordanian soldiers in the burial caves, so Sharar and Dentes took up positions high on the hill and shot inside the caves. Nachum joined in with the antitank gun and Chochima with two bazooka shells, one of them phosphorus.

Kritzman and Penso went inside the caves. Now the catacombs were indeed as quiet as the tomb. To make certain no more snipers were hiding there, they threw grenades into the dark caves, but were quickly satisfied that there were no living Jordanian soldiers left inside.

Sharar and Dentes killed a Jordanian soldier near their position, but Mussa complained over the radio that the fighting in the caves was taking too long; he wanted the company to press on.

In the meanwhile Uzi, with his staff, had come up along the street to find out what was happening. Ze'ev explained, and Uzi promised to send a recoilless-gun jeep to help in the evacuation of the wounded. Ze'ev then called on Sharar and Dentes to leave their position, as they had to go on.

Sharar replied that he had seen suspicious movements nearby, and just then they saw Dentes rolling down the hill, bullets following after him, and Sharar was seriously wounded at the same time. He was still high up on the hillside and no one could see where the Jordanian fire was coming from. Ze'ev thought that it was from the south, and looked in that direction and saw Ismirli lying at the crossroads. "His force probably fired in error," Ze'ev thought in agony. "I must go to them to stop it at once."

Yaron, the medic, climbed up the hill to attend to Sharar, and on his way looked around. Suddenly he saw two helmets on top of the mosque, and realized the Jordanian snipers were using the minaret. Stooping and twisting, he tried to get to Sharar, but a mighty blow on the back knocked him off his feet. He lay there for a while, thinking that his spine had been hit. Then he realized that he had been saved by a miracle, the bullet had hit his canteen. He was terrified that any moment he might get another bullet, but managed to crawl back without any further injury.

The *chevra* decided that the situation was desperate. Somehow they had to get Sharar out, and they still had to clean up the hill and the mosque. The battalion was coming along this axis; it had to be safe.

In the end Natanson, Kritzman, and Aryeh charged straight up the hill, bullets flying overhead. When they reached the top, a bullet got Natanson and he fell near a stone fence. Aryeh was hit in the knee as he lay close to a wall. When he and Kritzman tried to move, they were forced back by fire from a new direction. They realized that it was coming from the American Colony area.

The entire platoon fired everything they had at the mosque and the American Colony position of the Jordanians, until the shooting stopped and there was absolute silence. The *chevra* decided that now they could evacuate their wounded. From the

Wadi Joz road, the medic of another platoon joined them and together they brought down Kritzman, Penso, Aryeh, and Sharar. The recoiless-gun jeep arrived as promised to help them take the men back.

They had accomplished their mission: The mortar position had been destroyed and the area mopped up. But they had paid a heavy price: Few members of the platoon were left alive and unhurt.

Zamush's company crossed the Nablus Road and entered the Wadi Joz road. They advanced for some distance without encountering any enemy force. Mussa's company was in front of them, cleaning up the roads. From all sides came shots and the thunder of explosions. The *chevra* were tense but made no contact with the enemy.

Suddenly bursts of tracer bullets appeared from the left flank, nearby. Yoel, the section commander, sprinted forward, drawing his section with him. He placed the machine gunner next to a milestone and rushed ahead with the section toward the source of fire, up the edge of the wadi. They shot ferociously as they ran, and the Jordanian fire stopped. The paratroopers went up the street past the burning Jordanian truck, in which ammunition was still exploding. Then they passed the wounded Mag men. Near the crossroads at the garage, Zamush's company passed Mussa's, and now led the battalion.

Because of the speed of their advance, they had caught the Jordanians, and even themselves, completely by surprise, and they did not encounter any organized Jordanian formations. The advance of the company was undisturbed; they seemed to have gone beyond the war zone. It was an eerie feeling. Behind them fierce battles were being fought, but here at the front there was almost complete silence.

Zilche's section cleaned up several buildings facing Wadi Joz.

On reaching the entrance of one of the houses, Zilche saw a heap of branches lying to the left of the gate, so with a careful swing of the leg he spread the branches apart, and underneath found a sten gun and three magazines.

Zilche gave the sten to Musari, the platoon mortarman, and ordered him and Shmulik to cover the cleanup of the house. When they approached the door they shot covering bursts at the windows. The door then opened and an Arab family including four children came out. During the search of the house an English rifle was found.

Nevertheless the family was allowed to stay in their house, and the squad took up positions nearby. Suddenly a hand grenade fell near the paratroopers. With a mighty kick, Dani the medic sent it flying, and, in the same movement stretched out on the ground. The grenade exploded but no one was hurt. Rafi, the deputy company commander, and Dov, the sergeant, went to look for the person who had thrown it. On the roof they found a basket of old grenades, but no one there. Yet they knew the grenade could not have thrown itself.

Then they saw an armed Jordanian soldier trying to escape into the open area facing the wadi. Salvos of fire didn't touch him, and he entered a house one hundred and fifty meters away. Shmulik, a gun at the ready, waited patiently. When the Jordanian stuck his head out, an accurate bullet got him.

At the upper crossroads, a roadblock was placed under the command of Bitan. Its task was to secure the road in the direction of the Old City. The force consisted of two antitank rifles, a bazooka, and a machine gun. Before long, from the Old City and from the Rockefeller Museum, Jordanians were seen fleeing eastward. The range was long. *Chevra* from Reuven's force came to the roadblock. A Jordanian soldier crossed the road and a salvo of shots and antitank bombs dropped him. Two others followed, and they too fell beside him.

The company took up positions in the houses of the Wadi Joz neighborhood. From there they dominated the slopes of the Mount Scopus ridge, and the roads that lay north of Jerusalem and east of the Old City wall. In this way, the company cut off the main contact between the Old City and Jericho, and between Jerusalem and Ramallah.

It was true that Jordanian formations around the Auguste Victoria Hospital on Mount Scopus and Abu Tur had not yet been attacked, and were theoretically still in control of these areas. But the small Israeli garrison on Mount Scopus, permitted to be there as a police force under UN protection for the last nineteen years, under a system of changing convoys, was still holding out against the challenge from the Auguste Victoria.

With the establishment of physical communications between this small unit and the forces in the Hotel Ambassador sector, the Mount Scopus garrison was no longer in any danger: in fact it was the Jordanians at the Auguste Victoria who were in a precarious position, facing encirclement.

Nevertheless, the Jordanians' force was still large and formidable, and it had retained contact with the Jordanian army to the east toward the Heights of Edom. Although subjected to bombardment from the air by our Air Force and overland by our artillery, they were still functioning efficiently, and were able to control the area around the Rockefeller Museum below them. They could also fire at will on the men in the Wadi Joz and the American Colony neighborhood.

Zamush, who had set up the company command post at a point giving him a clear view of the wadi, suddenly noticed movements in the Jordanian formations and an increased concentration of forces at a particular point. He wondered whether this could mean that officers were engaged there in conference, perhaps planning a counterattack. So he reported his suspicions at once to Uzi and recommended heavy artillery fire. Uzi agreed, and a barrage was laid down immediately.

From his vantage point Zamush calmly gave reports to the gunners by radio, so that they soon got the range and shelled the target. The Jordanians scattered, the conference adjourned indefinitely.

Suddenly a jeep was seen rushing down the slope of the street from the Auguste Victoria crossroads toward the Old City. Paratroopers, busy clearing out snipers' nests, diverted their fire onto it. It was unclear whether the jeep contained officers in flight, or those trying to make contact with the Old City. The first shell did not hit it, so Amos, the mortarman of the platoon, dropped his mortar and picked up an Uzi he had taken earlier from one of the wounded. From Bitan's roadblock, set up in Wadi Joz above the Palace Hotel, they concentrated fire with all weapons on the jeep, which was hit and overturned into the wadi.

An open car came along the same road, and more bursts of fire sent it after the jeep. The *chevra* ran forward and found three dead Jordanians beside the vehicle.

Now the enemy contact between the Old City and the Auguste Victoria was almost completely severed, and only the road from Lions' Gate to Azaria village remained open to partial traffic. This too would soon be brought under control with fire, thus preventing operational traffic. The strategic aim of cutting off the Old City had been almost completely achieved. The time was 0500.

While the companies of Mussa and Zamush were advancing to take control of their targets, behind them the battles around the breach were still raging.

Eilat's company, after effecting the breach, assembled near the building-block area. Marico's company began to clean up the residential area known as "the ruins" in the Sheik Jarragh suburb. Amos's platoon secured the area toward the south.

From Samuel the Prophet Street, the heavy machine guns and the recoilless guns were firing constantly. They provided cover for the movement of the forces in front of the breach, including Battalion 28, and for the evacuation of the wounded to the rear.

Round the breach, men who had lost their units in the darkness and confusion were looking for them and for a chance to get a piece of the action. In the streets and houses, many wounded were waiting for medical attention and evacuation.

Uzi divided his staff in two. He himself went into the American Colony area. Reinitz remained in the area of the breach to bring up the recoilless guns, to supervise the evacuation of the wounded, and to try to introduce some order among the troops there.

At 0315 the recoilless gun platoon was the chief victim of the Jordanian barrage on the deployment area near Samuel the Prophet Street. Gideon, the commander of the platoon, was looking for new targets for his guns when suddenly the area was lit up by tracer shells. In their wake came a salvo of 81-mm shells from the Jordanian mortars.

The recoilless-gun jeep was hit and all the men were wounded. Fortunately some of them, including Dudik, the driver, found that their wounds were slight, and decided to move the jeep.

Ron and Shattner, who both fell out during the shelling, lay next to the jeep. Dudik pulled first Ron to shelter, then Shattner as well. Other men evacuated Keenes, who was badly hurt. In one blow the Jordanians had put half the platoon out of action.

The men who were comparatively fit organized anew. Quickly they loaded the jeep with the shells that had been neatly stacked to replace those used during the earlier barrage in support of the breakthrough.

* * *

Kapara's section, part of Zambush's A Company, had by then joined the recoilless-gun platoon. Before the attack began, they had been in Reinitz's bus, the bus that had gone astray and was only found at the last minute. But when the Jordanian shelling began and they were taken off the bus to move on foot, they lost their way again in the darkness. They had been trying to find their unit ever since, or at least to get into the battle together with some other unit.

Hearing the excited voices of men in the mortar platoon, they approached them hopefully, looking for a "job," any job. Raviv, commander of the platoon, was sorry for them, but he was too busy trying to find the range to attend to them, so he directed the lost sheep to Samuel the Prophet Street, where they might be able to link up with the Jerusalem Brigade.

They were not sure where they were going, but advanced hopefully toward the sound of heavy firing, on the theory that where there was shooting, that's where the war was. So they headed toward the noise. Very soon they came near to the Fagi houses. Here the shelling by the enemy was heavy, so they guessed that they were moving in the right direction. But they didn't know where or if they themselves should fire.

They worked out from the noises where the breach must be, and headed in that direction, asking everywhere for their missing unit.

"Who are you? What company?"

"28 Support . . ."

"Have you seen Zamush's company anywhere?"

"Sorry." The men moved off.

They looked everywhere. Everyone was too busy to bother about them. Nobody knew where Zamush was. They felt like children lost in a crowded stadium and looking for their mother, not paratroopers searching for a war.

Crushed, tired, and with frazzled nerves, they wondered what to do next. Salvos of shells were falling around them. They came upon numbers of wounded and, together with the reserves of Battalion 28, helped to evacuate them, for want of any other solution to their problem.

In the forward breach area, there was a dense concentration of men. Eilat, commander of the breakthrough force, assembled all his men not engaged in marking out the path for troops coming behind them to the breach, in the yard containing the building blocks.

Near him was Uzi, directing the companies on their way. Gradually, the supporting units of the battalion, part of the recoilless-gun platoon, the commando group, and the heavy machine-gun crews gathered there.

The men were scattered among the ruins of the houses, and in the olive trees, the building-blocks area, and in hollows of the ground.

Jordanian fire from the south had strengthened. Reinitz dispersed the men along the "terrace" and in the building blocks yard, where the piles of blocks provided both defense against enemy fire and possible vantage points from which to attack the Jordanians. The pitch blackness of the night was yielding to the first pale tints of dawn. A Jordanian heavy machine gun, apparently discovering the concentration of Israelis, became troublesome, although the fire was not very accurate.

Then, from a post somewhere in the vicinity of the white house, more machine-gun fire opened up. Movement in the field became very risky. Eilat went to Reinitz. "Let me take a bazooka man and give that heavy machine gun a crack!" Reinitz agreed.

Eilat took Atzmon and David with their bazookas. They selected firing positions. Range: 250 meters. Ammunition: anti-tank shells. Atzmon fired, but there was no sign of a hit. "Sorry, I have no night sight on my bazooka and can't aim accurately."

"No night sight? How can you aim at all?" David wondered,

aiming his own bazooka carefully. But again there was no hit, nor was a second shell luckier. They decided to try a high-explosive shell.

This time they saw a familiar ball of fire and heard a great explosion. Then silence from the machine gun.

Uzi instructed Reinitz to fetch the recoilless guns. By daylight they would be very good for shelling distant positions. Reinitz went at once. As he passed Zvika, he told him to widen the breach, so that the recoilless guns would be able to pass through. Zvika had just begun to widen the breach when Katz, commander of the commando platoon, came up. "You go to your platoon, Zvika," he suggested, "and I'll carry on here."

The bazooka had silenced the Jordanian heavy machine gun, but the light machine gun from the white house continued to fire constantly and efficiently. So Oded, the platoon commander in Marico's company, ordered David Natan to hit it with a bazooka shell. After each shell there was silence for a while, and they thought that David had knocked it out until it started firing again.

Uzi, the battalion commander, decided that it had to be put out of action once and for all. The best way to destroy it was to take the position and blow it up. "Any volunteers to tackle that post?"

All his staff officers volunteered, among them Barkai, the operations officer, and Barry, the intelligence officer. Bikel, commander of the support company, led them. Their place was really at the command post, but they were tempted by the prospect of hand-to-hand fighting. The officers were joined by Chaviv, the intelligence sergeant; Bikel's runner, James; and Yaakov Chai, Uzi's runner.

"Right, go on, but do it fast and come back here. We must move on to the advance companies," Uzi said.

David Natan turned to Eilat: "Should we hit the machine gun again?"

"No, no, David, not necessary. The officers have gone to finish it off."

The group of officers went past the casualty clearing station and through the narrow gate in the wall.

When they emerged on the Nablus Road, they realized that from there it was difficult to pinpoint the Jordanian posts, for between them and the bunkers there was a wall and a row of houses. The first was the house with the burning roof, and in the yard they could see a communication trench. They advanced along the wall of the house to its entrance, which faced the breach area. No fire was heard.

The officers and men went up to the veranda on the ground floor. Bikel took out a grenade and prepared to throw it. But there was no enemy to be seen. They decided to look for the machine gun in another building. In the side of the house facing Nablus road there was a door. A light push opened it, and they found themselves in a narrow maze between two houses. On the right was the two-storeyed house with the burning roof, and on the left the wall of a house with one floor. Carefully the officers went inside, but found nobody.

They returned to Nablus road and went on south. Barry took a grenade from Bikel and held it in his hand. Before they had gone ten meters they found a curve in the wall of the house there, and when they had gone round it, Barry suddenly came upon a Jordanian standing right next to him, pressed up against the wall, his weapon in his hand. His Uzi always at the ready in his right hand, Barry pressed the trigger, but there was no shot. Then he put out his left hand, stuck the grenade right on the Jordanian, and pushed his companions back round the bend.

The grenade exploded and the Jordanian fell, but Bikel, more exposed than the others, felt a searing sensation in various parts of his body and collapsed. Amos and Chaviv immediately dragged him to the rear. Ilan, the medic from C Company, rushed across the road, bandaged Bikel, and prepared him for evacuation. He was taken on a stretcher to the casualty clearing station.

Reinitz, the deputy battalion commander, brought the recoilless guns up to provide support for an attack on the Old City.

The darkness and the narrow lanes made driving difficult, as the enemy fire was still strong. Reinitz descended from his jeep and, walking slowly, led the guns.

Dudik's jeep got entangled in some wire, and at that moment a Jordanian tracer lighted up the area and immediately afterward a shell landed among the jeeps. Dudik's jeep jumped like an athlete and the camouflage net caught fire. But Dudik pressed hard down on the accelerator, and the jeep leapt forward. Rami, taken by surprise, was thrown out and remained lying on the ground. Nobody noticed him as the guns went on their way.

They went through the breach into the field of the building blocks. There the gunners looked for positions facing the white house. It was hard to find suitable sites for the guns. The piles of blocks provided good cover, but they also made it difficult to aim at the enemy positions.

Meanwhile, mortar shells, recoilless-gun shells, and bullets fell into the field, covering it with smoke and shrapnel. Eisner, sitting on a jeep, was hit in the eye and Lavie took him to shelter. Lerner climbed onto the jeep, moved it to a new firing position, loaded the recoilless gun, and fired. The Jordanian positions became quiet, but they still operated spasmodically.

Battalion 71, pouring through the breach onto the Nablus road, now passed the gunners. Men of the recoilless-gun platoon, who had lost their way earlier, now arrived at the field of the blocks. They had been operating as infantry under the command of their platoon sergeant, Yitzhak. With them came a heavy machine-gun section under Sergeant Avraham. Now the whole force was under the command of Gideon Levi, the deputy commander of the support company.

On the way they came across Rami, lying injured after his fall from the jeep. Yitzhak detailed men to evacuate him to the rear, and the others moved on to the breach, with single sniping shots sailing over their heads and even into the line among the men.

As soon as they reached the building-blocks field, nonstop accurate fire began to come at them from the south. Avraham spread the section out quickly behind a small hillock, and Apelbaum set up the heavy machine gun and at once opened fire. Gideon helped, standing among the blocks in a commanding position.

The recoilless-gun men took up positions all along the hillock, and they evacuated Eisener. Apelbaum fired the heavy machine gun, calmly ignoring the enemy fire, which was now only intermittent though still dangerous. Yitzhak and Masud brought the second gun into action, Gideon indicating targets to them.

Suddenly the Jordanians fired a heavy and accurate burst, and a recoilless gun shell exploded next to Gideon, who spun and fell. As the smoke cleared he called, "Don't bother about me. It's nothing."

Yitzhak and Avraham leapt toward him and saw that he had a wound next to his heart. Together they lifted him and pulled him to the shelter among the blocks. A jeep came pushing up and Gideon was taken back to the casualty clearing station, where he died.

Katz, who had been standing not far from Gideon, was found curled up as though asleep. He too was dead, and soldiers from his commando platoon evacuated his body.

Yitzhak and Avraham returned to their guns and continued the battle. It was getting light and enemy hits were more accurate. The *chevra* evacuated the wounded to a house on the left of the breach. Reinitz climbed on a recoilless-gun jeep and directed Gabi Lerner's fire on the heavy machine gun. Lavie and Ilan helped out. After two shells struck close, quiet reigned.

Reinitz went to look for a road so the recoilless guns from the building block field could get to Nablus Road. He found one, hidden behind a wall, running at an angle.

He got on to Goren's jeep and turned to Nablus Road. With him was Leizar, the operations sergeant. He sent Benny and Ben Yehuda to the command post with a request that the casualty clearing station should be brought forward to the new battlefield.

As he passed along the Wadi Joz road, he came across wounded but he did not stop for them; instead he went on, and at the garage crossroads caught up with Mussa and Zamush. On seeing the men spread thinly in the open space, he decided that it was necessary to bring Eilat's company forward, and Uzi confirmed this suggestion over the radio.

The medics decided to set up a kind of field ambulance post on the building-blocks field near the breach. Bernardo, Blumin, and Navaro took the wounded to a house they called the "antenna house" and turned it into a medical post.

Meanwhile, Uzi and his reduced staff were moving on foot toward the Nablus office. The officers who had volunteered to clean up the white house had not yet returned. From one of the houses snipers fired at the group, and the lust for combat suddenly gripped them. They ran into the first house, cleaned it up, moved to the second and finished that, but found that there was still sniping in the street. They were being drawn into the sector of Battalion 28, for in a house with pillars on Nablus Road, they met men of that battalion's A Company. They exchanged a few words, but had no time for a long conversation—that would all come later. At present there was too much to do.

Uzi and his staff went out along the Wadi Joz road. He maintained constant contact by radio with the companies and had to make snap decisions, give orders, and get to the van of his forces.

The companies of Mussa and Zamush were mopping up the Wadi Joz road while Eilat's company prepared to move on and Marico's C Company cleaned up the breakthrough area.

Gideon, commander of the second platoon in Marico's company, turned north toward the communication trench, but could not find it. He calculated that, according to the distance from the houses, he had to be in the right area. So he went on without result. There was no trench and no enemy. The men, organized so as to mop up trenches and bunkers, were perplexed. They felt they were wasting time.

So Gideon decided to clean up the houses dominating the open space. Running over an exposed area when the enemy was hiding behind houses and in alleys could be dangerous and costly. But he had to do something. The buildings looked more like ruins than houses. The yards were enclosed and connected with each other. Crossing from one to the other meant going through alleys, which were narrow and dark, without any cover. So they moved slowly and carefully, and only threw grenades at the higher buildings.

After a few minutes Gideon decided that he need worry only about the outermost houses, and need not go into those inside the suburb. The important thing was to secure passage across the open area.

On the left, in the direction of the breach, there was a high building. A group from the platoon went up to it to examine it from close quarters, because it dominated the open area. Inside the house they found men of the support company of the battalion, placed there to secure the flank of the advance. They separated and continued on their respective missions.

At the head of the platoon was a spearhead force, composed of Gideon in the middle, Ilan with a Mag on the left, and Peltz, the section commander, on the right. Behind them, the platoon moved in two groups, with not more than a few meters between them. When they reached the "ruins," they turned left and approached the corner house.

This was a square building, two-storeyed, with a red tiled roof. From there it was possible to fire at the whole of the breach area, and the area connecting it to Battalion 66, now operating in the north. At the outside corner was a concrete pillbox with shooting slits in the south and west walls. According to the photograph, the communication trench ran up to it. The platoon advanced on the pillbox from behind, where it was less strongly fortified.

Ilan was the first to see men next to the pillbox, he being on the extreme left with nothing to interfere with his field of vision. "Support force! Don't shoot!" he cried at the men he saw—he was convinced that they belonged to the force they had met earlier in the ruined house.

The men he saw were shocked and taken by surprise, and they stayed where they were. Peltz noticed that their helmets were flat, and that one of them was wearing a military tunic. Peltz emptied a magazine and a half at them. Gideon leapt to the left and threw a grenade at them. The grenade exploded. Ilan shot with the machine gun. The squad lay flat and the whole platoon pressed up against the fence of the house. Some of the Jordanians fell; others ran off.

When the paratroopers reached the house, they found three rifles, a machine gun, a bazooka, and ripped-open shell crates. Gideon decided to advance more carefully. He instructed Ilan to provide cover from above the wall of the pillbox, while he, at the head of the squad, entered the yard to mop it up. As they waited at the pillbox, Barash, the platoon sergeant, joined them. He had been at the back of the row, where he could not see what was happening, and had pushed forward with Sapir. After backing a few steps, Barash detected a Jordanian soldier at the back, inside the pillbox. From where he was standing he could do nothing. So he shouted, "Enemy in pillbox!"

Gideon turned and "threaded in" a grenade. Sapir added an Uzi burst. Barash looked to make sure there were no more Jordanians there. From the depths of the yard came a burst of bullets and the explosion of a grenade. Uri Maimon, the signaler, was hit in the tongue. Gideon went back to continue cleaning up the house.

As they renewed their advance, a burst of bullets struck from the yard, hitting the wall behind them and scattering stone splinters. No one was hurt, but nobody had managed to identify the source of the shooting. At the edge of the yard the stone wall continued, with a fig tree behind it. To the left of the tree there was another wall with a grove of pine trees behind that. On both sides of the fig tree were houses. Nowhere was the enemy to be seen, and no post could be identified.

Gideon decided to reinforce the spearhead with antitank weapons and to check the sector before moving on. The squad moved back to the crossing over the fence.

At the same time as Gideon was going forward, the back half of the platoon was fighting a battle with the neighboring house. Northeast of the "red house" stood the "white house." This was also two storeys high, but it had a flat roof. Its square windows controlled the lane that was the passage across the yard between the hut and the red house, and bursts shot from the white house into the passage divided the platoon into two parts, one close to the fence of the red house and the other, to the fence of the hut. The *chevra* returned fire to the white house, Steinfeld shooting toward the windows with his machine gun, Motti with his Uzi, Banishti his rifle, and Avi a bazooka.

Gideon moved Avi to his own squad. Then he decided to return and tackle the yard. Ilan stayed to gun down any enemy who might appear outside, with Barash, the sergeant, beside him. Sapir, Avi, and Peltz went inside the yard. Walking at the head of the squad, Sapir reached the corner of the house. Peeping to the right, he saw outside steps on the north wall of the house, going up to the second floor.

Suddenly a hand grenade dropped next to him and Sapir judged that it came from the direction of the steps. He threw two grenades, which exploded on the steps as he jumped behind the corner. At that moment a burst was fired at them and Avi fell, struck in the head. Gideon reckoned that the firing came from the pillbox and threw a grenade in that direction while Cheitzi, standing next to him, added another. The group collected round Avi, trying to save him, but in vain. Gideon turned round and called, "Amos! Where is Amos? Avi has been killed!" Fire still came from the white house.

Yuval, commander of the Mag, told Michael Steiner to take up his position with the Mag to silence the enemy. Michael took the machine gun and ran to the spot, but had only just entered the yard when he too was shot and fell. Amos went to Gideon, stopped beside him, and fired an antitank grenade into the pillbox. "I got it! A bull's eye!" Amos thought, until suddenly he felt as if a whole wall had fallen on him. He found that he had been knocked down by some powerful force and felt severe pain in his right side. He groped anxiously, but with immense relief found no blood, but that it was difficult to breathe.

He tried to shout, "Chevra, I'm wounded! Don't leave me alone!" He thought, "Oh, why did this have to happen to me?" Then he saw Peltz and gave him the antitank rifle and the cartridges. He began to feel much better, that he could breathe easier, could even stand.

Suddenly he saw Lippa running. The chevra shouted to Lippa to warn him to lie down, that the area was under fire. But it was too late. Lippa's body was contorted, blood spurted from him, and he fell opposite the lane of the white house. Amos made his way to him somehow, crawling, took the Uzi and two magazines, reached the concrete wall, and fired at the Jordanian position.

Steinfeld saw Lippa fall in the open area and, under cover from Eli and Banishti, went to him, picked him up, and pulled him to the shelter of the fence. When he returned to his post, Steinfeld saw Amos crawling toward them and shouted to him: "I'm covering you and pinning them down. Cross the open area!" He opened quick fire on the windows of the white house.

Pachpach tried to deal with Lippa, and felt his pulse. Gideon came, cast a glance at Lippa, and told Pachpach, "He is dead. Go into the trench." There were already three killed in the platoon and they still couldn't pinpoint the enemy, so it was essential to call for additional forces.

Gideon instructed his men to leave their posts and to enter the trench near the corner of "the ruins." Near the pillbox Cheitzi struggled with a soldier who had been thrown into a state of shock by the Jordanian shots and explosions. He was walking about in drunken fashion, trying to go toward the open area. Cheitzi directed him to the rear, to the point where the platoons had gathered.

Crossing the lane by himself, just next to Lippa, he was hit. His wound was not serious and he could go on. Beyond the crossing he noticed Amos, wounded. "What's with you, Amos?"

"Leave me. I'll get there myself," Amos replied, and the two wounded men went on, each one alone. But Amos returned to the trench and went on fighting despite his injury.

Barash, the sergeant, thought that everyone had retreated. He took Ilan the machine gunner with him, placed him in a position to cover the whole length of the barbed-wire fence, and went on to organize the platoon in the trench.

But Peltz and Sapir remained in the yard so did not hear the order to retreat. Suddenly they realized that they were alone, and decided to return to the platoon.

Amos saw them from the trench. Next to him lay two Jordanian rifles, but he preferred to use his own Uzi to cover their moves. So, as he put it, he knocked politely on the Arab door—with a burst of bullets—as Peltz and Sapir ran quickly to him. Peltz helped him to climb out of the trench while Shlomowitz bandaged him and put him on a stretcher.

Now the squad had to decide what to do next. The *chevra* made several suggestions to Gideon. They should get into the house somehow and kill everyone in it, if necessary with their bare hands; they should retreat, get reinforcements and return; they should contact Marico and explain the difficulties of the position. On one thing everyone was agreed: They could not remain where they were. The trench was too shallow and the Jordanian fire too accurate.

Gideon tried to get Marico on the radio, but failed. Pachpach suggested that he get to Marico somehow, and Gideon agreed to let him try. They fired to cover him as he ran out, and he got away, but before he had gone very far he met Peled, the deputy company commander, and told him: "We're in trouble; the position is serious. There are many wounded, and if we don't get help, it'll be no good."

When Brown reached Marico, near the casualty clearing station, he discovered that he had only six men with him.

The rest, it would emerge later, got cut off and remained with Peled near the tank. "Never mind, carry on," Maico said. "Tackle 'the ruins' and the trench alongside it."

Brown and his squad went off, but, like Gideon before him, Brown did not find the trench; instead, he and his men ran onto an open field. Yonaton suddenly called out, "Who's there?"

Brown turned and saw, close by, a Jordanian standing next to a pillbox at the entrance to the lane, outside "the ruins."

The Jordanian fired, but Yonaton was so close to him that he was able to push him by the shoulder with one hand and fire at him with the other. The Jordanian fell, but his shots had already hit Abutbul in the head and chest.

Before they could attend to him, Brown saw something else and roared, "Look out! Lie down! Grenade!" The Jordanian apparently had thrown or dropped a grenade right next to them.

The smoke faded and, finding that nobody else had been wounded, Ochna, Avi, Chaim, and Hagai carried Abutbul to the casualty clearing station.

Now Brown had hardly anyone left with whom to tackle "the ruins." He decided to report back to Marico that he was in trouble. They found Peled, Gideon, and Shmuel Katz at the brickyard. While they were discussing what to do, a burst was fired at them from beyond the burning house and Zvulon was hit in the leg, so they carried him to the casualty clearing station, where they also found Marico, wounded.

A few minutes after Marico had sent Brown to follow Gideon and clean up "the ruins" and the trench, the group that had been cut off arrived. So Marico had instructed them to join Brown, pointing in the direction of "the ruins," not knowing that Brown had already come back from there with Abutbul and was in the yard. The eight reinforcements entered the houses shooting, only to find, to their amazement, Gideon and Barash at the pillbox, organizing the platoon to withdraw from the red house.

Zafrir, Burman, and Yush joined Gideon, and took up positions to fire beside him. Yeruchum lay with the machine gun near the corner, and Shaike, the company medic, was behind him. Shaike tried to go forward, when a burst from the north hit him in the chest and back. Yerucham and Ilan helped him, and Marico pointed out to the squad where they should fire. A bullet hit his outstretched hand, so he went back to the casualty clearing station for attention. The trio left behind, who, with Gideon, were pressed up against the hill of sand, fired at the house on the north where the sniping was coming from.

This was the situation when Pachpach met Peled, the company commander: Marico was wounded. Avi, Lippa, Michael were killed. Abutbul had been evacuated, mortally wounded, as had several others. It was still difficult to identify the hidden enemy, who were hitting our men so efficiently. Two platoons were now mixed together, and Barkai, the operations officer, came up to see what was going on. The *chevra* told him about the wounded and pointed to the red and white houses as the center of enemy activity. Barkai took command. In the entrance to the lane in "the ruins," near the pillbox where Abutbul was hit, Barkai set up a pinning-down force consisting of Mags, bazookas, and anti-tank guns. Then, at the head of the force, he led an assault on the red house.

Baver shot antitank shells at the south windows controlling the open area, one for each window. Burman shot with an anti-tank gun at the west windows and the fig tree, which endangered the entry to the yard. Steinfeld joined in with a machine gun, Peltz with a bazooka, and Cohen, with an antitank rifle under the command of Barash, covered the white house. A Jordanian who came out of the entrance was shot and killed at once.

Near the pillbox at the red house entrance, Hagai, Yonaton, Zafri, and Ofer took their places as Barkai and two others broke into the house. From the bunker under the tree, a Jordanian emerged. Ofer hit him while Barkai went round the corner and up the steps, round a second corner and, with a leap, reached the door.

The door was locked, but on the right was a high window. Standing on the tips of his toes he dropped a grenade inside. He heard no movement, nor was any fire returned. Barkai decided that the house was clean, and gave the order to go back. When he reached Brown, he was told that a Jordanian soldier had been seen going up the outside steps. Taking Yonaton and Giladi with him, Barkai returned and this time broke open the door by shooting at the lock. The squad combed the house thoroughly but found no one.

"They are not operating from here. Come on. We'll go down."

They jumped down the steps, only to be met by a burst of bullets from the north. Giladi was hit in the chest and head and sank down and Yonaton was hit in the backside but went on running. Giladi was taken to shelter and got attention as Barkai returned to the force beside the hut. According to the information he had from the men, he judged that the fire came from the white house. Barkai organized another squad and Steinfeld shot the machine gun as rapidly as possible.

This squad burst into the lane where Michael had been hurt. Peltz shot the bazooka and Cohen antitank shells. This time they crossed the lane and went through the stone gate leading to the steps of the white house. As Yush and Avi stayed above to provide cover, Barkai and Zafrir went to the ground floor and burst in. Opposite them was a family clad in pyjamas.

"Stay where you are." Zafrir translated Barkai's order into Arabic and went out to join the unit. The two houses were now cleaned up. The Jordanians had retreated from the area and enemy fire had ceased. The passage of the forces through the breach was secure.

Brown, the Platoon commander, evacuated Giladi to the casualty station by making a stretcher out of a door taken off its hinges. A heavy machine-gun burst came from somewhere. They ran across the area fired upon and found Reinitz. Next to him were half-tracks with a doctor and medics. They were ready to go to the casualty station. There was no more firing from the Jordanians. Giladi received emergency treatment, but died.

The casualties had been very heavy, but at least they had not been in vain. All the objectives of the battalion had been achieved. Battalion 71 began its preparations for the next stage of the battle for Jerusalem.

Chapter VI

BATTALION 28 DROPS IN AT THE ROCKEFELLER

Battalion 28, according to the plan, was to follow Battalions 66 and 71 through the breach. Yossi P., the commander, watched the companies of Battalion 71 go through, one after the other, as they headed for the northern sector. Then his own A Company, commanded by Avidan, got ready to move, hard on the heels of the last company of Battalion 71.

The other companies of Battalion 28—Haggai's D Company, Alex's C Company, Katcha's support company, and the brigade reconnaissance company, commanded by Giora—moved slowly through the lanes of the Beit Samuel suburb.

Katcha organized the support forces at the corner of Reichman Street, in Beit Samuel. Then there was a sudden burst of Jordanian fire from the east and Ezra and Yitzhak, the machine gunners, were both wounded in the legs. They were dragged inside the lane, given treatment, and evacuated to the rear; Hans, the sergeant, took over the machine gun.

While waiting for the order to move, the men of Haggai's D Company, near Samuel the Prophet Street, knelt on both sides of the road, close to the houses. The recoilless-gun jeeps of Battalion

71 passed between them. These guns were set up near A Company in Samuel the Prophet Street, and launched the preliminary barrage before the breakthrough by Battalion 66.

Suddenly a Jordanian shell exploded among the waiting men, hitting a motorcycle, which exploded with a tremendous noise. The first reaction was shocked surprise that someone was shooting at them. The men pressed even closer to the walls as they sought at least the illusion of complete shelter.

A shell crashed in the middle of the D Company staff, hitting Avital, the deputy company commander, in the face with shrapnel. He screamed, "My face! My face;" From the top of the street came cries of "Doctor!" "Medic!"

Then these cries were swallowed up in the din of new explosions. Haggai ordered some men to evacuate Avital while the rest moved on. Pulchuk, who had also been hit, stayed to attend to Avital while the rest began to advance. Then another Jordanian salvo hit D Company very hard, and this time the street was so full of wounded that ten stretchers were needed.

There is a myth that two shells do not strike in the same place. Another Jordanian salvo proved that this legend is untrue. Again the casualties were heavy, and included all the men in the casualty clearing station, among them Dr. Eliraz.

Shai, the sergeant of C Company, saw that his friend Kinch had been wounded. He tried to get a medic, but those who were not injured were too busy to answer his call. He returned to Kinch. "Don't worry, Kinch, they'll come for you soon. Everything's going to be all right." Having no alternative, he left Kinch and went on.

Haggai reported to Yossi P., "We have more than thirty wounded." Yossi P. sent his deputy commander, Gedalia, to see what happened, and just then another salvo liquidated the battalion headquarters, but Yossi had luckily moved to the head of the battalion. Nonetheless, his operations office and intelligence officer were wounded, as was his second-in-command, Gedalia, on his way to Haggai.

Avi, commander of the engineering unit, was also hit, together with a large number of his men. Despite his injury, he remained in the field and helped evacuate those who were more seriously hurt; then he was hit a second time and had to agree to being evacuated himself.

Shells kept taking their toll, and Yossi P. ordered D Company to concentrate on getting out the wounded, asking the medics of C Company to come and help. The casualty clearing station of Battalion 71, which had been supposed to move after the breakthrough, stayed where it was to look after the wounded from Battalion 28. The brigade medical team also went into action. Vehicles began to run up and down the lines, and the evacuation went much faster.

One of the first men brought to the station was Yehuda, wounded in the jaw, his whole face covered with blood. Some of the medics had not yet seen so serious a wound, and it upset them. It was Yehuda who comforted them. "It's not so serious," he mumbled. "It looks worse than it is."

Battalion 71 was through the breach, and Yossi P. told his battalion to get through it, too, fast. He added that the best way to prevent the enemy's artillery hitting you was to get to it and smash it at close quarters.

Brave words, but he realized that he had to build up a new staff, so many of his officers had been hit. He ordered Katcha, commander of the support company, to report, but Katcha thought that the order applied to his entire company, and ordered them all to move.

This caused more disorder, over and above that made by the accurate enemy shelling. Katcha reached Yossi, who promoted him on the spot to the post of second-in-command, to replace the wounded Gedalia; the support company was taken over by his lieutenant, Micha Odem.

When the advance of the support company was halted, the men did not understand why they had been told to come forward at the double, and then stopped. The veterans among them reminded the youngsters cynically that that's what war was like. "All you need to know is that, if they tell you to go, go fast, and if they tell you to stop, stop at once."

Water gushed out of some pipes that had been hit. Benny thought, "What a waste of precious water! Maybe I should break ranks to switch off the main." But just then a strange order was issued to them: "Fix bayonets!" That was the first time they'd ever been told to do such a thing, and they didn't know how.

Suddenly Benny was knocked off his feet by an overwhelming blast. As he fell, he yelled, for some reason, "Take cover!" But he found that he had not been wounded and got back on his feet. He said to Haikin, next to him, "What the devil are we doing here, waiting like sitting ducks To hell with war . . ."

Shimon, the medic of platoon number two, went down the street, looking after the wounded and helping them to get into the shelter of a nearby building, where a number of civilians were sitting. The civilians gave him a hand by going upstairs to their apartments, despite the danger, to bring down shirts, napkins, sheets, and cloths, from which they improvised bandages.

Gershon got lost from his platoon and solved his problem in this way: "I'll run forward. They must be at the front somewhere." He headed at the double toward the breach and there, sure enough, was his plaoon. He felt happy and contented, like an exile returning home after spending years among strangers.

Sabach saw a piece of shrapnel flying through the air toward him. He tried to get out of the way, but it lodged in his chest muscle. A few minutes before he had noticed a sign, *Shelter*, so he made his way to it and found two other soldiers there already. The occupants of the house, very Orthodox, were tending to the injured. They tore up their old-fashioned underwear to make bandages.

Meletz, standing with his comrades next to the shelter, was hit in the arm by shrapnel. He put a dressing on with his good hand and Amos came across and tied the bandage for him. Around him he saw only wounded, and he rested a little because his head was spinning. When he got up his company had moved. He ran, but ended up in D Company, returned, ran in the other direction, and found his own company. "What a mess!" he muttered to himself.

The second-in-command of the reconnaissance company, Moshele, was wounded but insisted on carrying on. All the members of his platoon, including its commander, had been hit. Then Moshele was hit a second time, seriously, and had to be evacuated.

It was clear that D Company was in serious trouble, so Haggai alerted brigade headquarters.

Dov Carmi, the C Company medic, set up a collection point in one of the yards, for many wounded who were still lying in the street. Shlomo Epstein, another medic, moved along, attending to each man and then taking him to Dov. Shells seemed to pursue him, but he worked as calmly as if it were an exercise. One of the wounded was Yosef Hagoel. While Shlomo was treating him, a shell landed right next to them. Shlomo lay on Hagoel to protect him from the flying shrapnel with his own body, and was himself fatally wounded.

Shrapnel pierced the lung of Joshua Levy and he fell and crawled forward. Then darkness engulfed him. He woke up in the recovery room of the Hadassah Hospital, where the first person he saw was his father, looking very tragic. Joshua put his hand to his chest, and whispered, "We won, didn't we, Dad?" His father nodded. "That's all that matters. Don't look so sad."

Although Zvi Natan's wound was slight, according to him, the medics insisted that it was serious, and put him in a group waiting to be sent to the hospital. While they were busy with other wounded, he sneaked away. A member of the ultra-Orthodox movement, the Natorei Karta, directed him to the breach area, and he returned to the battle.

Dov Carmi's yard was about ten square meters in area and so full of men awaiting treatment there was no room to lie down. Uzi, C Company's second-in-command, stood at the door, directing the more seriously wounded inside while sending the more lightly injured up the street. As he treated them, Dov comforted them: "I know there's a lot of blood, but head wounds are like that, they bleed profusely and seem worse than they are . . . Don't worry, you'll be O.K. again in no time . . ."

Another medic, Leizer, wounded himself, sat on the side supporting his arm. When Dov came to him, he said, "I'm not so bad. Treat the others first." Dov passed on. Eventually he got back to Leizer. He found that a whole section of flesh had been torn away from the shattered arm.

The recoilless-gun jeep of Battalion 28 was hit and Moshele, the commander, and Simcha were wounded. Despite the damage to the jeep, Kusta, the driver, somehow got it going and evacuated them. The reconnaissance company jeep was also used to bring out the injured.

Doctors and medics from other units hurried to the casualty clearing station to help in the emergency. Some went out into the streets to treat the injured and bring them in, and in doing so one of the volunteers, Dr. Friedman, was himself hurt.

More and more wounded streamed in from the area around the breach. Chanan Samson, one of the battalion staff officers, having decided that he had finished his administrative duties for the time being, jumped into a civilian car and drove off to fetch the injured. He found that the car was full of cans, and as he threw them out, they clashed like exploding shells. A real shell falling near him smothered the sound; he was unhurt, but all the tires of his car were flat. He drove on regardless, picking up wounded.

Edward, the regimental sergeant major, organized stray paratroopers who had lost their units, and others not needed at the moment, into groups to fetch out the injured.

A truck brought a doctor to a group of wounded, the driver reversing as he approached them. When a shell landed next to them, the driver was badly hurt and fell on the wheel. The truck went on in reverse and seemed to be about to roll over the wounded, so Ochion, Kavas, and Dan hurled themselves at it, and brought it to a standstill by sheer strength, till David could get into the cab, push the driver aside, and take over the wheel.

Shells kept falling all the time. Eli Schechter, the company sergeant major, recorded the names of the injured with meticulous care, lest knowledge of what had happened to them be lost in the turmoil.

There were more and more wounded as the shells kept falling. Esther Arditi, the woman ambulance driver known as "The White Angel," drove her Magen David Adom ambulance right to the battlefield and there attended to the injured and drove them out again.

At 0340 dawn was breaking, but the area of the breakthrough was still covered with black clouds of smoke, the result of the preliminary bombardment by the mortars, so the thin gleams of the rising sun did not penetrate the man-made fog. The darkness was a blessing, hiding the men from Jordanian snipers and low-trajectory fire.

Now every second was precious. Soon the sun would be strong enough to pierce the dust and smoke, and the men would be subjected to fire while standing in an open field. But A Company couldn't move forward—Battalion 71 was still engaged in a fierce battle in front of them.

Yossi P. ordered Avidan, the company commander of A Company, to keep going, so Avidan changed the original plan and went with his company to the north, on the flank of Battalion 71. Opposite him was a wall. They groped along until at last they found an opening in it which led to the Nablus Road, and Avidan turned right, to the south, and stationed his men on both sides of the road. On their right was a long wall and on the left the tomb of Sheikh Jarragh, who had given the suburb its name.

In the pale tints of dawn they could now discern the outlines of buildings, some several storeys high, plus stone walls, iron fences, beautiful gardens containing old, shady trees, protruding balconies, and many, many windows. A fine city, but the worst place in the world in which to fight.

The sounds of battle had suddenly moved far away from them, and all around was the quiet of a newborn day. Shutters were closed and there was no sign of the enemy. But he had to be there, so their eyes searched every window, gate, and cranny.

Avidan looked about him. Everything seemed O.K., so he gave the command, "Advance!" Nachshon's platoon led the way on the right side of the road. Behind him was Ilan's platoon. On the left was a mixed force, consisting of some members of Gabi's platoon and some of Yermi's Mag platoon.

Suddenly bullets were flying around them, and it was difficult to pinpoint the sources of the fire. By night, flashes had betrayed such sources; by day they could not be seen, unless the fire was continuous; but these were single bullets or short bursts. Sometimes a mortar shell fell.

They suffered their first casualties, and the wounded were concentrated in a small hollow near a gas station. Because of it they enjoyed some protection from the north, south, and west.

To the east, Battalion 71 was already master of all important positions.

The air was rent by a long burst, but they couldn't tell where it had come from. Nachshon pointed—the fire was coming from the house with the burned roof, so the men pressed up against the wall. Then somebody saw a squad of Jordanians making for the house. Avidan grasped what was happening: The Jordanians were regrouping. They had realized that they had lost control of the breach area, and were preparing to fight for the streets of Arab Jerusalem. What had been positions in their rear would now become their front lines.

The Jordanian squad ran next to the wall and disappeared. Nachshon sent a squad to mop up the house. He did not know that this building had already been cleaned up by men from Battalion 71, and that the Jordanians had then gone back again.

Above the mopping-up squad was a high balcony. Udi took off his personal equipment so that Morene and George could lift him. He caught onto a drainpipe and climbed up onto the balcony. The door from the balcony to an inner room was open, and he threw in a grenade. After the explosion there was silence. They checked the rest of the house and found it clean.

Meanwhile, Avidan did not want to delay the advance of his company while they cleaned up every enemy position, as time was pressing. He sent Ilan's platoon on ahead of Nachshon's.

Battalion Headquarters got a report from the mortar platoon at the Sanhedria crossroads that the platoon had come under heavy fire. A recoilless-gun shell, fired from distant Shufa'at, had landed in the middle of the mortar team, killing Amnon Charudi and Yomtov Sharm. There were many wounded, and a medical team was treating them.

A Company continued to advance. A long burst came from the stone wall of the American College, close to the American Consulate. Shrapnel sprayed the men. Yermi, commander of the

Mag platoon, collapsed, severely wounded, a piece of shrapnel having penetrated his steel helmet and entered his head.

The paratroopers took cover below the wall, knelt, and returned the fire. Bursts passed over their heads and struck the wall. From the height of the fire, it seemed that the enemy positions were high up, or that a wall prevented their shooting low down the street, and the men noted this useful knowledge.

Amos Gul supported Yermi till David, the medic, was able to reach them. David held up Yermi's head lest he should choke on blood flowing into his lungs. With difficulty David spread open a stretcher as Yochi, another medic, went across to help. Gabi, commander of the other platoon. ordered his men to provide heavy covering fire from the other side of the street. The *chevra* helped David to remove Yermi's equipment carefully and then they carried him, as gently as possible, back to the yard of the petrol filling station, where he died.

Ilan and his platoon were already fighting farther up the road, attacking the fortified house they called "the house of the yard," which, they found out later, was the headquarters of the Moslem Council. Fire was opened on them from the gate.

Mordi, second-in-command of the company, went past Ilan and rushed to the south side of the gate. From there he tried to fire inside with his Uzi but was forced back by accurate bursts.

The yard was very large. In the middle of it was the beginning of the communication trench with stone walls which stretched westward. The building had two floors and the second storey was fortified with concrete and sandbags.

The paratroopers fired antitank grenades at the concrete fortification and hurled grenades as well. Herzi threw a grenade at the entrance to the communication trench.

Dan Rimalt, with the antitank rifle, scored some direct hits. The squad burst into the yard—Ilan, Herzi, Alon, Nahmias, and Muallem. On the step in front of the door of the house they saw a number of Jordanians with a bazooka. A salvo of Israeli bullets wiped them out.

Quiet reigned. Apparently it was all over, and they had to go on. So Ilan led his men out of the building and they ran on to the south, not knowing that they had left behind them communication trenches and bunkers with more Jordanian soldiers hiding in them. In any event, their duty was to go forward and to clear the road for the company to advance.

Shortly after Ilan and his squad had left the Moslem Council building, fire again came from its top storey. Gabi, commander of the platoon following Ilan's, told Sharabi to tackle the house. When Sharabi got to the gate, they fired at him from the trench, so he jumped onto the wall and threw a grenade at the opening to the trench. A Jordanian climbed out and ran towards the house, so Sharabi fired a burst at him and he fell.

In the meanwhile Nachshon had finished mopping up the house with the burned roof. He and his platoon caught up with Gabi at the gate of the Moslem Council building. Gabi was waiting for orders from Avidan as to whether he should go forward after Ilan. Then two mortar shells exploded in the middle of the street and shrapnel hit Gabi and several of his men. Their comrades evacuated them to the filling station. The ranks were thinning.

Ilan's squad went on under the cover of the wall. They they stopped for a few moments, realizing that they had used up so much ammunition that they had to refill their magazines and reorganize the weapons at their disposal. Unknown to them, on the other side of the stone wall Jordanians occupied hidden trenches and subterranean bunkers.

Nachshon's squad went up the road after Ilan. When they passed the gate of the Moslem Council building, now officially cleaned up twice, they were shot at again. Amos was hit, but managed to crawl right up to the gate. Chico, right behind him, looked in the gate, and was also wounded. He crawled to a hut on the south, inside the wall, and Nachshon leapt forward and dragged Amos back, under the wall on the north side of the gate.

Selek and Herzi took up positions on the south side of the gate. Amos seemed to be dead, and Chico was spitting blood and appeared to be dying. Avidan rushed to the south side of the gate, followed by Alfandri, his runner. Suddenly Alfrandi dropped, as though dragged down by an invisible hand.

They worked out that there were three Jordanians firing at them—one from the trench in the yard, another from the right of the building near the wall, the third from the second storey. The last posed the most danger, so Nachshon hurled a grenade at him. It exploded on the wall of the house, and the Jordanian vanished inside the building.

Kochavi took a stand across the road, and shot with his Mag into the yard, hoping to hit every Jordanian lying there, and any enemy who tried to get at Chico in the hut.

Herzi decided that he must rescue Chico, whatever happened. He could not leave a wounded friend alone like that. Before he could move, Reuven stopped him—he had seen a Jordanian in the opening of the trench. Reuven threw a grenade, which exploded. The Jordanian disappeared, and Yitzhak jumped inside the gate and threw another grenade. Nachshon threw another at the second floor, and they entered the yard and pulled Chico out. The house and the yard seemed to be completely quiet again. Herzi had a slight wound and he was very pale from loss of blood, but, after being bandaged, carried on.

At the top of the road, Ilan's platoon was soon involved in new battles. The road remained quiet for precisely the length of one building.

After filling their magazines again and getting up to go on, the men happened to look over the wall and there they saw Jordanians running to the south. The paratroopers opened fire and the Jordanians scattered. One fell.

The platoon went on, Mordi sprinting to the other side of the street, taking with him a squad to provide covering fire for Ilan. They went to what they called "the house with the pillars" and there, next to a great pile of stones among the pillars, took up positions. Behind them they heard shots. They worried in case somebody was shooting from the American Colony Hotel at the backs of Nachshon and his squad. Meir turned in that direction with his machine gun, but the fire stopped. Ronny, Arbilli, and Amos entered the yard of the hotel and combed it, but found no soldiers.

Nachshon's platoon came up. It seened that the Moslem Council house had been conquered once and for all, so Nachshon joined Mordi. Soon Yossi P. and Avidan also came to "the house of the pillars" and Mordi went up to the top floor to make certain that the building was safe before going forward to join Ilan.

The others discussed what they should do when they had attained all their objectives. Because of the casualties and the absence of medics, who were busy evacuating the wounded, Avidan had to reorganize the platoons.

Ilan advanced to the south, and suddenly fire poured out at them from a house to the right, about ten meters from the road. The paratroopers huddled close to the wall and returned the fire. While some were shooting, others prepared to throw grenades. When a Legionnaire appeared in the yard of the house, a salvo of grenades was thrown at him, exploding and filling the yard with shrapnel and smoke. The Jordanian vanished into some bushes in the garden next to the yard and without bothering to find out whether he was dead or wounded, they pressed on.

Then they made a mistake. They missed the fork to Saladin Street and continued up Nablus Road. They had never seen the area and were relying only on a photograph, so the error was a natural one.

On the other side of the road, next to the wall of St. George's

Cathedral, Kochavi and Hoffman advanced with the Mag, keeping parallel to Ilan's platoon. Through the gate of St. George's School, Hoffman saw a squad of Jordanian soldiers, and he and Kochavi opened fire.

Mordi and Ilan kept going forward. In a section of the wall there was some latticework, through which Apallelo saw the same Jordanians Hoffman and Kochavi had seen. The memory of what had happened to Amos and Chico was still very fresh so, shouting to his friends to halt, he threaded his Uzi through the delicate latticework and fired. One of his bullets hit a Legionnaire.

In the meantime, Aryeh, Shaggai, Meir, and Gadi had come around the building from the side. Shaggai helped Meir get up to the top of the wall and from there he fired his Uzi at the Legionnaires. In the meantime the others broke into the yard and hurled grenades, killing the Jordanians.

Under cover of this fire, and that from the Mag, Ilan and Muallem also rushed inside. They saw another squad of Jordanians coming up and wiped them out with a rapid salvo of bullets. The paratroopers discovered that these had been two bazooka squads, so their destruction was very timely, since Rafi and his tanks were on the way.

While waiting at "the house of the pillars" for orders, Nachshon sent a squad from his platoon to secure the road that went to the east, which he believed was Saladin Street. On the right the squad saw a wrecked recoilless gun, destroyed during the preparatory bombardment. This was in fact Saladin Street, the road which Ilan had missed.

A Jordanian Land Rover came from the continuation of the road and tried to cross into Nablus Road. Itzik hit it with a shot from his Mag and the Land Rover stopped and a Jordanian jumped out and ran back along the road. He was shot and fell, and the street was quiet for a moment.

Then Nachshon came after the squad with the rest of his platoon. They moved down Saladin Street and he went to the left side with most of the platoon, while Menachem Ben-Ari took a section to the other side. They advanced until they reached the jeep, where Menachem stopped while Nachshon sent a squad to get onto the roof of a house on the corner to cover their further advance.

The squad found the entrance to the corner house closed by a heavy iron gate, which was also locked. An explosive charge failed to break down the gate, and a second charge only damaged it. So Nachshon sent another squad into the lane at the back of the house to try to get in from the outside. Udi, Yoav, and Henry entered the lane. On their left was a stone wall, behind it the Tomb of the Kings, and here too there was an iron gate. They put a load of two kilograms of explosives next to it, ran some distance away, hugging the wall, and detonated the explosive.

A tremendous blast reverberated, the gate flew off, and the squad rushed in. They found themselves in a beautiful, tranquil garden. In the center was an ornamental summerhouse and all around were hothouses. It was the inner courtyard of a hotel, and the war seemed a million miles away.

In Saladin Street a burst of fire came from an unidentified Jordanian position and Menachem Ben-Ari was hit in the head and killed on the spot.

The squad in the flower garden climbed quickly onto the roof of the hotel. But they found that it was too low to serve as a good observation post, so they reported back to Nachshon.

In the meanwhile, Nachshon had himself received new orders—to go back and join Yossi P. and Avidan, who were going after Ilan in what they believed was Saladin Street. In fact they were wrong; it was the Nablus Road; it had been Nachshon who had taken the right road. But he went back to join them.

Carmon, the medic, went forward with Ilan's spearhead platoon. On both sides of the street there were wounded, with some soldiers helping to dress light wounds and others helping the seriously wounded to get back to the rear.

Whenever the advance stopped for some reason, such as for a squad to mop a building or a snipers' nest, other paratroopers not concerned in the immediate action tried to help their injured mates. But while in a prolonged, continuous fight, they could not take time off to help the wounded, however close to them they might be; they had to leave them and hope for the best. But they seized every opportunity to do something for them.

The wounded who required major attention were sent back to the filling station, and from there they were evacuated to the Casualty Clearing Station.

At 0500, there was a lull for a few minutes. Most of the forces were gathered close to the walls on the right, in Nablus Street, though some men were still mopping up a row of houses from which there had been signs of resistance.

The area in which they were huddled seemed to be a dead one as far as enemy artillery was concerned. No shells were landing, but occasionally isolated bullets flew dangerously close. Paratroopers say that nothing is worse than to catch a single bullet when everything is quiet. Single bullets are usually well aimed and hit their targets. With salvoes they have a sporting chance.

They found the suspense wearing, sapping their will. As one man bent down to bandage a friend, suddenly a bullet would whistle by his ear or a ricochet bounce off the pavement at him. If he stood under a wall he might suddenly be spattered with shrapnel or stone slivers. It was better to keep moving, for when a man is on the go he doesn't think of such things.

The delay was caused by Yossi P.'s decision to get some help from the tanks. When Yossi P. reported to Brigade Headquarters about his street battles, Rafi's tanks were waiting for orders at the crossroads of the hospitals and the Hotel Ambassador. I instructed Rafi to go down Nablus Road and help the men fighting in the streets of Arab Jerusalem. As they moved along the road, the tanks fired at any targets they could find, although they knew that thereby they might attract fire on themselves. In fact, as they passed "the house with the burned roof," a shell exploded near Arzi's tank. Arzi had been travelling along with half his body outside the tank. But, although shrapnel sprayed up at him, he carried on.

The paratroopers welcomed the approaching tanks with happy laughter and sighs of relief as Rafi stopped for a briefing with Yossi P. The plan was that the tanks should advance along the road firing at nests of resistance, but without getting involved in long, drawn-out battles, as the aim was to reach the Rockefeller Museum as soon as possible.

Rafi listened and nodded. Everything was clear and he passed the orders on to the other tanks. As they moved south, enemy snipers fired at them and it seemed to Rafi that the fire was coming from a wall with embrasures around the cathedral. The turrets swung around and after a few shells and machine-gun bullets the sniping ceased.

The appearance of the tanks changed the life style of the paratroopers. Until now all the enemy fire had been aimed at them, but now it was concentrated on the advancing tanks. The paratroopers' morale soared. They no longer needed to hunt through the houses with Uzis and grenades. And they knew that the will to resist of the Jordanians would wane when they saw the iron monsters on the march toward them.

When the tanks fired their first shells the thunder was deafening, for the mighty sound waves of the explosions echoed and reechoed with terrifying force among the high stone houses lining the narrow streets. Accustomed to the lesser sounds of small arms fire and bazooka shells, they were almost stunned by the blast.

But they pulled themselves quickly together, for they knew that it was not pleasant for the tanks to be in such streets, where walls and houses served as enemy strongpoints, from which might come bazooka shells or antitank grenades or snipers' bullets aimed at the tank commanders.

The infantry were essential to protect the tanks from such fire, and the presence of the tanks meant that remote Jordanian posts could be crushed before they could fire on the paratroopers.

Ilan's platoon and Rafi's tank went up the street side by side, Ilan next to the wall. An antitank grenade fell in front of the tank tracks, but no harm was done. And Rafi then spotted the snipers' nest from which the shot had come, and directed his machine-gun fire at it.

Communication between the infantry and the tanks was very difficult, almost impossible. The men on foot wanted to point out choice targets, but the telephones linking the tanks to the outside world were either unusable because the cable had been cut by shrapnel or bullets or else these external telephones had had to be switched off so the tank commanders could concentrate on the internal phones, on which came a stream of orders throughout the tumult of the fighting.

The paratroopers tried shooting, but could not be heard. Then they tried waving their hands, holding their helmets, but these indications were misunderstood as often as they were interpreted correctly. So the joy of working in partnership was marred somewhat by the frustration caused by the inability to communicate.

An antitank shell came from the right and exploded in the street near the tanks, and after it came a long burst of bullets from the same direction.

Avidan sent a newly made officer, Peled, and Sergeant Weiner to examine the yard on the right. They found that it contained piles of chiseled stones and a large excavation, apparently for a new building. Beyond was a wall containing firing slits;

they watched these slits for a while but saw no fire or any sign of life. So they advanced to check the slits. Although they found no one, it still seemed probable that the firing had come from there.

They realized that the slits faced the wall that divided Jerusalem and the Mandelbaum Gate. Presumably they had been planned to enable the Jordanians to fire on Jewish Jerusalem. Whoever had been there was gone, so they returned to report to Avidan.

Yoska Balagan signed to Albez's tank to open fire on a yard, and Albez did so. Suddenly he put a hand to his face. He had been wounded in the jaw, so he jumped down from the tank and was treated.

Meanwhile, Ilan's platoon advanced. It had shrunk considerably in size, several men having been wounded while others were somewhere behind them, still involved in mopping-up operations. On their right was the great East Jerusalem YMCA building. A bazooka shell and an antitank grenade fired from a rifle exploded near Rafi's tank, but inflicted no damage. The platoon fired in the direction from which the shots came as did the tank.

They ran into the YMCA building and found a dead Jordanian lying on the steps, but nothing else of interest, so they went on.

Heavy fire came from the direction of the American Consulate ahead of them, and also from the wall facing the Mandelbaum Gate. Ilan climbed up onto Rafi's tank to indicate the sources of fire. Rafi nodded and Ilan jumped down again.

The tanks took firing positions; at the same time Rafi contacted Avidan and asked him to cover the crossroads and positions near the tanks. Avidan in turn contacted Ilan.

Ilan and his squad tried to get into the American Consulate, but the gate was locked. Ofer hung half a kilo of explosive on the gate and the men moved back for the explosion. The gate flew off and some of the men rushed in. The tank soldiers, who were not advised of the plan to blow open the gate, were shaken and thought for a while that their tank had been hit, but Ilan calmed them down. "It's nothing, only us."

Ofer and the others in Ilan's squad cleaned up the consulate yard. Then they took up positions along the wall, which bordered on Mandelbaum Road. From here they could see the whole length of the road, as far as Mandelbaum Gate, on the border between the two Jerusalems. They realized what a powerful position it was. Communication trenches ran all the way along the road, with hidden bunkers in the yards. From these positions the Jordanians had been firing shells and grenades at the tanks and small arms fire at the paratroopers.

Ilan's force opened fire with all available weapons. Avioam fired three antitank shells; one hit a post, another the wall, and the third went astray and passed Mandelbaum Gate into Israel. But the intense fire of the paratroopers was effective and the Jordanian attack withered away.

The tanks advanced, Rafi's reaching the crossroads near the mosque, so he turned around and went to within five yards of the Mandelbaum wall. The tank was so close to the Jordanian positions that some of them were in a dead area below the minimum range of the cannon.

From the consulate, Ilan threw stones at the Jordanian strongpoints to help the tanks to pinpoint targets. The gunners lined up, one after the other, and knocked them out.

Behind Rafi, Shaul's tank stuck opposite the YMCA and wouldn't start. Arzi overtook it, gave it a tow, and got it started. Arzi went on and took up his position at the crossroads. The tanks of Shlain, Shaul and Nizan stopped opposite the YMCA. Gilboa and Albez came at the end of the line.

Ilan's platoon lay close to the stone wall of the consulate. The Jordanians shot at them from the northern part of the building, so Shlain's tank was signaled to fire at the building. The tank had to maneuver to get the range and Appallelo directed it by hand signs where to shoot, standing underneath the gun and blocking his ears.

From outside the yard, antitank shells crashed down near the tank and the blast threw Appallelo into the air and then onto the ground. One of his friends fell on top of him and shrapnel sprayed the yard, killing Nahmias and Alon and wounding Dubi.

Another antitank shell exploded in the command post of the company commander. Avidan was hurled forward and lost his senses for a few minutes. Feier, the communications sergeant, was wounded and Selek, the antitank gunner, was hit in the legs. For some moments there was no company command—battalion command, which was right next to Avidan's post, had to take over and direct the company. Yochi attended to the wounded and the men threw him extra dressings and bandages.

From somewhere in Arab Jerusalem, the Jordanians fired at the tanks with a heavy machine gun, and Nizan's tank returned the fire. The ammunition box on the outside of the tank was hit and began to burn and the machine gun was damaged. Nizan, standing exposed on the turret and giving orders, told Adri to put out the fire and deal with the machine gun, so Adri jumped out and extinguished the fire, and then pulled the machine gun and its base outside the tank. Nizan started to ask for a weapon to replace the machine gun, but at that very moment was hit and dropped down into the tank, dead. Mazliach took over the command and withdrew the tank to evacuate Nizan to the rear.

The fire from the consulate and the positions along the wall had stopped, so Ilan and his platoon left the consulate yard and went back to the Nablus Road. Rafi's tank returned to the crossroads. From time to time this still drew enemy fire from all directions, particularly from the east.

Avidan sent Mordi to look for a way to outflank the crossroads from the east and to attack the source of fire from that direction. Mordi took a few men and they went past the tennis court to the back of the houses controlling the Nablus Road.

They were hampered by shots from snipers, but managed to get to a gate to a road from which they could reach the open square east of the mosque. The gate was locked, and when Mordi tried to smash it with a shot it still didn't open. They called for wire-cutters, and with the speed and precision of burglars cut their way through.

Katcha, who had served as Yossi P.'s second-in-command ever since Gedaliah had been wounded, suspected that some mistake had been made, that Avidan's company had gone down the wrong road. But Avidan was firmly convinced that they had gone right, and Yossi decided that they should carry on. Just then the battle for the mosque square began.

Here the Jordanians had organized a very formidable system of defenses. Communication trenches ran along the length and breadth of a small hill north of the mosque. In the middle of the hill was a large concrete bunker. Its slits provided clear views of the crossroads and the approach roads from the north, from Mandelbaum Gate and from Nablus Road. In the mosque square they had built a concrete bunker to control the western part of Arab Jerusalem, facing Israel and the crossroads. Nearby, the communication trench began to run to the south, to the Jordanian Command's bunker for the sector. The communication trench was dotted with strongpoints.

The tanks of Rafi and Arzi stood at the crossroads, at the corner of the American Consulate and Mandelbaum Road. Moshe's tank was at the consulate. Ilan's platoon organized under the wall of the consulate, close to Moshe's tank. Battalion Command and company command went forward to join him in preparations for the next stage of the advance, as did Ilan's platoon.

As soon as the platoon left the shelter of the consulate wall and came into the open, it came under heavy fire from the main Jordanian bunker in the mosque square. Believing that the Jordanian positions along the wall had been completely liquidated by Rafi's tank, Ilan decided to try a frontal assault against the bunker. The first two tanks, Rafi's and Arzi's opened fire, while Moshe's tank came forward to cover the area around the petrol station. Mordi with Kochavi's Mag squad provided cover against any attack from the road to the east.

Ilan's platoon got across to the other side of the crossroads without any casualties. But the fire from the mosque and the bunker continued unabated. They advanced closer to the bunker.

A Legionnaire emerged. Ilan threw a grenade, so did the Jordanian. Ilan was wounded, dropped to the ground, and crawled back to a tree—a kilometer of continuous battle had ended for him. Mualem was wounded in the ear. Uri, who had been wounded earlier in the shelling, ran right up to the bunker and threw a grenade inside.

Ofer and Leiserke, who had come to the steps of the mosque through their outflanking move, changed direction and rushed straight to the bunker. Ofer threw two grenades inside. Then the two of them dashed in, shooting with Uzis in all directions inside it.

Uri took Ilan on his back and carried him back to the consulate. Mualem, holding his injured ear, went back as well, and Elisha bandaged them.

A Legionnaire came out of the trench near the bunker. Roni, advancing toward the mosque, threw a grenade, as did the Legionnaire. Roni scored a hit, and the Arab missed; so it was the Arab who fell. Roni, running up, found a basket of grenades next to the Jordanian and tossed two of them into the bunker. Two explosions followed hard upon each other, and clouds of dust and smoke rose from the bunker.

When the smoke cleared, Roni saw two Jordanians fleeing

down the communication trench to the south. He fired a burst and one was killed, but the other, although wounded, got away.

Roni mounted to the minaret of the mosque, which the Jordanians had been using as a snipers' nest and observation tower. Meanwhile the tanks continued south, up the road toward the mosque, and Avidan and his staff went forward to the filling station, opposite the mosque. As Battalion Command moved into position, Avidan prepared his company to go forward. A little behind them, Alex's C Company was approaching along the Nablus Road.

At 0330, despite the heavy shelling and the casualties his company had suffered, Alex was still following the original plan. He had left Uzi, his second-in-command, some medics, and the wounded in the rear. There was still considerable disorder because of the shelling and the mistaken arrival of the entire support company when Yossi P. had called only for its commander, but somehow Alex got the company to move forward.

They reached the open field in the breakthrough area while it was still dark. Sounds of battle came from in front of them and enemy marksmen sniped at them from the right. The paratroopers, moving along the concrete wall next to the breach area, were also exposed to fire from the north and south. They kept close to the wall and only ran forward when there was a break in the Jordanian fire, caused probably by the need to change the magazines of rifles and the belts of machine guns.

These precautions didn't help. Dan's engineers were hugging the wall when a shell exploded next to them, killing Chanan Book and mortally wounding Chanan Levin. As he was trying to get to them, Dan was hit by a bullet, and when Alfrandri also tried, he too was wounded.

Six 81-millimeter shells dropped on Benny's platoon, causing Gideon to say to Yigal, "You know, I don't think I like this war. In fact, I'm beginning to hate it." It took the platoon some time to recover.

When they got their advance going again, they were met with another salvo of shells and more wounded. Snipers from the south and east now had their rifles trained on the opening in the Nablus Road wall, next to the eucalyptus trees.

Benny's platoon ran up Nablus Road, but saw nobody. A Company seemed to have disappeared, though they searched anxiously in all directions. On the Wadi Joz road, the road to the Ambassador Hotel, they found no sign of life. Then, from somewhere, a communications section materialized and came to their rescue. They told Benny that the company had moved south, so Benny headed in that direction down the Nablus Road. They found Battalion Command at the American Colony Hotel and they got close to the wall and waited.

As Alex's company was advancing, a salvo of 52-millimeter shells pulverized the road. Yosef Yachmi, the radioman, was wounded badly in the leg, which upset everyone because he was a well-known soccer star. Yachmi gave the radio to Giora. Alex himself was also wounded by shrapnel in the leg, but he bandaged it and went on.

As they passed the burned-out recoilless-gun jeep, shells in it were still exploding. The *chevra* chuckled. "That's good to see— the Arab recoilless gun fighting itself." They crouched, holding their breath, but there was no explosion. Then they were told to stop, so they sat close to the wall and waited. Ahead of them A Company was fighting.

From the north came the sound of tanks and they looked up fearfully, but Alex reassured them: "Don't worry—they're ours."

The tanks rolled by and the men got up and went on again, soon passing the wounded of A Company, among them Gabi, the platoon commander, whom everybody knew well, so they stopped to exchange a few words. Gabi smiled and encouraged them, and Alex detailed a few men to help in the evacuation of the wounded from the petrol station to the casualty clearing station. By the time they had finished, the company had gone way ahead of them and was engaged in bitter fighting, as the van reached the house with the yard, the building of the Moslem Council, where Yermi had been killed.

In fact, the building had been twice mopped up, once by Amos's platoon and again by Ilan's, but the Jordanians had come back through the communication trench and reoccupied it. Alex's company, of course, knew nothing of these events. When the shots came from the right, Moshe Mazer and several men leapt to the left, with a Mag, and took up positions to fire from the yard of the hotel. They pinpointed the source of the fire as the second floor.

The tanks of Gilboa and Albez were nearby so they called Albez and, with hand signals, indicated the target. The turret turned ponderously around and the gunner aimed at the balcony. Despite all the fire to which it had been subjected, the fortifications still stood intact. The gunner fired two shells, the earth shook, and the balcony was split in two. In the quiet that followed the tank moved south.

So the *chevra* stood up. But then once more came the sniping fire from the same house. Yigal Botnik scored a hit with an antitank grenade beneath the windowsill, but it was still not enough.

Platoon number two, commanded by Uri, was at the continuation of the wall. With Uri was Ephraim Holetz, who had been wounded during the shelling but insisted on carrying on. Now he was holding an antitank rifle in a steady hand. "Put it through the window," Uri said to him.

Ephraim lifted the rifle and as he did so pressed the trigger, almost instinctively, like the hero of a Western. "Bull's-eye!" cried the *chevra* in admiration. "Ephraim, give them another!"

He put in another grenade, swung, fired... "Bull's-eye

again!" they cried, cheering. He decided not to try a third time, lest he miss and spoil his reputation for supermarksmanship.

Now there was real quiet and the men took advantage of it to press on. Alex reached the YMCA and there were bursts of machine-gun fire from the left side of the street. Close to the wall of the house, near the tennis court, lay the wounded of A Company; around the gate of the American Consulate were more wounded and some dead. Yossi P., who had previously told Alex to advance without stopping, now changed his mind, and said that they should first mop up the YMCA.

Uri heard Yossi giving the orders to Alex, and at once ran into the YMCA courtyard, sure that his platoon was coming in behind him. But nobody else had heard Yossi's orders so, finding himself alone, Uri looked back and returned.

This time he organized more carefully. He arranged that Ron Levy and his section would rush straight for the main door of the building while Shai and Elisha would go along the wall and then work their way around to the door. The rest of the *chevra* would take up positions along the fence to provide cover.

The tanks were standing along the street, waiting for new assignments. Uri arranged with Rafi that they should fire on the upper storey of the building until he signaled them to stop.

Covering fire came from the tank and Ron raced to a giant flowerpot standing in the middle of the yard, and from there leapt to the wall of the house. Others followed him while Shai and Elisha went along the wall to the right wing.

Uri and Uzi rushed through the door of the building. A dying Jordanian, hit by A Company, lay beside the stairs. A burst came from somewhere and hit Uzi in his right thigh. Shai and Elisha got in and mopped up the ground floor. Then they went up the stairs. Shai and Elisha went to the right wing, Ron to the left. They found long passages with rooms opening onto them from both sides, every one a potential trap. But as they burst into each in turn, they saw no one.

They went up the stairs, taking the turns very carefully, as one shot might be enough to kill one of them. But there was nobody on the stairs.

Uri signaled to Rafi that the tanks should stop firing. They went from room to room, and Amos Brin, bursting into a room with his Uzi at his hip, caught a glimpse of a terrifying enemy facing him, a weapon at his side, all set to kill. Amos ripped off a burst and a mirror smashed to smithereens. Giora ran in—"What happened?" They looked at the shattered mirror and laughed. Amos wondered, "Do I really look like that?"

They went up the stairs to the third floor as if they were dancing on eggs, but no one was there. However, in one of the rooms they found the base of a machine gun. So the Jordanian who had fired at Uzi must be somewhere. There was an attic and as they reached the stairwell a burst cut in front of their legs. Shai prepared a hand grenade, but a bullet struck right ahead of him. He was scared to throw the grenade up the steps in case it rolled down on top of them.

Deciding that a frontal assault on a man armed with a machine gun on top of the stairs would be fatal, they moved a curtain aside to glance out of a window, and immediately attracted fire from both the Jordanians and the Israelis in Jewish Jerusalem. "To hell with this! On top of all our other troubles, our own men are firing at us!" To reinforce this impression, a tank shell shook the building. Apparently Rafi hadn't got Uri's message to stop shooting.

Elisha and Ephraim found other stairs leading to a skylight in the roof, and through the skylight they could see a Jordanian firing into the street. They each fired and the Jordanian disappeared. But it was impossible to know whether he had been hit, so they decided that using the skylight was a poor strategy.

As they returned to the *chevra* at the main stairwell, a bullet sliced through the air and got Shai in the hand. Amazed, he cried out, "Hey! I've been hit," but investigation showed that the wound was slight. A burst from above came close to them—the bullets going into the wall right next to them. They withdrew down the passage for a conference and in the end decided to go down and tell the tank to aim at the roof.

They stood next to the wall of the building. Any approach to the tank was very hazardous. Now and then a bullet struck it and ricocheted off with a whistle. They tried to attract the attention of the tank crew by screaming like banshees, but got no response. Then they whirled their arms in frantic signals—still no response. It was clear that somebody had to brave the sniper on the roof and go across the yard and the street to the tank. They looked at each other to decide which it was going to be. Without waiting for any discussion, Yoska Balagan, one of the older men, walked across to the tank.

The young soldiers were full of admiration. "Hey, just look at Yoska Balagan strolling around as if this were Dizengoff Street." Inspired by his example, Ron and Elisha dashed across to the tank and tried to get the attention of the crew, without result. In the end Ron clambered up the side of the tank and got face to face with the astonished tank commander, Shaul. "Quickly—shoot at the roof, at once!"

Even before he had climbed off the tank again, the first shell was fired, followed by three more. The Jordanian machine gun was silenced at last, never to fire again. Two injured Jordanians were found on the roof; a third got away by climbing down a scaffolding at the back of the building.

In the meantime two wounded men, Uzi with his thigh wound and Albaz, shot in the jaw, made their way disconsolately to the rear. Uzi hopped along, Albaz walked, holding his face in his hand. The pain was fearful. They gradually came closer to the casualty clearing station. Paratroopers, watching their slow progress down the street, whispered to each other, "Just look at those two . . . For them the war is over . . ."

After exchanging compliments with the tank crew, the platoon went back into the building, where all was now serene.

Kuchak, the reconnaissance officer of the battalion, now serving as operations officer, arrived and instructed Uri to link up at once with the rest of the company, which had already advanced south beyond the courtyard of the mosque.

While Uri's platoon was still fighting at the YMCA, the main part of the company arrived at the gas station. They decided that the yard of the station was a good place in which to reorganize, because there was a wall on the southern side between them and the enemy. But very soon they found that there was no safe place and no front line in a built-up area. Bursts of bullets sprayed the area from the east, the north, and even the west, the zone through which they had already passed. They identified the main sources of fire as the American Consulate and high buildings to the east, in the vicinity of Saladin Street. The paratroopers took up their positions at the corners of the yard and huddled along the wall. Nevertheless, Avinoam, Moshe, Ilan, and Gideon were hit, one after the other, and were placed in the courtyard of the monastery.

Avinoam was unconscious and when he woke up in hospital, found wounded Jordanian POWs on either side of him. Military police came in to interrogate the Jordanians, and a nurse pointed to the three wounded men. "Hey! Not me!" Avinoam shouted.

Yigal fired three antitank shells at the consulate and Aaron shot with his rifle, but it was difficult to pinpoint the Jordanian positions. Alex was wounded again.

Moshe Mazer brought Moshe Levi's tank up to the yard. The tank commander was an old friend of his. He directed the tank to a position opposite the YMCA and the American Consulate. The first shell bored a large hole in the upper part of the southern wall of the YMCA. The building shook, and at that moment something exploded between the tanks, wounding both Rafi and Moshe. They went to the yard of the monastery and as they entered it a burst hit Mazer in the neck. He was sure at first that his throat had been cut open, but Dalit, the sergeant, reassured him; he was bandaged, and helped Zvi Friedman to guard some Jordanian POWs in the yard.

Uzi, Eli Riback, Gutman and Yankele huddled under the wall and talked for a few moments. Eli said that he had a strange foreboding that he would not survive the war, and began to talk about his little daughter, whom he loved very much. Uzi stopped him. "That's quite enough. After the war's over, you can talk about your forebodings and then I'll be prepared to listen. But not now."

The shots of the snipers continued. In a little while they would have to get up and move on again. It was 0630.

Earlier, at 0500, two of our objectives had already been attained: The Police School was in our hands, and had become a strongpoint of ours in the rear, and on Ammunition Hill we were masters of the position, although mopping-up operations were still in progress. The companies of Giora and Gabi had established bases at the crossroads of the hospitals, and in the Hotel Ambassador and its vicinity; they had begun to spread out toward the lower Sheikh Jarragh suburb. The forces in contact with the enemy at Givat Hamivtar prevented Jordanian reinforcements making their way to the city, and were also preparing to link up with the garrison on Mount Scopus.

In the central sector, the position was also satisfactory. The area of the breach was now secure, and we dominated the American Colony and Wadi Joz suburbs, including the slopes going down to the Kidron Stream. We also controlled the vital cross-roads near the Rockefeller Museum.

No further Jordanian attempts had been made to get down from the Augusta Victoria ridge to relieve Arab Jerusalem or the Old City. The artillery bombardment of the northwest slopes seemed to have ended any danger of a counterattack. Zamush's company was now in a position to fire on the road from the ridge.

Major objectives not yet in our hands were the Rockefeller Museum itself and the group of buildings opposite Herod's Gate.

Yossi P. of Battalion 28 had reported that he was in the area beyond the YMCA. This report did not yet raise any suspicion that they had taken the wrong road. Nobody knew that the YMCA was on Nablus Road and not in Saladin Street, where Yossi was supposed to be.

We had done astonishingly well. Within a period of only four hours we had broken through the main Jordanian lines. We were still waiting for permission to invade the Old City, so the delay in taking the buildings opposite Herod's Gate did not matter so much.

So far, so good. But some of the men at Headquarters searched the aerial photograph for the YMCA building on Saladin Street and they didn't find it. They knew the system of Jordanian fortifications very well, and the network of buildings used as key positions. The YMCA was not one of them.

Slowly the staff officers began to think that something had gone wrong, and urged me to intervene. But I did not agree with them. Yossi sounded so confident and sure of himself on the radio that I did not believe he needed our help.

In reality, Battalion 28 was in a delicate situation. D Company, hard hit by the Jordanian shelling before the battalion moved, had still not rejoined it. The support company had been cut off going through the barricades and was now making its way on its own toward the Rockefeller. A and C Companies had been engaged in savage fighting for two hours, and the tempo had not decreased—if anything, it had intensified.

Despite these difficulties, Yossi had no doubt that his battalion would carry out all its missions.

The tank company in its entirety was operating inside Arab Jerusalem, and helping the infantry wherever needed and possible. The artillery and Air Force were striking accurately and swiftly at every target allocated to them. So, looking at the overall situation, we had every reason to be elated; we were doing better than we had ever dared to hope. But, for the infantry, the battles in the Arab city were still ferocious and costly.

At 0630, A Company was ready to advance, but movement in the middle of the street was impossible, for Jordanian fire from the buildings and the wall of the Old City to the south covered it effectively. Avidan ordered his men to move forward cautiously, clinging closely to the walls.

The white stone wall of the monastery courtyard ran along the left-hand side of the road, to the east. The mosque, with an empty plot behind it, was on the right. Beyond the empty plot were two buildings, then another empty plot.

Mordi advanced along the monastery wall, accompanied by Kochavi's Mag squad. On the other side of the road, Leiserke was next to the wall, Ofer to his left nearer the road, and Yigal behind them. Then came Avidan and the command group. The advance command group of the battalion was at the mosque, and the tanks were close by.

When the squads reached the bend in the wall of the monastery, they came under heavy fire. Echoes of the shots reverberated in the alley and it was hard to determine where they were coming from. Avidan told Weiner to take a squad into the monastery yard, and attack anyone shooting into the alley from behind.

Leiserke saw snipers to the left and shouted to the *chevra*, while Ofer shot a burst into the building. Then came a telltale knock—ammunition finished. Ofer moved back, and at that moment a grenade was flung at them and a hail of bullets fired from the monastery wall. Ofer was wounded by shrapnel and Leiserke fell, hit by a bullet.

Yigal, a meter behind them, thought that the fire was coming from ahead of them in the alley; he went forward, grenade in hand, but was hit in the arm by a grenade from an antitank gun before he could throw his grenade, and his leg was hit by shrapnel. He fell, calling for a medic.

Mordi, Kochavi, and Micha all ran to the help of their comrades. They pulled Leiserke and Ofer back, but Leiserke died almost at once. Kochavi applied a tourniquet to Yigal's leg.

The first tank, commanded by Rafi, stood next to the mosque, and Avidan sent it forward. When the tank reached the entrance to the alley, an antitank grenade passed under the belly of the tank and exploded behind it, spraying shrapnel on the turret. Suddenly, from a hidden Jordanian post to the left, strong fire was opened on the command group from behind.

Avidan called Rafi to return with the tank to deal with the new threat, so Rafi came back, shooting in the direction from which the Jordanian fire had come, although he was not sure of the exact place. Then, from the turret, he identified a Jordanian post and smashed it with a tank shell.

The paratroopers rushed forward and found that there was a communication trench running from the mosque to the vicinity of the alley, parallel to the road.

To Mordi every second seemed to last an hour. He went back to Avidan and said bitterly, "I've lost Leiserke. We've got to do

something. They must pay for this." The others called him down:
"The tank's coming soon." But he was not prepared to wait; Leiserke, his friend, was lying there dead. He rushed back to the
entrance to the alley, grenade in hand. To throw it he had to
expose half his body. A burst knocked him down, and he fell
beside his comrade, Leiserke.

Weiner's squad mopped up the stone wall and the pine grove
next to the monastery. He placed Itzik at the gate of the gas station to provide cover for him and Yoska Balagan. They were running along the stone wall when they suddenly saw a post ahead
of them and threw in a grenade, only to rouse two rabbits with
the explosion!

Itzik noticed shots coming from the monastery, so he fired his
Mag in the direction, but could not pinpoint the sniper's position.

Yossi P. joined the men of A Company. He found the bodies
of Mordi and Leiserke and saw that Yigal and Ofer were being
treated for their wounds. He decided that A Company had done
enough for the time being and that he should bring C Company
forward, so he told Avidan to take his remaining men back to the
monastery yard to reorganize.

But there was to be no rest for them yet, for they still came
under sniping fire from the roof of the monastery. Avidan sent
Gadi with a squad to clean up the roof, and there they found two
Jordanians, who surrendered.

But the sniping still continued, and they could not identify
the source. Shlomo Cohen said to Avidan, "I'll run into the open
area. The Jordanians will fire at me. As soon as you see the
flashes, fire." Avidan turned down the suggestion.

He decided that they could live with the sniping; they found a
protected position in the yard and took a few minutes to rest. They
ate, refilled their magazines, and discussed their experiences.

The mood was very black. Mordi, the company's second-in-
command, was dead, together with three others; several men

were wounded, including Gabi and Ilan, platoon commanders. They had practically no ammunition left.

Avidan took the aerial photograph out of his pocket to check his position. He found that the photograph looked like a sieve— little pieces of shrapnel had pierced his pocket and the picture.

Alex designated two groups to mop up the alley. Shaul Chugim was to move along the right hand side of the road; he had with him Yehoshua Diamant with a Mag, Eli Rieback and Dani Frishman. Chanoch's number three platoon was to move along the left hand side. Rafi's tank would help. The source of the fire was still not clear.

(Only after the war did they discover how strong the Jordanian position had been. A network of trenches and bunkers ran from Mandelbaum Gate through the mosque, across the open area, up to the end of the "alley of death," which had a concrete bunker running along its entire length.)

Chugim led the squad into the alley. His Uzi jammed and he went back to fix it, but the others went on. When they were ten meters inside the alley, they came under violent and accurate fire, and Diamant and Frishman were killed. Berko was wounded, got through the gate of a building, and found shelter. Eli Riebeck ran back and joined Chugim, who realized that it was hopeless to try to advance straight down the alley.

Berko, although his wound was bleeding profusely, shouted a warning, "Be careful—sniping!"

Rafi's tank and Nachshon's platoon came from the direction of the mosque. Alex signalled to Rafi to go into the alley. Nachshon directed the tank.

The tank advanced slowly. Bullets cut into the armor, and an antitank grenade went under it. Rafi aimed the cannon. The explosion seemed to shake the entire suburb. A second shell and the bunker was completely liquidated.

Now the alley of death could be traversed. It had earned the grim name given to it by the paratroopers.

At 0700, back at Brigade Headquarters, I contacted Uzi of the 71st. "I'm afraid that Yossi P. has run into difficulties. Can you help him to take the Rockefeller?"

"Of course. It'll be a pleasure."

"Then coordinate the action between you. If you need me, I'm always at your disposal." But I doubted whether they would require any help from us. Most of the tanks were already fighting with them, and they could always activate the artillery directly.

I noticed that my staff officers did not agree with my decision not to interfere. They suspected that Yossi P. was exaggerating his problems, and that our appearance in the battalion would change the situation immediately.

Even I myself was not sure that I was right to leave matters to the battalion commanders. We had not received a detailed report from Yossi P., but we gathered that he had had a very hard time and might not be able to carry out his mission. So we felt uncertain and depressed.

But in the field it never entered Yossi's head for a moment that he could not execute the assignment. While we were wrestling gloomily with his difficulties, he and his staff were eating biscuits and planning the next stage of the operation. Despite the losses, they were in high spirits, as they knew that D Company was heading toward the Rockefeller, and they had no doubt about the ability of A and C Companies to go on fighting till the cows came home.

Two of my staff officers, Amos and Arik, had personal reasons for wanting to join Yossi. Until a few months ago Amos had commanded A Company; he had led it for many years, and concern for his old comrades was now eating him up. They were in trouble, and he was on a roof in the rear, offering them advice.

Both he and Arik feared that they might go through the whole war without firing a shot or storming a position. That all those years spent in commando training would result in giving advice to others was not to be borne. They had been too young to take part in the retaliation raids of the fifties—and now they might miss this chance for combat because they were too old. They didn't know how they would be able to look the *chevra* in the eyes.

Moshele, my second-in-command, supported their view that we should go to the help of the 28th, but he did not press his opinion. More experienced than they, he was more restrained. He knew that I had to make the decision.

I faced a very difficult problem. Both from my experience and from my knowledge of military theory, I believed that it was sound policy for a commander to rush to the help of a subordinate in trouble.

On the other hand, leaving a command post and running the danger of losing contact and control of the fighting in other areas seemed to be contrary to the dictates of good sense. I did not detect any sign of panic in Yossi's voice over the radio. I had given him tanks and artillery, and he could call on me if he needed more help.

From our roof we had contacts both with the battalions in the field and Central Command. We had selected the roof because it provided us with a clear view of the entire battlefield. An effecitve reaction to any counterattack by the Jordanians made central control essential. Fighting through the streets and running the risk of losing all these contacts would have definitely been a mistake. In fact, we had proved the value of being where we were by getting Uzi's battalion to join with Yossi P.'s in the attack on the Rockefeller.

So I overruled Amos and Arik and decided to remain where I was. But I made a concession to Moshele; I sent him to coordinate the joint action of the two battalions and to deal on the spot with any problems that might arise. It is an accepted principle that the second-in-command of a brigade should take over the command when more than one battalion is involved. It would give Moshele a chance to show his mettle. Orni quickly organized communications and Moshele prepared an advance command group.

Rafi reported that the stocks of ammunition and fuel of his tanks were running out. Moshele contacted Kotik, the ordnance officer, who was still at Bet Hakerem, and asked him to send the necessary supplies in a hurry. When he set out to get the ammunition and fuel, he found that the trucks bringing them for the tanks had disappeared when the brigade rushed up to Jerusalem. He rushed around Schneller, frantically collecting supplies, and managed to load ten trucks; to speed the work, he even loaded them personally. Suddenly he saw ten other trucks standing at the side of the road inside the Schneller compound. He made inquiries and found that they were fully loaded—they were in fact the missing trucks from the convoy. He instructed Jackie to take these vehicles to Fagi at once, beyond the Police School, while he himself brought the others behind them.

Moshele instructed Rafi to send somebody to the Police School to take delivery there and to bring the supplies up to the tanks in the battle area. This would obviate the need to pull the tanks back to refuel and to reload.

We were hoping to get permission at any minute to attack the Old City, and we wanted to be sure that the tanks would be ready the moment we got that all-important order.

From a cemetery near to Herod's Gate, Uri's platoon was exchanging fire with the Jordanians on the Old City wall, when he got an order from Yossi P. that he had to take what Yossi called "the building with the blue shutters opposite the gate." This was, in fact, the post office.

Still subjected to heavy fire, they crawled between the gravestones until they reached an alley leading to some broad steps between the buildings, at the end of which was a road. They got into a tangle of buildings and shops, and entered one building to check for snipers. A woman shrieked in Hebrew, "Don't shoot! My little daughter is here!" "How do you know Hebrew?" "I grew up among Jews." She helped them gather all the women and children from the area and put them in a safe place and they went on across the road.

Uri realized that they seemed to have gone too far, and went back. They reached another road. Something was definitely wrong, so they turned back again and came to the road they had crossed. At the end of it, they saw the Old City wall: diagonally opposite, on the corner facing the wall, was the Hotel Rivoli. Uri realized that this would be an ideal site from which to dominate Herod's Gate.

Heavy fire was opened at them from the wall. At Herod's Gate they saw a group of Jordanian soldiers; Arele, the signaler, brought down one with a burst from his Uzi. Somebody yelled, "Grenade! Run." There was smoke everywhere. Uri led the platoon at the double across the street and into the hotel. Nobody was hurt.

Elisha took a squad up to the roof, where they set up a bazooka and a machine gun facing Herod's Gate. The others dispersed through the hotel and took up positions facing the Old City. They realized that the Jordanians had posts all along the wall. Uri reported the position to Yossi P. It was 0800.

At 0330 hours the support company was given its target—the Rockefeller Museum—the most dramatic of all objectives outside the Old City, apart from the linkup to Mount Scopus. Everyone had seen photographs of the imposing concrete structure, just outside the Old City walls. To take it was obviously all-important for tactical reasons: It was an ideal springboard for an attack on the Old City through Herod's Gate.

Unfortunately, the company suffered heavy losses from the Jordanian guns while it was waiting to go into action. Many of the men got scattered, so, by 1500 hours, Odem, the company commander, had only half his company left. Something was wrong with the communications system—he could not get hold of Yossi P. to confirm or change his orders. Nevertheless, he decided to go on and take "the Rock" with the forces he had at his disposal.

He assumed that so prominent a landmark would be easy to find, although none of his men knew where it was. So he set off south, in the general direction of the museum, cutting through fences, climbing walls, crossing yards. They saw no enemy—and no Israelis either. They were alone and Odem wondered where everybody had gone.

At long last they met some men of Battalion 71's D Company. "Where's the Rockefeller?" "Somewhere in that direction." He felt like a tourist trying to find a museum that simply *must* be seen. A Jerusalemite reassured him and gave him more detailed directions.

All of a sudden they found themselves close to a great white, squat concrete building, with a huge rectangular tower rising above them. "The Rock!" And it looked rather like the Rock of Gibraltar.

He divided his company into two squads, one under Amnon, the other under his own direct command. Amnon's squad raced across to the courtyard of the museum while Odem's provided cover; then Amnon gave them cover while they rushed over. They found a door to the courtyard ajar, went through, and ran up to the great bronze door of the museum. It was locked.

Heavy fire was opened on them from the wall of the Old City. Three hand grenades were hurled at them but they missed. "We're lucky they're so poorly trained in grenade throwing," somebody said. Gabai threw two Mills bombs. One went over the wall and exploded on the far side, one fell in the street. The Jordanian fire stopped for a moment, then resumed.

Amnon took no notice. "Break down the door and let's get inside," he shouted. He hurled a phosphorus grenade at the Wall. Burning pieces of shrapnel and smoke scattered in all directions and the firing stopped. He took advantage of the opportunity to fire a burst from his Uzi at the lock of the door. It did not help; the door would not open.

The way they got into the building was anticlimactic, ludicrously simple. Other members of Amnon's squad, checking the yard, found a number of Arab workers hiding there. The Israelis asked how they could get into the museum. One of the workers produced a key. So they went in like visiting archaeologists or tourists.

Ashat rushed up to the roof, where the Jordanian flag was flying from a flagpole, and pulled it down. Kopel found a piece of cloth and a fountain pen: he painted a blue-black Shield of David on the cloth.

They hauled up the flag. The Jordanians responded by hurling every kind of explosive imaginable at them—bullets, shells, grenades. They went inside the tower. It was still impossible to contact Yossi P. and tell him the great news—Israel held "the Rock"!

But the word got around somehow. The army apparently did not rely solely on its modern communications system. Good news travels fast.

Haggai's D Company suffered heavily in the shelling by the Jordanians. Nevertheless he gathered together the men he had left, as well as other forces that had become separated from their units for some reason or another. Thus he got some machine gunners under Moshe from the support company, and some ammunition bearers under Yoram. They set off in the general direction of the Old City, their aim being to attack the Rockefeller Museum.

Near the casualty clearing station he met Uzi, commander of Battalion 71. Uzi advised Haggai to go along the Wadi Joz road, already taken by the 71st. But, he added, he had heard that the 28th had already taken the museum, although he was not absolutely sure.

Haggai went on. Near "the read house," his mixed force met men from the support company, who told him that the Rockefeller had been in Israeli hands for some time. Delighted, they went on, entered the courtyard of the museum, and went up to the great bronze door of the building. As they were about to enter, Uzi, second-in-command of C Company, who had stayed with Haggai after helping in the evacuation of the wounded, glanced back to make sure that everyone was safe.

To his amazement, he saw six Jordanian soldiers marching into the courtyard. He fired a magazine of his Uzi at them; three dropped to the ground, two ran into the olive grove, and the third escaped through the gate. But one of them managed to fire at Uzi, and he was wounded in the hand and evacuated to the rear.

Odem and Haggai, two company commanders, went into the courtyard together to plan the defense of the museum against counterattack, and its use as a springboard from which to carry on the battle. They placed a platoon on the southeast corner of the yard, controlling the Kidron Valley, the road going up to the Augusta Victoria ridge, and the street running alongside the wall to Lions' Gate. The recoilless-gun platoon went up to the tower. The rest of the men took up positions in rooms inside the museum.

At 0630, because of the heavy losses Battalion 28 had sustained and the manner in which the companies had gotten scattered, I ordered Giora's brigade reconnaissance unit to link up with the battalion and help it. They went along Nablus Road without encountering any resistance, and when they reached the museum, found that it was firmly in Israeli hands, so Giora decided to comb the yards and buildings in the vicinity, and in the yard of "the white house" took two Legionnaires prisoner.

Kaposta was also looking for work for his reconnaissance company, so I sent him to reinforce the 28th as well. My aim was to bring the battalion up to full fighting strength for the attack on the Old City.

On the way to the museum, they came under sniper fire, so they broke into the building the fire was coming from and killed the sniper. Farther on, they came face to face with a Jordanian 52-millimeter mortar squad and stormed it, killing two Jordanians and capturing two. When they reached the Rockefeller, they found everything under control, and Kaposta put his men in strategic buildings in the vicinity.

The sniping battle between the wall and the museum continued unabated. The Jordanians had the advantage—they could fire from anywhere along the wall, while the Israelis could only fire from the museum's windows, of which there were very few. The Jordanians blanketed every window wtih fire. It was impossible to move in the yard. The paratroopers crawled along the stone wall and kept changing their positions, at the same time trying not to expose themselves. Avihu Peled, raising his head for a second to shoot, was hit by a bullet and killed.

Stacking sandbags next to the windows, essential if these were to be used as firing posts, was also a dangerous task, for the sacks were at once riddled with shots. Gradually, however, about a hundred sacks were placed around the windows and a machine gun was set up in the library, directly opposite the wall. But it was only beginning to operate when it was hit by a shell and the gunner wounded.

Ami, with a recoilless gun, began to hit the Jordanian positions one by one and Moshe and Yehuda's accurate sniping began to weaken the Jordanian fire a little.

Yisrael treated the wounded, going from position to position to see who was hit. From time to time, he went to the rear to collect more medical equipment. The number of wounded rose.

At 0715, when Uri reported to Yossi P. that he was in the Rivoli Hotel, opposite Herod's Gate, Yossi decided that it would constitute an ideal headquarters for the battalion. He and his staff made their way through the cemetery, ran in front of the hotel, where they came under fire from the wall, and then dashed into the hotel. Yossi reported to me the good news that he had moved his headquarters to the Rivoli, directly opposite Herod's Gate.

But those inside the Rivoli found that they were not free to enjoy a vacation in a luxury hotel. Some Jordanians had hidden between the walls of the alley and the post office, and anybody shooting at them came under fire from the Jordanians on the wall. Then the Jordanians from the alley managed to make a dash for it and got through Herod's Gate.

Eli, the company sergeant major, had spread his men in the buildings across the road from the museum. He decided to move across to "the Rock." As they crossed the open space, they encountered two Jordanians, one armed with a submachine gun, the other with a rifle. Eli killed them both, but they managed to hit Yoram in the thigh. They dragged him to safety and entered the museum.

There they found long halls lined with exhibits, and the amateur archaeologists among them forgot the war. Cupboard after cupboard was crammed with antiques, and they moved reverently from exhibit to exhibit, purring like cats over the treasures, while less-cultured paratroopers snatched a quick nap in the cool halls.

Now and then they could hear a shell, but most stayed where they were, only the snipers at the shooting slits changing place from time to time.

Soon life took a distinct turn for the better at the Rivoli.

Amos Manker, the radio technician, adapted the telephone system of the hotel so that they had communication with all posts. The *chevra* decided that it was high time the hotel restaurant served meals, and went off to investigate the food situation. They produced an alfresco banquet, laced with champagne. Then they shaved and washed, cleaning themselves of the dirt, the blood, the smells of war, and felt like new men.

Yossi P. got in touch with the companies and obtained confirmation that "the Rock" was in Israeli hands, and that the *chevra* were in good shape, in fact longing to take a crack at the Old City. All they needed was the green light.

At 0747 Yossi reported to me: "All our objectives are in our hands. When do we go into the Old City?"

Meanwhile the other Yossi was organizing at the crossroads of the hospitals. He stationed tanks, recoilless guns, and heavy machine guns opposite Givat Hamivtar. At the crossroads was part of A Company, Squads of men with Mags and heavy machine guns were ordered to the roofs and in the tower, from which points they could both shoot and observe. The Jordanians fired systematically and persistently from Givat Hamivtar.

Suddenly the *chevra* saw a Jordanian Land Rover coming along the street from the direction of Givat Hamivtar. Gilad scored a bull's-eye with a bazooka shell, and the jeep began to burn. The driver was killed and two other men wounded.

During a moment of quiet, Gadi hoisted the flag of Israel on the flagpole on the tower of the hospital. The tower became a major objective for Jordanian fire, but no one was hit and the flag remained.

Doron, the second-in-command of the Battalion, decided that the time had come to liquidate the Jordanian positions on Givat Hamivtar. He called for artillery fire and the tanks and recoilless guns joined in. Givat Hamivtar was covered with fire and smoke and Jordanians were seen in headlong flight.

Jordanians were still shooting from bunkers and trenches in the area between Mandelbaum Gate and Nablus Road. They had to be mopped up to make free movement of traffic to the Old City from Mandelbaum Gate along the main road, Nablus Road, possible, so A Company was charged with finishing off the job. As Mualem went toward Mandelbaum Gate, a wounded Jordanian surrendered to him. Suddenly two armed Jordanians came out of a post. Mualem was first with a quick burst and they fell. He went on, saw two more armed Jordanians in a communication trench, and with a hand grenade dispatched them as well.

Sniping continued from the buildings on either side of the "alley of death." Machson, now second-in-command of the company in place of the dead Mordi, assigned the task of disposing of the problem to the sappers attached to the company. Giora blew open a locked door with explosive and threw in a grenade. They rushed through the building, firing. There would be no more sniping from that building.

Iran fired a recoilless-gun shell at another building that had been giving trouble, and the door was split open. They ran from room to room, firing. On the roof they found the sandbags of a machine-gun position and crates of ammunition. But the Jordanian gunners had fled, taking the gun with them.

The "alley of death" was clean, the road to the Damascus Gate wide open.

Chapter VII

THE PEAK OF MOUNT SCOPUS

The reports from the battlefront had lost the tension they had had at the time of the breakthrough; by now the paratroopers were cleaning up the area around the hotels, liquidating pockets of resistance and snipers' nests in the American Colony area, and gaining complete control of Ammunition Hill.

Contact with the remaining Jordanians on Ammunition Hill and at the Augusta Victoria Hospital had been reduced to exchanges of intermittent fire, and there were no signs of a Jordanian intention to counterattack.

The two battalion commanders laid down preventive artillery fire in their sectors and were ready, if necessary, to intensify it. Ziklag, commander of the artillery, selected objectives and set ranges for the guns. He wanted to be certain that no shells were wasted.

Reuven, the adjutant, set out on a tour of the casualty clearing stations. They had had a very hard time. The evacuation of wounded from the battlefield had proceeded at great speed, and the doctors and orderlies had their hands full of work and blood.

At 0700 three civilians arrived at Brigade Command. Their faces were familiar and several people interested in archeology identified them at once as Professors Avigad, Biran, and Aviram. We shook hands and they asked to be allowed to join us during the attack on the Rockefeller Museum. The archeological treasures there were of very great importance, and they wanted to make certain that not a single item vanished mysteriously into thin air.

We looked at them in astonishment mixed with admiration. The museum was not yet taken, there might be heavy fighting for it, but they were prepared to risk their lives to protect the cultural inventory.

We would have to take them with us in the two half-tracks assigned to the brigade commander's group. We could not go into the firing line in soft-skinned vehicles. They understood and said courteously: "If you refuse us, we won't be angry." But their eyes pleaded and I finally answered, "All right, we'll take you." They sat on one side and waited.

We heard the hum of planes in the sky. Our planes were bombing the Jordanian artillery positions east of Mount Scopus; the Air Force had been brought into action at the request of Uzi Narkiss. We watched the planes and the antiaircraft fire directed against them in the heavens and our morale was as high as the planes themselves.

Suddenly we held our breath. One plane was hit, and anxious eyes followed it westward, hoping it would reach the field.

At 1720 we were waiting for Battalion 28 to report that it had taken up positions opposite Herod's Gate and the Rockefeller Museum. Gaining control of these key points would end the first stage of the battle for Jerusalem. Then we could begin the liberation of the Old City.

Kotik, the quartermaster, had reached Fagi. Moshele told him to get to the Police School, where one of the tank officers was waiting for him.

The Center Command medical officer, Lieutenant Colonel Michaeli, and the brigade doctor, Dr. King, were mobilizing ambulances and other vehicles to evacuate the wounded and were rushing to get supplies to replace those used during the battles.

The residents of the house came up on the roof and stuffed us with the best of home delicacies: hot drinks, eggs, vegetables, and cooked dishes. An elderly man came up, pistol in hand, and asked me to give him some job to do. We explained patiently that we did not really need him or his weapon. He went off sadly, but returned happily, carrying food instead.

Everyone was in excellent spirits. For practical purposes, Jerusalem was already in our hands. It was hard to believe we had accomplished so much in a few hours.

Top officers came to say the traditional blessing: "Blessed art Thou, our Lord our God, King of the Universe, who hast kept us in life, and hast preserved us, and enabled us to reach this day." We shook hands and embraced each other.

Davidi, chief parachutist officer, and Dudik, his adjutant, separated. They were going to join different units in action. Opposite us, in the open area in front of the Police School, men were marching in Indian file. It was Kaposta's reconnaissance group.

Suddenly a cloud of smoke and dust rose in the middle of the group. Not sure whether it was a shell or antipersonnel mine, we looked anxiously through the glasses and saw first one wounded man being evacuated to the rear, then another.

The sun rose. The cold seemed to have penetrated to our bones during the night, but now we thawed out, as the operational picture became clear.

Although the minutes were slipping away, I was not pressuring my battalion commanders to hurry. I relied on their judgment in the field. To us, on the roof, time seemed to be rolling at headlong speed, but to the *chevra* fighting in the field, every minute was a lifetime. We restrained our impatience by remembering that, in our most optimistic planning, we had never dreamed we could finish the battle so quickly. There was still no authorization for us to invade the Old City. Nor had the Armored Brigade finished encircling the city from the north, and Jerusalem Brigade had not yet closed the circle from the southwest. It was only the idea that we might get to the Temple Mount today that seemed a spur to instant action.

We waited, our main task now to help in the swift reorganization of forces, the evacuation of the wounded, the provision of fresh supplies, the replacement of wounded officers.

Moshele, the deputy brigade commander, reported that he wanted his group to join Uzi's battalion. He had got back his half-track, used to evacuate the wounded of Battalion 66, and he went off in the direction of Rockefeller Museum.

At 0725 I instructed Yossi, of Battalion 66, to move with two complete companies toward the Rockefeller Mueseum. He himself was still at the Hotel Rivoli, but would be at our disposal to complete the conquest of Arab Jerusalem. The area around the Rockefeller Museum was particularly important, for it would provide the springboard for the attack on the Old City. Then at 0730 Yossi P. of the 28th reported that he was at Hotel Rivoli opposite Herod's Gate and the other Yossi reported that, as ordered, he was beginning to move with two companies toward the Rockefeller. At 0747 Yossi reported that we held the Rockefeller Museum. He himself was still at the Hotel Rivoli, but his two companies were at Rockefeller and he was in communication with them.

Arab Jerusalem, outside the Old City walls, was in our hands! Now the Old City lay before us! I gave orders to prepare the advance command group to move.

At 0804 Uzi Narkiss came again to our roof, where he could observe both our brigade and the Armored Brigade attacking the Shufa'at sector, en route to Givat Hamivtar. The half-tracks which would take us to the front arrived, but they still had to be checked. Orni, the communications officer, went down with a band of radio technicians to overhaul them. We stayed on the roof. From here we would give the command to proceed with the attack.

At 0830 I begged Uzi Narkiss again to authorize my entry into the Old City. He sent in a request to the Chief of Staff, and while we waited for the reply, we took another careful look at the aerial photograph to plan the attack.

At this stage it seemed that our first plan to break through Herod's Gate and the Moslem quarter was still good. General Chorev, who had been on the roof with us for some time, interrupted the discussion, suggesting that perhaps it would be a good idea to capture the southern gates in the wall so as to be able to enter the Old City from two directions. Recalling the 1948 War of Independence, he cited the possibility of making a feint of an attack from Mount Zion with the object of misleading the enemy, thus making it easier to get in with fewer losses. Arik, the intelligence officer, favored an assault from a gate that permitted the passage of vehicles. We all agreed that it was desirable to avoid fighting on foot in a built-up area. I preferred Herod's Gate, as we could shell the Moslem Quarter of the Old City and advance between it and the wall.

Uri, the commander of the Armored Brigade, reported to Uzi that he would shortly begin the attack on Shufa'at and on French Hill. And Yossi reported that he was near the Rockefeller and I ordered him to deploy his forces there and to await further orders.

By 0855 Uzi Narkiss gave instructions that our forces should leave the Police School and Ammunition Hill; they would be replaced by men of the Jerusalem Brigade and the exchange would take place by noon.

At 0900 Uri, commander of the Armored Brigade, reported to Uzi Narkiss: "Beginning the attack on Tel-el-Pul."

Far to the northeast, near the new palace being built for King Hussein, the first tanks of the Harel Brigade appeared. This was an encouraging sight; it meant that the Jordanian forces in

Jerusalem were now cut off from the north. The famous defense system in Shufa'at, French Hill, and Givat Hamivtar would fall into our hands in a few hours. Because the road to Hebron was already blocked by forces of the Jerusalem Brigade, there was no alternative left for the Jordanians in the Old City but to assume that they would be completely surrounded and their line of retreat to the east cut off, a development that gave immediate relief to our forces in the area.

At 0915 Uri, commander of the Armored Brigade, reported: "Tel-el-Pul in our hands. We are about to attack Shufa'at."

At this point Uzi Narkiss decided to free our brigade from maintenance tasks in the liberated area. His order was: "When Uri and his tank forces arrive, we shall leave some of them here. You take the force out of the Police School and assemble in Sheikh Jarragh, for further advance. Eliezer, commander of the Jerusalem Brigade, will take over the Police School and French Hill, and link up with Mount Scopus." Still no word about our going to the Temple Mount.

By 0922 Yush, from the General Staff, advised Uzi Narkiss that as yet our entry into the Old City was not authorized. Uzi was furious: "If we don't enter it, history will lay the blame on us," he declared. Yush stressed again that we were not to move into the Old City.

But we all knew that this had to be the next stage. History demanded it.

At 0930 Orni advised that the half-tracks were now in good condition, and that we could move.

I called Moshele Yossi, Uzi, and Yossi P. on the radios and told them that the advance command group was moving forward, and that, if contact was cut while we were on the move, Moshele would take over the command. I asked the battalion commanders to meet me at the museum for a commanders' discussion on the next stage of the action.

Yossi and Uzi confirmed, but Yossi P. was doubtful about his ability to reach the museum. Jordanian snipers from the wall had absolute control of the entrance to the Rivoli Hotel, and every attempt to go in or out had met with accurate, deadly fire. The position in the hotel was gloomy. Inside were seventeen men in all—a few of them wounded, including Alex, the company commander. Yossi expressed his opinion that it was a good idea at that stage for him to stay with the *chevra* at the hotel. I told him to use his own judgment and then Moshele took over command while we went down and got into the half-tracks.

In the street, the air was that of rest after action, the joy of quiet after noise. Many people were walking about, happy, with bright faces. The nightmare of living right on a dangerous border, at the mercy of the trigger finger of a Jordanian soldier, was over. The tension of the last few days, due to the shelling, had vanished entirely. One could also see how tired they were. Citizens who had helped in the early hours of the morning in the evacuation of casualties came up to us to express their feelings, to say how shocked they were by the face of war. They opened stores and filled the half-tracks with delicacies for the men in the front. The Orthodox mumbled prayers over us, others wished us luck. "May God guard you and keep you from all evil!" One of the men coming from the synagogue asked us to raise a glass of wine with him and to say the *Shehecheyanu* blessing. "Who hast kept us alive, and preserved us, and brought us to this time!"

Signs of the night's shelling were evident on every wall and window. From the top of "our" roof, we already realized that the other roofs round about must have suffered a similar fate, with huge black holes showing in the slanting surfaces of their red tiles.

Generals Narkiss and Chorev joined our group in Uzi's jeep. In my half-track were Amos, an ordnance officer; Arik, the intelligence officer; Orni, the communications officer. Other soldiers were Yablu, Francis, Yisrael, Chanania, Arbib. In the second half-track were the adjutant with the three professors. In the third were the linesmen from the signal company.

We turned left in Yoel Street, and right on one of the streets going down to Samuel the Prophet Street. In front of us was the battlefield where the breakthrough battalions had fought so grimly. Now the area was relatively quiet. From time to time shots were heard in the distance; the war was already being fought far to the east. I sat next to the driver, whom I did not know. The officers and radio technicians were behind, some standing, some seated. Amos and Arik, microphones in hand, continued to maintain contact with the units. We heard the battalion commanders talking to each other. Nothing of importance had happened and we were not asked to do anything. I recognized Moshele's voice discussing supplies with Kotik.

We reached the Sanhedria corner. Next to the Fagi houses, a long convoy of trucks and vans, loaded with ammunition and tank fuel, had come to a standstill. Kotik was at the head of it and we were glad to meet—we had not seen each other since noon the day before. Kotik told us briefly what had happened during the night and morning hours. In his opinion there were enough supplies, except that he was somewhat short of medical materials. But the doctors were already dealing with this. We parted and went on.

Because the convoy blocked the main road, we tried to go round by way of the Old Fagi neighborhood. We found that the way was unusable; so we turned back on our tracks. In the meantime, the first section of the convoy started up again and took a route prepared by Yod-Bet's engineering company. An ammunition carrier in the square of the Police School had exploded a few seconds earlier. It had received a direct hit, had caught fire, and the shells inside it were exploded in every direction, endangering the convoy.

Rafi, commander of the tank company, wanted to retire to reorganize under more convenient conditions, as the number of tanks hit and the nature of the damage to them required full and careful attention. The open space at Nablus Road was not suitable for this work and he suggested the square of the Police School.

I did not agree at first, but asked him to wait for the meeting of the officers at Rockefeller, as perhaps we might still launch an immediate attack on the Old City.

The traffic moved sluggishly. Early in the morning the tanks had raced along the route, and later the wounded had been evacuated over it. So the road had taken a beating and there had been no time to smooth over the ditches and ruts.

Suddenly there was an explosion underneath the caterpillar to our right; but as there was no damage, we went on.

Between the fences stood Yod-Bet, smiling as usual, but there was a grimness to his welcome. Many of his men were casualties, some killed, some wounded. The wait in the field from three in the morning until now—about six hours—under continuous enemy fire and in one place, had not passed without leaving its mark. On both sides of the road a white ribbon had been stretched, and men were still busy removing mines.

We exchanged a few words and greetings. But I could not stop for more than a few seconds; it was nearly ten o'clock. At the school square we came across Micha Kaposta and Meir Bar-Zion. These two unfortunate warriors had been looking for a piece of the action since the small hours of the morning, but had not yet found it.

A group of officers and men stood on the left and Uzi Narkiss got out of his jeep and went up to them. Yod-Bet joined the group and we exchanged but a few words, because time was pressing. Once again we got into our vehicles and listened to reports that the open area between the school and the hospitals was under fire from Givat Hamivtar. So we organized our convoy that the "soft" vehicles enjoyed the protection of the half-tracks and drove as fast as possible through the dangerous area.

But all seemed to be quiet, the odd shot and distant volley evoking a feeling that the battle was over. I breathed deeply and inhaled the perfume in the air; nothing can compare to the purity of an early Jerusalem morning. There was no smell of gunpowder or blood or death.

I recalled other engagements, in particular the smell of the battles at Bir-Aslug, before the first truce in the 1948 War of Liberation. A jeep had gone over a mine and its men were slaughtered; a police station full of soldiers had been demolished. In the field were enemy corpses; the air was heavy, a dreadful mixture of blood, smoke, gunpowder, nausea, death, and decay.

The present case was quite different, despite the ferocious fighting. On our left was Ammunition Hill. On our right, Sheikh Jarragh. In front of us the road to Nablus and Wadi Joz, all battlefields. But the air—the unique air of the Holy City—was pure and untainted.

We passed by the hospitals and on the roofs, in the yards, at the windows, and saw paratroopers. We waved happily and they responded triumphantly but it was difficult to distinguish their faces.

We went on down the slope of the road to the Hotel Ambassador—*the* hotel of Sheikh Jarragh, surrounded by Arab embassies. Normally, a flag flew from every other building—but now the flags were conspicuous by their absence. For some reason this brought home to us the extent of our victory.

Straight to the left was the road to Mount Scopus, and in a distant corner we saw the famous double line of "dragon's teeth." This barricade had always been one of the danger spots when the convoys went through to Mount Scopus. Crossing between the two rows was very slow; at times the drivers had to maneuver the heavily loaded vehicles back and forth and thus were very vulnerable to a Jordanian attack.

We carried on down the narrow, steep road and came to Nablus Road. On our left was Wadi Joz and above was a hill of white rocks, a strong military position. Above that, on the horizon, was Mount Scopus. A little to the left we saw French Hill and the southern end of Givat Hamivtar.

On our right was the white chiseled stone wall dividing the Sheikh Jarragh neighborhood on the west from Nablus Road. The Jordanians had erected this as protection against Israeli fire from our side of the dividing wall, from Samuel the Prophet Street and Mandelbaum Gate.

I remembered one discussion with the then commander of the Central Area, General Yosska Geva, about a breakthrough in this area. We had been sitting on the Hill of the Pool at Romema, together with Lezer Amitai, today commander of the Jerusalem Brigade, then an officer on the staff, and Itzik N., the intelligence officer. Itzik had pulled out a panoramic photograph of the whole of the white wall and explained its structure. The question we had been considering was whether tanks could destroy the wall by crashing into it or, if not, what else would be needed to demolish it.

Now we were on the other side of the wall. I studied the heavy supporting pillars and the discrepancies in height between the wall and the street. The question of a breakthrough had been solved. Our recoilless gun jeeps had gone through the gap extending from the building-block works to the Nablus Road without our having had to smash down the wall. The infantry had broken in through the eucalyptus—exactly as we planned it back in 1962.

At the crossroads we left Nablus Road and turned left, to the Wadi Joz road, cleaned up by Battalion 71. This was our road to the Rockefeller. The streets were empty and everything was quiet.

Suddenly the caterpillar on our half-track split apart. We stopped and the *chevra* jumped off and took up positions in case we were attacked.

It was clear that the repair would take a long time, so I instructed them to transfer everything needed by the advance command group to the second half-track. Some of us would go on, while the rest would wait for the half-track to be fixed or for another vehicle to come. Uzi Narkiss left us and went back to Police School. The battle of the Armored Brigade on Givat Hamivtar had not yet ended, and he wanted to follow it from close at hand.

Orni came up to me. "Motta, what about the professors? There isn't room for all of them." I hesitated a moment, wondering if we should try to squeeze them onto our vehicle. There was no room, but on the other hand—to bring them this far and not to let them enter the museum would have been almost criminal. "O.K. Let them get on, somehow with us." So we crowded into one half-track and set off for the Rockefeller.

Reuven, the adjutant, and Dudu, the signals officer, remained with the group of radio technicians. As we started off, they tried in vain to move the half-track without a caterpillar. There was nothing to do but wait, and to organize a defensive position. Dudu placed Pollack, my runner, on the wall next to the street. One squad mounted guard facing the crossroads, and another squad was opposite the Wadi. Next to them stood a Mercedes motorcar which they tried to start without success.

Suddenly, Botnik, standing close to the wall of the hotel, detected three soldiers descending into the wadi. "They could be men from the Jerusalem Brigade. Their helmets are similar," he said. He and Dudu looked carefully, and became convinced that the men were Jordanians. The range was about two hundred meters—and the radio technicians only had Uzis. If they had let the Jordanians get down below in the wadi, they could have attacked the squad. So they opened fire with Uzis and hit one, who fell, while the other two ran into the wadi.

Zohar and Shai chased after them until they saw a camouflaged Jordanian truck among the trees. A kind of channel crossed the area. While Zohar and Shai were searching beside the truck, two Jordanians came out from the channel. The *chevra* shot quickly at a range of one hundred yards. One Jordanian fell and the second went on running. In the distance, on the slope of the road, more Jordanians were seen. But the range was much too far; there was no sense in firing.

They returned to the half-track. After a while, a jeep arrived, as well as the station wagon of the signal company. So the group went on to the Rockefeller.

While they were playing hide and seek in the wadi, we continued on the single half-track along the Wadi Joz until we arrived at the Workshop Crossroads, where Mussa's company had installed itself. I was very pleased to find the *chevra* looking fresh and prepared for further action.

We also passed Zamush's company, and they too were in fine fettle.

The road began to climb very steeply. Looking to the left, and through the spaces between the houses, we could see the Valley of Kidron and above it the Augusta Victoria Hospital.

We went past the last building. On the left lay the valley, on the right an olive grove with a row of houses above it. This was the upper road of the American Colony neighborhood. Any moment now we would reach the intersection near the Rockefeller.

Suddenly the corner of the Old City wall jutted out before us. "Stop! Reverse!" I called to the driver. He did not understand. "Back! Faster!" I had heard the clink of weapons ready to fire above me.

The half-track slid slowly backward and we got around the

corner. The wall disappeared and there were no shots. "Turn right!" I told the driver, "and get on to the road to the Museum."

The half-track climbed slowly up the slope of the road. We sighed with relief, and laughed. The joke would have been on us— the Brigade Command in a clash with the wall! To our left rose the museum and on its turret flew the Israeli flag. To the right was the olive grove and a group of buildings: "the red house," "the white house," the museum square. Around us were private vehicles of Jordanians, "mobilized" by our people.

Moshele's half-track was parked on the square. He greeted us. "What's the position?" I asked.

"All right. Do you want to go inside? All the *chevra* are there resting a little and looking at the antiquities."

"Are the battalion commanders already here?"

"Uzi and Yossi Y. are already here. Yossi P. is still at Rivoli."

"Good. Let's go in."

We jumped out of the half-tracks and I cast a glance at the Augusta Victoria ridge. It was exposed to us and we to it, and as we got out a machine gun cut through the air. We stooped and moved toward the gate of the yard.

"Careful," Moshele cautioned. "The area here is exposed to the wall and you have to go through at the double." The door was just opposite the wall.

"Why take a chance?" I said. "Let's go in the back."

We moved along the wall of the building, inspecting it as we went. We touched the stone. It was still hard to take in that we held the Rockefeller. Bullets passed overhead, some of them sticking in the walls of the building across the road. Some of them went on to distant targets or were lost in the sky. From the behavior of the *chevra* I noticed that they had become accustomed to the place, and knew exactly where they could walk in safety, and where they could look out. They were already war veterans.

The museum had a special gate for vehicles. Through its iron bars, we saw in front of us an inner courtyard. The gate was closed with a chain and lock. On the other side of it was a white station wagon. Orni raised his Uzi to shoot the lock so as to open it.

"Be careful of the car!" the *chevra* called. Two shots, the chain was loosened and we entered the courtyard. At the edge of the left wing was a green door. In the courtyard area there were some stone and marble heads of pillars, some planks and work tools. This, it seemed, was a back yard where work and repairs were done. We went through the green door into a dark corridor, turned right, and passed two doors. We looked to the left—a room with glass cupboards. We looked right—a long passage, part in shadow, part lit. There was a spacious, circular hall with a giant stone pillar in the middle, and everywhere paratroopers were stretched out, sleeping or resting.

We went on, our helmets in our left hands, our Uzis hanging from our right shoulders. The radio technicians were pleased that the ceiling was so high that they did not need to fold the antennae.

I greeted the *chevra*. "Shalom, Shalom. Nu, how was it?"

"All right." Some of them were still wearing their equipment as they lay down; some had their equipment next to them. Some lay on their backs, their weapons on their stomachs; some dozed on their sides, their weapons between their legs. I stopped for a while to chat with old acquaintances. It was hard to talk about the comrades who had fallen, about war and death, about our dreams for peace in the future.

Here and there men walked round among the exhibits. Already, at first glance, it was apparent that there had been no looting. Some glass tables and cupboards had been smashed in the explosions, but the contents were untouched. Archeology is a passion and a hobby in Israel, and respect for the glories of the past was deeply embedded in the soldiers, who were impressed by all the newly discovered antiquities.

They recognized the professors at once and bombarded them with eager questions. The "veterans" in the building, who had already managed to investigate the whole place, volunteered to direct the professors through the long corridors and the numerous rooms.

"Fine. Where can we sit down and start work?"

Uzi and Yossi came toward us. Here, in front of all the *chevra*, we tried to conceal our feelings and shook hands calmly. Both of them were covered with dust, and while Uzi had a light stubble of beard, almost unnoticeable, Yossi's two-day growth was black, obvious. Uzi held his helmet under his arm. Yossi's was on his head, with the chin strap loose. Uzi looked quite relaxed, Yossi showed that he had gone through a profound experience.

To the left was a small room with writing desk and armchairs, presumably the director's. We went in and I sat down on a chair behind the table and made myself comfortable. The glass on the table was dusty, and on the right were sheets of writing paper, with addresses in Arabic and in English.

Books lay on the desk, as if someone had just been using them. On the wall were pictures and maps of digs.

The company commanders, Haggai and Odem, came toward us, less ebullient than they had been, as the sight of the wounded from the morning's shelling had colored their feeling of satisfaction about their victories.

We settled down to talk. The battalion commanders began to report: Dead, wounded, ammunition used, medical equipment used . . . I urged Orni, "What about Yossi P. Is he coming?"

"I'm sorry, sir, but it is impossible to make contact with him from inside the room. We will have to set up communications outside and arrange long-distance contact into here."

"No, there's no need. If you can't get him from here, we'll go outside. It's pleasant here—but there is no point in staying. Come on. Outside!"

Rather reluctantly and slowly they got out of the comfortable chairs, and we returned to the small courtyard, where we sat at the gate of the open space outside the museum, settling ourselves next to the wall.

"Yossi P. Calling you to the radio," Arbib told me, and handed me the microphone.

"Speaking. What's happening?"

Yossi P. reported that he could not come to the discussion because the exit was still dangerous. He asked us to send a vehicle to rescue a wounded man who was losing blood, and who, if he did not obtain treatment, might go into shock.

"Right. We'll send something! And otherwise?"

"All right. Quite quiet. There are seventeen of us here, and I don't want to leave the men at this stage."

"O.K. We'll contact you later." I returned the microphone to Arbib.

I turned to the group around me. "We have to send a half-track to Yossi at the Rivoli to evacuate a man there. The hotel is opposite Herod's Gate. They're shooting there and whoever goes must be very careful."

Amos, the general staff officer, took out a large aerial photograph and indicated the Hotel Rivoli to Uzi the operations officer. In the museum courtyard there were several vehicles, and Uzi took a half-track and a munitions carrier and set out for the Rivoli.

The two battalion commanders reported to me and my staff. Yossi had many killed and wounded in Battalion 66. He still did not know the exact number. Some of them were evacuated to hospitals, and there was no report as yet. The breakthrough had gone off excellently but the battle for Ammunition Hill had been tough. Shells had fallen on the mortar platoon and more than half the men killed or wounded.

They were also very short of equipment: hand grenades, antitank grenades, Uzi bullets, and medical dressings—almost everything.

The companies of Giora and Gabi were ready to go, but more time was needed to reorganize the companies of Dubi and Dudik.

The position was better in Battalion 71. The companies of Zamush and Mussa had been hardly hit at all. Uzi's company had been hit but had already reorganized. Marico's company had suffered badly, and he himself had been wounded, but the battalion as a whole could continue to function more or less as an intact body.

The summation of the overall situation confirmed that we had suffered heavy losses. Well, we had known it would be difficult, that it would not be like taking candy from children. It was precisely because a hard battle was expected that we had been chosen for the attack on Arab Jerusalem. And we had conquered it and were at the Rockefeller. The bullets that whistled constantly overhead were coming from the Old City, and soon we would liberate the Temple Mount. This was no mere retaliatory raid. This time there would be no going back.

Yet the magnitude of the accomplishment did not resign us to our losses. Although we had expected them, the expectation was not as cruel as reality.

"What is the position of the tanks?"

Amos reported that most of them were opposite the Damascus Gate. Rafi told us that every tank had no more than one of two shells left, and fuel too was almost exhausted. Repairs to the communications systems, hit in the shelling, were essential. He suggested doing the repairs at a site where he could personally supervise them, and remain in contact with his battalion. It seemed to him that the Police School was a good place for the repairs. He also needed commanders to replace the wounded.

"How much time will the repairs take?"

"At least two hours."

"O.K. Anyway, it will take two hours to reorganize the battalions. Apart from this, there is still no authority for me to attack the Old City. So return with the tanks to the Police School and fix them up. But don't waste time—we may get the go-ahead signal at any moment."

Hagai told us that the fire from the Old City wall was accurate and deadly. At first he had placed men in posts facing the wall. But the Jordanians sniped at every window, and in one or two cases even gun barrels that stuck out were hit, and the *chevra* wounded. Up to now they had taken up to the posts about a hundred sacks of sand, and were trying, by careful observation, to pinpoint the enemy positions.

I turned to Ziklag. "Can you do something with the artillery?"

"Very sorry, but I'm afraid not. I have already examined the position. We have enough weapons. But, in the first place, our shells will fall into the Old City. If you give the O.K. that's fine. Secondly, shells will fall on our own positions as well, because the distance between us and the wall is very short. What we are already doing is finding the range for the whole of Augusta Victoria ridge. We are also preparing assignments for defense. But, Motta, you're the boss—if you give the order we can begin firing at once against the wall as well."

"No. Not now. What we should do now is to prepare objectives. If we get sudden authorization to break into the Old City, you will be the sole support for the infantry. Uzi with Battalion 71 will be ready any minute to go into the Old City. We have no tanks, but anyway they can't get through Herod's Gate. The battle is going to depend entirely on infantry with artillery support only. You had better prepare for this. Battalion 28 and Battalion 66 will reorganize as quickly as possible. Meanwhile, for purposes of the reorganization, we shall stay more or less in our present sectors: Battalion 66 in the Hotel Ambassador area; Battalion 71, in Wadi Joz; Battalion 28 at Rockefeller and up to the Damascus Gate."

While I was talking, Amos, the general staff officer, began to mark out the boundaries of the sectors in red pencil on the aerial photograph. The battalion commanders bent over the photograph and suggested some corrections from their knowledge of the actual dispersion of their forces. Everything was clear.

Reuven, the adjutant, asked the commanders to be strict about compiling lists of wounded, and to report with these as quickly as possible. Moshele told them supplies for them were on their way. He had already instructed Kotik by radio to come as far as the Police School. In the first stage, ammunition would arrive. During the night, Kotik organized the ammunition which came from the command on trucks in such a way that each truck would bring all kinds of bullets, shells, and grenades.

To bring food and water forward was not urgent at this stage, Reuven added. It was possible to make do with what they had. Yossi and Uzi smiled. They had been "making do" forever, it seemed to them. Central Command was rushing bandages, dressings, and medical supplies to us both from Jerusalem and from outside the capital.

The time was 1130 and all seemed clear. I summed up: "Hurry with the reorganization. As soon as I get the green light from Uzi, I'll contact you fast. Until then—*Lehitraot!*"

The battalion commanders separated and returned to their units. Moshele got up. "Motta," he said, "I think Amos and I should go back to the city to make sure we are getting all the supplies we need. If necessary, we can hurry them along. Otherwise there may be a holdup."

"O.K. I'm staying here. We may get permission to advance into the Old City at any minute: I want to get the order from Uzi myself. Arik will stay with me, and we'll plan what we're to do next."

The group broke up and I rose. The place where we had been sitting was in the open, and near the gate was a much more pleasant spot, with a leafy tree and bushes providing shade and some greenery. I sent the radio technicians there, but admonished them to be on the alert for a message from Uzi.

Prisoners were being brought in from every quarter. Some of them were in civilian clothes, some in half military, half civilian garb. Among them were smartly dressed business and professional men. There were also many prisoners wearing traditional Arab clothes, a copious *abaya* enveloping the body, a white *keffiyeh* covering the head.

The prisoners stood with their faces to the wall while our men searched them and important documents were put into a special basket, while normal papers were returned to their owners. Most of the prisoners were sent home, but suspects were kept for further investigation.

One old Arab, dressed in a blue *abaya*, complained to me, shouting that his money had been taken from him. He contended that he had had some hundreds of pounds in his pocket and that it had been stolen while he was being searched.

Foxie, the assistant to the operations officer responsible for the investigation, tried to take him away, but the old man kept returning, never ceasing to complain about his wrongs.

"Why shouldn't we give him back his money?" I asked Foxie.

"Because the war hasn't ended yet."

My first thought was that Foxie was right—we had more important matters to worry about. But a moment later I added: "Nevertheless, see he gets back his money. We won't win the war by taking it. And he is an old man."

Yossi P. called me on the radio because the half-track to evacuate the wounded man from the Rivoli Hotel had not arrived. True, they had seen it coming, but at the corner of the road it had disappeared. Although the wounded man was not in mortal danger, his condition was getting worse.

Arik, my intelligence officer, went off to find out what had happened and to send out another rescue party to the Rivoli, while I nagged the radio technicians to find out if there was still no go-ahead order from Uzi.

When Uzi, the operations officer, returned from the rescue operation, he reported, "I traveled along the main road till we got to the mosque. There I met a group under Nachshon; they had three killed and a few wounded. I thought that they were the men I'd been sent to help, so I gave them the half-track, and Nachshon evacuated the wounded. I went on walking down Saladin Street. An Arab came toward me with his hands up. Then, behind a pillar on the other side of the road, I saw one of our soldiers. He shouted and signed to me not to cross the road; it was under fire from the wall. He explained in shouts that this was the Rivoli, and that they were waiting for the half-track. So I realized I had made a mistake; still, Nachshon needed it the worst way. Now we must have another half-track for the Rivoli."

Precious time had been lost. The calls from the *chevra* at the Rivoli to hasten evacuation of the wounded were now coming thick and fast. Amos, the general staff officer, turned to Uzi: "Take one of Kaposta's platoons and rescue them on foot." Kaposta detailed Yoram's platoon for the mission.

Moving swiftly, they passed along the winding path through the yards of the houses and soon reached the entrance opposite the Rivoli.

Yoram placed machine guns close to the street and Uzi made contact with Yossi P. They agreed that, at a certain moment, the machine guns would open covering fire, a smoke grenade would be thrown, and Yossi's group would cross the road on the double, bringing the wounded with them.

The signal was given and the machine guns opened fire. Yossi's group went out into the street. In a "liberated" red private car, Mor traveled at lightning speed along the road, put the seriously wounded man inside, and came back. The enemy did not shoot. Yossi P. was on his way to us at last.

Then from the top of our street we heard a short burst. Kaposta had sent a force from his reconnaissance company to the city to bring vehicles for the next stage of the advance. Yishai, the platoon commander, went with a team. Walking along the street, they met three armed Jordanians marching in the middle of the road. At the order, "Halt!" the Jordanians tried to run away. After a short shooting match, two Jordanians were wounded and one fled. The team confiscated a Jordanian car and continued with its job.

We went into the showrooms of the museum. Now that things had eased off a bit and we were waiting for orders, we had time to look at the exhibits. But I found that I could not concentrate on archeology. I was not just waiting for orders, I was waiting for *the* order, the green light to recover the Temple Mount for the Jewish people. I felt as if time and history were slipping through my fingers like sand.

We went back and sat next to the communication men and took out the aerial photograph to examine once more the planned axis for the advance through Herod's Gate. A tractor with explosives had to be brought forward. True, Herod's Gate could be broken down with only a small charge, but we could not rely on this.

The use of artillery was going to be very complicated. The wall was a very small target, and difficult to hit. Pinpointing where our shells fell in the Old City would be very hard, and the rangefinding likely to take a long time, with mixed results. Because the *chevra* were so near to the wall, they might be in danger from our own shells, unless we moved back a little. But we didn't want to leave the museum. We could instruct the *chevra* to go down to the lower floors and collect there in inside rooms. This too was not simple, and might be too dangerous. We also had to take great care not to hit the holy places. Luckily for us, most of these were situated in the southern neighborhoods of the Old City.

When we went into the Old City we were likely to suffer heavy casualties. If we broke in according to the original plan, between the wall and the end houses of the Moslem Quarter, we would run into endless cleanup fights in the houses and yards, along a route that was more than a kilometer in length. We had already learned the hard way that this kind of fighting should be avoided if possible.

Tanks and other vehicles could only get through Lions' Gate. This meant that a subsidiary attack on the wall was essential, this one from the east. From the topographical point of view, attacking from this direction was most difficult. It was true that we could place the tanks outside the wall to shoot over it—but how would this affect the infantry fighting inside?

To sum up, what seemed best at this stage was that we should break in through Herod's Gate with infantry supported by artillery. The tanks, if they arrived, would provide support only for the breakthrough through Herod's Gate. The artillery would bombard the entire path of the advance. We could ask for planes, but the prospect of getting them at present seemed nil. It was hard to believe that they would decide to use bombers in an area densely crowded with civilians and containing so many holy places.

Central Command told us that the Jerusalem Brigade was going to attack Abu Tor in the afternoon. This was a key site in south Jerusalem. Conquering it would complete the encirclement of the Old City and sever Arab Jerusalem from its neighbor to the south. The prospect of being completely surrounded might induce the defenders of the Old City to surrender. Alternatively, even if they fought on, they would be compelled to spread their forces thinly so as to meet an attack from the south as well as ours from the north.

Arik contacted Intelligence at Central Command, and asked if they could give us any more information about the strength of the Jordanian forces in the Old City. As far as Intelligence could tell, the Jordanian strength remained what it had been estimated at at the beginning of the war—between two companies and a battalion. They might have been reinforced by men running away after our attack on Arab Jerusalem and by men running from the Abu Tor battle. There was no accurate information.

But this information about what forces we had to fight did not seem to me to be very important. I recalled the answer given by the great Russian general, Suvarov, when he was besieging a city, and somebody said that there were so many enemies inside that he should delay his attack until he had identified his foes. "Gentlemen," he had said, "we have not come here to count them, but to destroy them."

We had come to liberate Jerusalem, not to conduct a census.

Yossi P. arrived at last, breathless, and gave me a quick roport. Many had been killed, and many wounded. It had been very tough, but the *chevra* had worked splendidly. "But what now? What's the plan? What about the Old City?"

I smiled because I knew very well what was bothering him. Under the original plan, his battalion was to be the first to enter the Old City. Now that the 28th had suffered so many casualties, he worried that the privilege would be given to somebody else.

Trying to console him as best I could, I said, "Look, so far we haven't got permission to advance into the Old City, and it's by no means certain that we'll ever get it. So the question of who is in the vanguard is academic at the moment. You concentrate on reorganizing as rapidly as possible. As things stand at present, I won't be using you just yet. The 71st is going into action against the Augusta Victoria; their units are almost complete. If you've reorganized by the time I get the order to attack the Old City—*if* I get the order—I promise you that you'll be the first."

Yossi thanked me and went off to see those of his men who were in the Rockefeller. We stayed outside.

Moshele was in the Bet Hakerem headquarters with Amos and the other staff officers, and had taken Amos and the three professors with him from the Rockefeller. The professors, convinced that the paratroopers were respecting the treasures of the museum, had gone to report that there were no casualties among the antiques.

They hoped to return with "reinforcements." Moshele took a half-track with him, followed by two captured Jordanian jeeps, loaded with booty for the Intelligence boys—files of documents and certificates. In one of the jeeps sat a captured Jordanian officer who was being taken back for interrogation, as well as an officer from our mortar battalion, who was to bring back the mortars from Bet-Hakerem to us.

The journey of the convoy through the streets of Jewish Jerusalem was like a miniature victory parade: the Jordanian jeeps, driven by paratroopers, earned stormy applause. The *chevra* smiled broadly and waved at the cheering crowds ...

In Bet Hakerem, they entered the telephone cellar—the civil defense shelter—which had served as staff headquarters.

Kotik arrived there and they sat down to snatch a moment's quiet. Kotik told them what had happened to him: After he had fixed up the ammunition column for the tanks, he had been on his way to us at the Rockefeller on a half-track when he had met Uzi, the operations officer, and had given him the half-track to evacuate the wounded from the Rivoli.

On his way back to the Police School, he had seen a huge, red

Impala car standing idle. With him was Zachik, a Battalion 66 officer, who earlier had volunteered to show Kotik the way to us, and who now wanted to return to his battalion. Neither of them knew how to drive such a splendid car, so a driver offered to take them. Zachik and the driver got into the car while Kotik and Sergeant Major Lavie stopped a little way behind to finish a conversation. A volley from the Augusta Victoria had hit the car, covering the face of the driver with splinters. A bullet had caught Zachik in the chest. The driver had run to the rear, his hands covering his face, which was streaming with blood, and Zachik had collapsed. When Kotik and Lavie had seen that Zachik was hit, they had run across to him and pulled him into a protected corner where medics had dealt with him immediately.

Then a recoilless gun under Bash, Uzi's company commander at Headquarters, had come up from below and Kotik had rushed Zachik to him, and Bash had taken him to the Police School. The wounded had been evacuated in the half-track to the hospital. In the Police School, Kotik had "borrowed" a car and gone to Bet Hakerem to collect supplies for our men. "So here I am!"

Moshele held a staff meeting, short and to the point. His instructions were to hasten the supply of ammunition and medical dressings. There was a plentiful supply of food and water. The adjutant had to tour the units and hospitals to compile a register of all the wounded. These were the main subjects under discussion.

Outside, crowding the doors, were men of the mortar units and antitank units. During the breakthrough, they had had a vital function. Now that objectives had changed, they had been left "unemployed." So they had left their mortars and guns and were demanding the right to participate as infantry in the attack on the Old City. All of them, beginning with Ziklag, their battalion commander, and ending with the newest recruit, had brought pressure to bear on us to let them share the action.

In the parachute brigade, every man was trained first and foremost to be a combat soldier. Many of the *chevra* went through a severe emotional crisis when they were transferred from the first line of shock troops to auxiliary forces helping in the "rear," as it were. And now they could see a never-to-be-repeated opportunity to get into the van without being handicapped by their usual heavy weapons.

Moshele, my second-in-command, had thought of them. The battalions had suffered heavy losses. True, we did not yet know how great the blow had been, but it was clear that the ranks had been thinned out. If we were to take the Old City by storm, we would have to introduce additional fresh forces. So he welcomed the volunteers. In fact, when he had left the Rockefeller, he had already taken with him an officer of the mortar battalion to bring men from Bet Hakerem to the vicinity of the museum.

Moshele agreed to put the volunteers into battle immediately. He coordinated the transfer of the troops with the staff officers and arranged the route through the liberated areas.

Reuven, the adjutant, got in touch with command headquarters and asked for medics and medical supplies. We were all very worried about the shortage of medics, many of whom had been hit in the morning's battles, for it was clear, unfortunately, that our need for them was likely to increase, not diminish.

Reuven learned that medical supplies had already been dispatched to the casualty clearing stations and the other medical teams. Some supplies had even reached the medics in the front lines. Dr. Michaeli, the Central Command medical officer, had personally dispatched an extra truck loaded with equipment.

The conference broke up and Reuven then went round the hospitals and medical stations to ensure that the evacuation of the wounded was going ahead at full speed, and that accurate lists of the casualties were being compiled.

Kotik organized convoys of ammunition. Moshele decided to

go through the battalions to see for himself whether the hard hand-to-hand fighting had in any way affected the morale of the men. On his way, he stopped to talk to Dr. King, the brigade doctor, and repeated an order, already given by Reuven, that the medical teams should go into the Rockefeller area.

From there Kotik went to the Police School breakthrough passage, meeting with Yod-Bet, who he instructed to broaden the track used by the supply vehicles. The great number of vehicles on the path made orderly work very difficult, but Yod-Bet promised Moshele that he would do everything possible. Moshele entered the yard of the school to find out what was happening to the tank companies.

Apart from lacking ammunition and fuel, the tank soldiers faced three main problems: they had to repair tracks and the wheels; they had to repair and at times change the communication networks, especially those parts outside the armor, such as antennae; finally, they needed new tank commanders to replace those who had fallen.

Rafi contacted his battalion headquarters to get help, and even went there to hasten the process. Moshele went on to Battalion 66 command at the Ambassador Hotel.

By 1330 I was nagging Central Command again about the order to enter the Old City; they assured me that I should get it any minute. Uzi Narkiss had gone with Moshe Dayan, the Minister of Defense, on a tour of Mount Scopus. Doron, the second-in-command of Battalion 66, who had been left in charge of the battalion in the Ambassador Hotel area while Yossi was with me, had joined Uzi and Moshe on the tour. They promised to give me my orders very soon.

At 1340 Uzi Narkiss called on the radio, but instead of the longed-for go-ahead, he had bad news for me. The Government wouldn't authorize an attack on the Old City. There were political considerations, for they were not at all certain we would be allowed to remain there after taking it—and there was no point in sacrificing men for nothing.

"I understand," I said gloomily, "but it is a bad decision, I must tell you. Very bad."

Thoughts raced through my mind as I left the radio. I recalled discussions we had held in the past about invading the Old City. One suggestion then had been that we should take only the gates, and this possibility had been mentioned again this morning. I wondered if I should suggest it to Uzi, or take a chance and do it on my own.

I faced the hardest challenge of my entire life. If I ordered an attack on the gates only, arguing that it was not a full-scale assault, although it could be used as a springboard for the subsequent liberation of the whole Old City, I would be acting in defiance of clear orders. There was no doubt that a top-level commander was sometimes forced to make critical decisions that were not in accordance with official orders, and I remembered that Nelson had been immortalized and universally acclaimed for ignoring Parker's order to withdraw at the battle of Copenhagen. Besides it was more than possible that, in obeying the order not to enter the Old City, I would incur contempt for the Israel Defense Forces, and be the cause of weeping anew for generations. I would be despised for ever as the man who stood outside the Temple Mount and had not entered it because he was too timid to act on his own.

On the other hand, the nation's leaders knew all the international complications better than I did. They had full knowledge of how well-placed we were to seize the incredible opportunity we now had, and might never have again, so I could not claim that I knew the situation better than my superior officers, nor suggest that there had been some misunderstanding.

But I wondered if I dared to take on myself, with the eyes of the whole world on the Holy City, the decision to invade—a field commander take the responsibility and not the government. Yet . . . to lose so rich a prize, after all our sacrifices, was unthinkable.

These thoughts churned round and round in my mind. They were brought to an abrupt stop by new orders from Uzi. "We have decided to surround the Old City, so as to create a situation which will force them to surrender. Alternatively, if they don't, and if we get the green light, we will have a perfect springboard for the assault. So your brigade must now conquer the Auguste Victoria—Abu Tor ridge as far south as possible. Finish it this afternoon, if you can. You'll get an additional company of tanks from the Harel Brigade to help you."

Uzi went on, "The tank company is being organized on Givat Hamivtar. Send somebody to get it. Uri's Brigade is going on to Rammallah, and from there to Nablus or Jericho. Lezer's brigade will attack the Abu-Tor suburb in the afternoon. All clear?"

"Absolutely clear. We'll do it. Have you any new reports about the enemy dispositions on the Augusta Victoria ridge?"

"Wait."

I instructed Arik to contact the intelligence officer at Headquarters, and after a few seconds, Uzi called me again. "No. No new information, but there are no reports of their getting additional forces there. There is a rumor of an order for a general retreat by the Jordanians, but we don't know if this is correct."

"I understand. Thanks."

I looked around the group of officers and men as I finished talking to Uzi. Everyone was staring at me, tense anticipation in their eyes. Some already guessed from my expression that I had been turned down, but they didn't want to believe what they suspected.

"Sorry, boys. No permission yet to tackle the Old City. Instead we're to go for the Augusta Victoria. But it is not really so terrible," I said over their groans, although not convinced myself. "The hour of the Old City will come. Almost all the conquerors of Jerusalem in history began by gaining control of the ridges around the city, especially Mount Scopus. By encircling the Old City, we may drive the Jordanians to despair, and then the city will fall into our hands like a ripe fruit."

Arik's investigation had not produced any important new facts. We estimated that there were about two Jordanian companies stationed on the ridge, that men who had fled from the night's battle might have joined them, and that they might have been reinforced from the east, but we had no information about these possibilities.

I sent a message to Uzi to report to me at once. Then I told Ziklag, standing next to me, to shell both sides of the street that ascended from the market in the Kidron Valley to the Augusta Victoria. I sent Giora, our reconnaissance officer, to Givat Hamivtar, to find our what had become of our company of Harel Brigade tanks. And I sent a message to Rafi to find out when his tanks would be ready to go into action again.

Arik and I sat down together next to the museum wall to plan the next phase of the war. We would have liked to move out into the open road to survey the scene where the fighting would take place, but the area was under constant and accurate sniping fire from the corner of the Old City wall and from the ridge. Still, without exposing ourselves overmuch, we managed to get an adequate view of the entire area up to the ridge. We also studied the aerial photograph with great care.

Around us sat the radio technicians, and many of the more curious *chevra* strolled over to hear what was in the wind. Ziklag issued orders to his gunners and hurried back; he wanted to participate in the planning and make sure that his ideas for a barrage agreed with ours. While we were talking, Uzi came from Battalion 71 to join in the session.

We had a choice of two alternatives. We could launch a frontal attack from Mount Scopus, where the garrison that had held out so long had now been fully integrated into Jewish-held Jerusalem, or we could climb up the long, steep road from the market to the Augusta Victoria ridge, which linked the hospital to Abu Tor. It was also possible, of course, to attack from both positions simultaneously.

The advantages of mounting the assault from Mount Scopus were two. We were at the peak of the mountain, on the same level as the enemy strongholds at the Augusta Victoria and the distance to be covered was very short—only two hundred meters.

But there was one drawback. For nineteen years the Jordanians had fortified the side of the Augusta Victoria facing Mount Scopus, and so, we feared, the *chevra* would have to cross minefields, barbed-wire fences, communication trenches, and bunkers. The cost might be heavy.

An attack from the direction of the Kidron Valley would be a flank action, aimed at the enemy's "soft underbelly." It was a considerable distance from the wall that divided the two Jerusalems, where the Jordanians had set up such a strong system of fortifications; in fact, we were already on the far side of the Old City and of Arab Jerusalem. As a result, it was an area entirely in Arab territory, which they had never bothered to fortify. Their nearest defenses were on the Abu Tor ridge, a kilometer away, designed to block the Jerusalem-Jericho road. This system could do only negligible damage to forces moving up the hill to the Augusta Victoria from the Kidron Valley.

The disadvantage of the attack from the flank was that it involved a long, hard climb from the valley to the ridge, with our backs exposed to fire from the walls of the Old City.

I opted for the second alternative for the opening attack and instructed Uzi to deploy Batallion 71 on the Wadi Joz neighborhood. They would go up the road past the Palace Hotel to the

Legion's cluster of barracks at the top of the ridge, near the Augusta Victoria hospital.

Uri rushed off without waiting to hear final details of the plan. He had much to do and little time to do it.

I felt a pair of laser beams boring into my back and turned my head; they were Kaposta's eyes. He pleaded: "Motta, we in the reconnaissance company are just the men for this job. We've got jeeps with machine guns and jeeps with recoilless guns; we also have weapons carriers. After the mess we got into last night, give us a chance to do something. This time we've got a full house."

"O.K., we'll see. You've certainly got a case. But I can't send you in just because you're here—we'll have to work it out. Wait till we finish the planning."

Giora came back. He said that the tanks of Givat Hamivtar would not be ready before 1630, as their equipment had disappeared and they had not yet begun to refuel. Rafi's tank company was also not ready. There were still a number of essential repairs to execute, and they needed to load more ammunition before they could get going again.

"Good. Sit down. We'll see in a little while."

The rangefinding shells began to fall, and with every blast the mountain seemed to tremble and the houses shake from shock. The echoes rolled in waves. I had no difficulty distinguishing between the types of shells, especially as the 120-magnum are phosphorus shells. From the left wing the 81-magnum rangefinding of Battalion 71 began. The bullets of Jordanian snipers passed above our heads, and our snipers fired in reply.

We summed up the situation. We knew nothing about the Jordanian artillery. Either it had been destroyed or their gunners were hiding from our planes. They might only begin to function when we launched our attack. We had to draw them out somehow as soon as possible in order to identify their positions.

Generally, we had not pinpointed the weapons of the enemy

accurately. Our people had been in contact with snipers and heavy machine gunners all morning, but we still remembered very vividly what had happened the previous day. Toward evening, most of their weapons ceased operating and some people believed that they had fled. The battle had proved that this evaluation was unfounded. Now too, we could not permit ourselves to assume that we had pinpointed all their weapons. It was better to force them to put all their cards on the table.

The only axis permitting free movement of tanks was the street. There were neither mines nor roadblocks there. Going up the road might mean that our columns would present obvious targets, but it would be incomparably easier, without a doubt, than struggling slowly up the terraces that ran across the slope of the steep hill. Furthermore, going by road would result in very fast progress almost to the back of the Augusta Victoria position, and this might well demoralize the enemy.

There were some houses on the slope, especially on the south side of the road. We had no information as to whether there were snipers' nests or other forces located there, but it was safest to assume that there were.

So our plan crystallized. We would open with an intense preliminary bombardment of the whole area on both sides of the long road. One tank company would spread out in the area on both sides of the long road. One tank company would spread out in the area around the Rockefeller and fire on any post, bunker, nest, or force that dared to show itself.

The second tank company would move along past the market and begin to mount the ridge by the road. Kaposta's company would follow the tanks up the street, after we knew the enemy's reaction, particularly the response of his artillery. Then would come Battalion 71, and I would give the orders where they were to go.

Our planes would be put into action against Jordanian

artillery if called upon. As soon as the tanks were ready to go, we would attack.

I explained to Uzi and Kaposta that, if it turned out that the enemy was using effective artillery fire against the tanks, I would not put their units in at all. In that case, we would content ourselves with the tank attack, for the time being, and would review the situation afterwards.

After completing the technical arrangements, we turned to the question of when we could expect the tanks from Givat Hamivtar. Giora said that they had been involved in heavy fighting throughout the night, and as a result, in his words, "the tanks' bellies were empty"—meaning that they had to get full supplies of fuel and ammunition. Since the Harel Brigade had moved on toward Ramallah, the company commander of our tanks was having difficulty finding somebody to reequip him. But he was now busy refueling and rearming with whatever supplies he could locate, and hoped to get all he needed shortly. He reckoned that by 1630 he would be ready.

I realized that I would have to accept this.

Ziklag reported on the rangefinding. He recommended continuing from time to time to shell the enemy, to prevent his reorganizing, to check the range, and to keep the *chevra* busy beside the guns, and I agreed.

Another convoy of prisoners arrived for interrogation. Foxie, the operations officer's assistant, came up to me and reported that one of them, a Jordanian major, claimed that he was a representative at the Israeli-Jordanian Armistice-Truce Commission and asked if I wanted to talk to him.

At first I thought not, for I had nothing to say to him, but in fact, since I was marking time, I let him come.

He and I shook hands and went into the inner courtyard of the museum where we sat on two steps leading up to the entrance door.

The Jordanian major was perplexed. Yes, he said, he was a minor representative on the Armistice-Truce Commission, but had nothing more to offer. When I asked was the war necessary, he replied that he was an officer and didn't deal with politics, but thought that King Hussein did not want war. Queried if he had expected we would conquer Jerusalem so quickly, he did not answer.

I thanked him and again we shook hands. He sighed with relief and turned to sit on a heap of planks at the side—apart from the other prisoners. He was an officer.

The *chevra* stared at him inquisitively. He bowed his head and lowered his eyes.

Photographers and journalists invaded the square; Yachin took photographs, Elimelech taped, Shimshi wrote.

Rabbi Goren arrived with a Shofar and a Scroll of the Law. "Take note, Motta, that it says in the General Staff's order that I must be the first man at the Western Wall."

"Sorry, Rabbi. We haven't got permission to go in. Maybe you can get it for us?"

"What, what, no permission? And I was certain that we were already going in."

"I'll go like a shot if you get me the order. Perhaps you'll use your pull to get me permission."

"Are you serious? Really, no permission? What is it? What's happened? What's gone wrong?"

"I don't know, but there are clear orders. We are not going in. Instead we're marching on Augusta Victoria."

"But this is terrible. I don't understand." A moment later: "Maybe, just the same. Motta, after all, you're not afraid to take chances . . . We could fix it up afterwards . . . What do you say?"

"Rabbi! Really! We paratroopers are disciplined. After all, you should know—"

"Listen, it's a scandal! You're joking?"

"It's too serious to laugh about, Rabbi. That's it. We are waiting outside the gates, and we're not going in."

The rabbi's expression was very grave.

"Maybe the order will still come. I'll stay here with you."

"I wouldn't recommend it, Rabbi. Real war will start very soon, and there's no point in getting hurt for nothing. If I get the order, I'll call you. I promise on my honor."

"*Nu!* What do you think, that I'm afraid of war? I'm staying here. We'll wait and see."

We discussed a Jew's duty during war. Rabbi Stiglitz, the paratrooper chaplain, involved Rabbi Goren in a discussion and Rabbi Goren declared: "According to Jewish law, this is the only time when a man is commanded to give his life, fully aware of what he is doing." He told us that yesterday, near Gaza, he had been saved by a miracle, when the weapons carrier in which he was traveling came under heavy fire. All the men around him had been wounded.

The discussion was at times serious, at times light, mixed with quotations from the Pentateuch. Every now and then, Rabbi Goren returned to the theme of the Old City. "History will never forgive you, Motta, being here and not entering!" Just what I had been thinking. It is not often that temptation comes dressed as a rabbi . . .

Suddenly we had a pleasant surprise. An armored corps company commander arrived from Givat Hamivtar with the word that soon we could begin the attack. It was so unexpected that I expressed my amazement—we had not expected him for some time.

"Yes, I'm the company commander of the tanks attached to you. That's right, from the Harel Brigade."

"Where are your tanks?"

"Here, just behind me, on the slope of the street."

"Excellent. Just in the right place. Come, I'll show you the plan."

Arik told Kaposta that his company should take up positions behind the tanks. We began to go down in the direction of the olive grove.

"How many tanks do you have?"

"The whole company."

"Very good!"

"Your name?"

"Chaim. Chaim Luz."

Our spirits soared. Chaim and the Rabbi had cheered us up. And it was good to think we would soon be on the move again.

I showed Chaim the plan. "You'll spread your tanks out here along the road. Hit every enemy you see. Rafi, with his tanks, will advance. You'll join in later."

Everything seemed to be as simple and clear as daylight, although we knew that nothing ever turns out in battle exactly as planned. Still, the range was short and the whole of the battle-field seemed to lie in the palm of my hand.

Then we found that we already had a problem—contact between the tanks. Rafi's tanks and Chaim's were Shermans of different vintages, and had different communications networks, which were not correlated. It was clear that they could not function together in the usual way. Something had to be worked out so that contact could be maintained, at least, between Rafi and Chaim.

Orni had already anticipated the problem, and had improvised a communications system. He distributed the instruments. Since the signal company had arrived about two hours before, there was no lack of instruments, equipment, or men to do the job. Orni thought the system would work.

I gave Uzi the order, "Get ready."

The companies in Battalion 71 got ready to advance. Ziklag

went on firing freely at enemy targets. Bullets fired by snipers in the city wall flew overhead and stuck in the walls. Moshele and Amos returned.

Chaim went off to prepare his tanks for the operation. We sat down to complete the final details and asked them to tell Rafi to hurry; now we were waiting for him.

Uzi, who was following developments closely, went off to brief his men at the Rockefeller and in the surrounding area. Kaposta organized his vehicles and arranged the distribution of his forces, giving special assignments to men in his platoons.

Suddenly Chaim came running up at great speed, panting. "They've stolen my tanks! Somebody has stolen my tanks! They've disappeared!"

We burst out laughing. "What do you mean, your tanks are stolen?"

Chaim did not laugh. "It's no joke. They're not where I left them. Somebody has taken them."

We cast amused glances at each other: "We didn't take them or even move them. Must be a shoplifter." Chaim ran back and returned after a few minutes: "I'm awfully sorry, but I made a great mistake. My tanks are not yours at all. I contacted my head-quarters. You're to get other tanks. A column of our brigade passed and took my tanks with them. They've gone and I'm stuck here. They are going to Ramallah. They certainly need me—I can't stay here. I must catch up with them. Please help me, please."

In spite of the seriousness of the matter, we could not stop laughing. Somebody had stolen his tanks! I gave instructions that Chaim should be taken by jeep until he caught up with his company. We parted with a handshake and a smile. But we had stopped laughing—the joke was on us. Here we had had an attack all set and suddenly *our* tanks disappeared.

The hours passed and we disbanded the forces. I sent Giora

again to Givat Hamivtar and to the Police School to see what had happened to the tanks that were really ours.

Moshele reported on the arrangements he had made in the rear and on the position of the units he had inspected.

We were worried about the situation on the roads and the dense crowding of men and supplies. The road at the Police School had been cleared of the truck stuck here, but because of the mines and the pressure of the traffic, preparing it for use was going very slowly. The supplies of the Harel Brigade had been diverted by the ordnance officer of the command through the Mandelbaum Gate. But, in trying to hasten the passage of the columns, some of the vehicles got onto the Police School road. This intensified the pressure on all roads in the area, so the ordnance officer sent the brigade back to the Mandelbaum Gate. And we finally learned it was because of the traffic in the streets of East Jerusalem in the direction of Ramallah that the "stolen" tanks of Chaim Luz had reached us, while our own were still waiting for supplies.

Ammunition and medical dressings had already been distributed and the infantry were ready.

Reuven returned from his round of the hospitals and medical stations. It seemed that we had at least forty killed and more than one hundred and fifty wounded.

By 1730 Giora had returned from still another trip to get our tanks. The company on Givat Hamivtar had just received the ammunition and fuel, but would not be ready till dusk. Rafi's company was also not ready. Shells and fuel had been put into the tanks, but the truck with the light ammunition had not yet arrived and several men needed for vital tasks were also still missing.

I asked Moshele to hurry things as much as possible, and to instruct Rafi to advance even if his preparations weren't complete.

Because of the late hour it seemed logical to postpone the attack till night. The Jordanian soldiers on the wall of the Old City would not be able then to interfere so easily with the movements of infantry, or hit the tanks when they were on the sharp turn facing the Valley of Kidron.

But it was important that the tank company commanders should inspect the field while there was still daylight.

It was nearly 1800. The suburb of Abu-Tor had already been conquered by Micha Paikess's battalion of the Jerusalem Brigade. And at 1800, at last, Rafi and his tanks arrived. He had washed his face of the morning's bloodstains, and looked serene and relaxed as usual. Without wasting a precious moment, I outlined the plan to him. In a few short words he explained the delays, but I did not pay much attention. He was the kind of person who did not waste time. If he had been delayed, it was for a good reason.

We tried to descend to the olive grove, for from there we would be able to see the road for the advance very clearly. But the sniping from the corner of the Old City wall forced us to give up the idea, and so we leaned instead on the wall around the museum. We saw the rise to the ridge, and the valley, but could not see the streets below us nor the turn at the corner of the Wall.

We had the aerial photograph, and, since the distances were short, it did not seem that there would be any difficulty pinpointing the traffic axis. The distance from the corner of the fence to the turn at the corner of the wall was not more than a hundred meters. Rafi said that the truck with light ammunition would arrive within twenty minutes and he begged us not to begin before they could load the machine guns with ammunition. He believed that filling the kits from well-organized crates would not take long and that it was certainly worthwhile to wait.

I agreed, but urged him to hurry. Rafi briefed his men and prepared them for the operation. The tanks took up their positions in the open road opposite the entrance to the museum. One tank was placed close to the wall of the museum; a second descended to the vicinity of the "red house"; and a third was put close to the "white house."

Rabbi Goren organized *Mincha*—the evening prayer.

The bright light of the afternoon began to wane into the soft glow of the evening twilight.

Suddenly one of the tanks fired a shell at a point on the rise to the Augusta Victoria ridge. The tank commander, Karni, had identified a tank or an armored post hidden under a tree halfway up the ridge. Little time was left before darkness fell. If the enemy had indeed placed antitank weapons in the area, they might hit the tanks advancing up the hill. So I gave orders to the tanks around the Rockefeller that they should fire at every likely target, and Rafi's tank, near the museum, also joined in.

We raised our field glasses and looked for targets. I instructed Ziklag to get his gunners to shell the area where Karni had seen the movement. A few minutes later the gunners found the new range and we saw shells exploding. Since we were looking for targets, we found at least three points that roused our suspicions. The gunners set our fears to rest by some accurate, intensive shelling.

At long last the truck arrived with the ammunition for the tanks' machine guns, and the bullets were transferred at great speed. Then Dr. King reported that his medical team was in the next street. He had doctors, medical supplies, and even vehicles to evacuate the wounded.

Everything was set—all we were short of was our company of tanks from the Harel Brigade. At that very minute an officer from the armored corps arrived; he introduced himself as Eytan, commander of the missing tank company. This time there was no mistake: he was the real thing. He had come literally at the last moment—there were only a few minutes of daylight left.

Rafi, Eytan, and I went down to the spot near Karni's tank,

close to the "red house," and I went over the plan with them. We saw the two streets below us. I explained to Eytan that he must spread his tanks out on the upper road and cover Rafi's movement on the lower road up the slope of the Augusta Victoria ridge. Eytan understood. Like Rafi, he was quiet and soft-spoken. Orni hurried to set the radio connections in order. The differences between the tanks made coordination of their instruments difficult, but a partial and reasonable solution was worked out.

Rafi and Eytan went back to their companies to brief them. Rafi returned with two platoon commanders, Shaul and Gilboa, to Karni's tank, and briefed them while they inspected the terrain.

Eytan came back and also went down with his tank commanders to brief them. The platoon commanders with Rafi returned to their platoons and began to move their tanks in column formation for the operation.

Eytan's tanks took up their places in the museum square, on the edge of the olive grove. As soon as the tanks were in position, the tank crews sank into a deep sleep, worn out by their efforts of the past twenty-four hours. The artillery rangefinding stopped. Ziklag reported that he had enough guns and ammunition for any purpose, and Kaposta that all his vehicles were in position, ready to move, with Yishai's platoon at their head.

Uzi received and issued final orders, and prebattle excitement mounted. I assured Rabbi Goren that we would call him the moment we got permission to tackle the Old City, and I told him to move to a place that was safer than the museum. He shook his head sadly, but agreed. I assumed that this would mean he would be leaving, but in fact he remained at the museum, close to the soldiers and the battlefield.

Eytan reported that only four of his tanks had arrived. There was no time to investigate why, and we could not wait any longer. I explained to Eytan that we were starting: "We don't count tanks. From our point of view, you are a company, and will also operate as an independent force. While the operation is going on, you must find your missing tanks and bring them forward."

Officers of the brigade stood on the distant roofs and watched the operation.

By 1930, in the darkness, the Augusta Victoria ridge turned into a crude, gloomy shape, without any recognizable landmarks. Only a fire at the top of the hill, result of either rangefinding or pinning-down fire, served as an accurate and obvious marker. We stopped the shelling and ordered the tanks to halt. After the barrage of the past hour, it was important to have silence: The Jordanians would wonder what our intentions were, and they might think that we would be satisfied with the blows already struck by the artillery, and that we were not going to launch an infantry assault. So we changed our plan and decided to hold back a little, in the hope of gaining tactical surprise.

We reported to Command that we were beginning the attack and received permission to go ahead.

A group of radio technicians were attached to me. In the square also stood the station wagon of Chakim with direct communication to Uzi Narkiss, and Noah's weapons carrier, which had a very powerful instrument covering our entire network.

Yablo, the radio officer, was still rushing from tank to tank to put the communication systems in order. The instruments of the platoon commander's tank were not working yet, and Yablo was trying to connect them, each one separately, to the network. Zohar was working hard to link the tanks up to the network, and Yisrael attended to the connection with the reconnaissance company and with Battalion 71.

Orni reported at last that the instruments were "more or less" in order. Noah was linked to the battalion commanders, and the two company commanders of the tanks could hear and be heard.

Uzi reported that Battalion 71 was ready to go.

We began to feel the chill of night. There was great excitement. All those who had nothing to do came to do it next to us so they could listen to the communications networks.

On the Augusta Victoria ridge a great flame soared higher and higher. It seemed that a shell had struck a storeroom containing inflammable material. The familiar block of the hospital stood out sharply against the background of the flames.

Amos checked the operational network. I surveyed the sector and the organization of the force through field glasses. "Everything ready," Amos reported to me.

"Instruct Rafi to start," I answered, and followed the tanks with my eyes.

Rafi confirmed: "I'm off."

Over the radio we heard his order to his company, "Move!"

They departed in thick darkness. The driver could hardly see the road, and Rafi directed him. They reached a circle, but Rafi worked out that it was too close to their starting point and certainly could not be the circle where he was expected to turn left. Nevertheless, there was a slight turn in the street. He went on traveling downwards, his eyes scanning the surroundings, suspecting that something was wrong.

Suddenly he asked for me on the radio and I took the microphone.

"I think I've made a mistake about the street," he said.

"Do you think you know where you are now?" I asked, and we all ran forward to the observation post near the olive grove.

"No," Rafi replied, "but I turned left."

"Switch on the searchlights of the tank so that we can identify you," I ordered and instructed the staff officers to watch from all sides.

I was sure that Rafi had made a mistake by turning left too soon, and that he had gone into the Arab city and not down into the valley.

While talking, Rafi continued down the slope of the street.

He saw a hill on his right, and in front of him the street went up. (Later it transpired that this was the street to Lions' Gate.) As Rafi's searchlight was out of order, he ordered Arzi to go past him with his tank and switch on his searchlight. Arzi went past, only to find that his searchlight too was out of order. They had all been hit in the morning's shelling near the Police School and the tank crews had not managed to repair them.

Suddenly fire was opened on them from the right and projectiles hit the sides of the tanks while glowing splinters rose on high. We heard shooting.

"I am sorry," came Rafi's voice, "but the searchlights aren't working. They were hit this morning."

"All right," I answered. "We'll put on our big searchlights, and you can orientate yourself by them."

A Jordanian bullet grazed Rafi. Blood flowed over his eye so that his eye glasses were covered with blood and it was hard to see. The darkness made it worse, but the tanks continued to advance.

Ziklag ordered the big searchlights to be switched on. After a few seconds, giant beams of light passed overhead, remaining fixed on the ridge, a soft glow covering the white houses. Panes and sheet metal glinted like torches, but no tanks could be seen on the road to the ridge.

Two tanks beside us opened fire. Adler, the tank company commander, arrived at the building in the middle of the ridge, from which there was a white flash which he took for a volley of shots. He fired four shells at the building, but the flash did not stop. A fifth shell apparently scored a hit and the flash could not be seen. Adler ordered them to stop firing and change the position of his tank.

Chuyun, commander of the second tank, selected other targets. A soft-voiced man, he explained that his policy was never to shoot first, but if anybody fired at him, then he let go! Targets were now visible on the ridge, and there were flashes, so the tanks kept firing.

For a while we tried to pinpont the origin of shots fired in our direction, but could not. We were not even sure they were aiming at us.

I decided to try Rafi again and got him on the instrument. "Rafi, do you know where you are?"

"No. I don't think so."

"Then turn round and go back to your point of departure."

I was now convinced that he had gone wrong, or the illumination from the searchlights would have helped him find his position. So I decided to send Kaposta to him, to help him to return quickly, and ordered them to call Kaposta to me.

Eytan's tanks continued to shoot. I wanted to order him to slow down the firing rate and to shoot only at specific targets, at the same time controlling maximum fire. But I couldn't get him on the radio. Orni ran down to pass on the order personally. Eytan tried to pass it on over his communications network to his other tanks, but there were hitches. He leapt out of his tank and passed between the others to regulate the fire by word of mouth.

Orni stayed to help him in the same way, passing among the nearby group of tanks. In each, he lifted the back telephone and called inside: "Stop! If you hear, wave your hand!" The tank commander waved his hand, and Orni continued to the next one.

Kaposta arrived. I explained to him what I thought had happened. "I figure that Rafi made a mistake at the turn. He turned left at the first crossing instead of going to the crossing near the corner of the wall. Go after him, bring him back, and take him to the right place."

Kaposta hesitated. He had not seen the area very well in daylight, and was not at all sure that he could find the right roads. "Come, let us go up and study the photograph," I said. Arik spread out the photograph and somebody lighted a torch. From the direction of the wall shots were heard, but there was no further report from Rafi.

Meanwhile Arzi's tank, which was leading, reached a sharp turn to the left. Rafi was behind him, wondering if it was possible that they were at the proper place after all. His eye was completely covered with blood. It didn't seem to be a serious wound, but it was irritating. Suddenly there was another turn to the right. Rafi strained his eyes. In front of him stretched a wide double-lane street. Now there could be no doubt. He had made a mistake. He raised the microphone to his mouth: "Stop! All stop! Turn round! Each one turn round where he is!"

The tanks were spread along the slope of the street. The last one was still near the Rockefeller. "Arzi," Rafi ordered, "pass me and then turn round and go back." Rafi stopped where he was, but ordered the driver to keep moving so that they should not present a stationary target.

Arzi turned round, reached Rafi, and passed him, so that Rafi remained at the end. Arzi approached the bridge, and along the street the other tanks began to turn round.

The officers of the staff gathered round my jeep, and I explained to Kaposta, who stood next to me, where I wanted him to go. Kaposta understood and turned to brief Yishai, commander of the reconnaissance spearhead platoon. Yishai, one of our veteran reconnaissance men since 1954, studied the photograph intently and confirmed that everything was clear.

Their jeeps moved slowly, without lights, down the slope of the square. When they reached the street that went along the wall, they were stopped by Eytan's tanks, which were standing there and shooting at the ridge. The jeeps came to a standstill. We tried to make contact with Rafi again, but there was no response.

I realized that somehow we had to reach him as quickly as

possible. In the meantime we ran forward to Kaposta to help him get past Eytan's tanks. Amos and Arik climbed on the tanks and ordered their commanders to move a little to one side so as to leave the street clear for the jeeps to pass. Eytan tried to deliver the message through his internal communication, but the process was too slow. Chuyun heard the order on the communications, but Eytan had to send Frika, the platoon commander, to Adler and Zisman to tell them by word of mouth what to do. We took the jeeps up onto the pavement, and directed them by hand signals, as if we were attendants in a parking lot. But progress was difficult, and the pitch darkness made it worse. Somehow they got past.

When I saw that matters were improving, I hurried above to try to make contact with Rafi on the big communications radio that was on the munitions carrier.

I trembled in a way that I could not control. This trembling came from the excitement and fear of the beginning of battle, and this time the evening cold of Jerusalem had aggravated it. My fears were intensified by anxiety about the fate of the tanks.

Noah, the radio technician, said in disgust: "All the time I've been talking to them and just when you come, the contact breaks down!"

I gave him back the microphone, but I remained beside the munitions carrier. "Keep trying to get them."

As the reconnaissance company continued on its way, Yishai's jeep was first in line and took the same incorrect left turn that Rafi had taken.

Kaposta, traveling behind the platoon, got the impression that they were descending too far and contacted Yishai. "Yishai! I think you're going wrong."

"I think so too, but since it's still quiet, we'll go on to check."

Benny, Yishai's driver, continued to go down, his attention

focused on passing the tanks. He discerned, a little distance in front of him, a sharp turn to the left. Suddenly rockets and tracer bullets were fired at them from the Old City wall, illuminating their surroundings. They realized they had gone wrong.

"Stop!" Kaposta roared. "Stop! All back! Back!"

As Arzi stared into the darkness, all of a sudden a red river of tracer bullets flew right at him. Some of them struck in the street in front of him, and ricocheted off at an angle. Fire poured down at them. By the light from the tracers, he saw the wall of the Old City beyond a hill covered with graves.

He urged the driver to hurry.

On the other side of the bridge, Rafi turned his tank around. The road was narrow. Rafi gave the order to the driver: "Back—Left—Back." The tank hit a bell tower. Rafi realized that the wound in his eye was making it difficult for him to function efficiently, so he called Nechama, the loader-signaler, to the turret to direct Amitai the driver. But when the order was given, "Driver, forward," the tank lurched instead to the left.

Rafi shouted with all his might, "Stop! Stop!" But the tank smashed the stone rail of the bridge and began to turn over down into the wadi. Amitai tried to stop it, but was unsuccessful. Rafi and Nechama managed to pull their heads back into the turret, just as the weight of the tank overturned it and plunged them down to the wadi bed ten meters below.

Near the bridge, the distance between Yishai's jeep and Arzi's tank had been reduced to nil. Fragments flew up from the stones of the wall of the bridge. Benny drove forward, and suddenly Yishai was wounded in the hand. "I'm hit," he cried. But there was no time to attend to him. Then, opposite them, a tank loomed up. Yishai shot half a magazine until he saw that it was a Sherman—ours! He stopped. "Benny—reverse!" he roared.

He looked back and saw that others in the jeep had also been wounded. Reuven Sadeh was hit in the back. Benny managed to turn the jeep around on the bridge and they drove back. Then Benny swung the jeep violently left and got to the edge of the pavement. "Stop! Reverse! Swing! Stop! First Gear! Gas full on, and hard turn with the steering wheel." The wheels screamed and bullets flew around them. Everyone bent down and Benny pressed hard on the accelerator—and entered the cover of the hill and drove at top speed to the doctor.

Arzi brought his tank over the bridge, reached a spot under cover of the hill which was protected from fire from the wall.

We of the advance command group were standing beside the weapons carrier trying to contact Rafi, as we also assessed the position. Then we heard the horn of a jeep and the shouts we feared so much: "Doctor! Doctor!"

We rushed to the jeep. "What is the matter? What's happened?"

"They laid an ambush and they're giving the *chevra* a hard time."

"Where?"

"They're shooting from the whole wall."

Reuven Sadeh had been very seriously wounded, and Yishai himself was also hurt.

Bitan treated Yishai, and Orni did his best for Reuven. A doctor came, but it was too late—Reuven died in Orni's arms. "What on earth were they doing near the wall?" I asked myself in anger and perplexity as I ran down to the edge of the olive grove. On the right, from the area of the wall, we heard continuous bursts and saw red rockets and tracer bullets. By the reddish light we saw the corner of the wall and its eastern side, above the cemetery.

On the bridge, a full-scale battle had developed. When the jeep commanders had seen Yishai's jeep turning round, they too had ordered a turnabout. Uri Arbel, the driver, slowed down and tried to turn, but the jeep behind smashed into him. Alex, taken by surprise by Uri's movement, did not manage to stop, and collided into Uri's jeep, stalling his engine, which he then couldn't get started again.

The fourth jeep stopped dead because Reuven Shacham, who had been driving it, was wounded in the hand and had fallen onto the steering wheel. The hail of bullets continued and the men in the jeeps were hit, one after the other. Three vehicles stood in the middle of the bridge, close to each other, all facing in different directions.

The first jeep was jammed into the wall of the bridge. Uri Arbel, the driver, jumped out and sought shelter behind a heap of stones nearby. Yoel, the jeep commander, was wounded in the arm and ran to the rear. Gabai and Aryeh Golan were sitting in the back of the jeep when a tracer bullet struck the reserve gasoline tank, spraying burning gasoline over the jeep. Aryeh Golan was set on fire and rushed to a heap of gravel near them, his clothes alight. Gabi was wounded and crawled slowly back along the street. Jordanian rockets lighted up the area. Uri Arbel detected the sources of the fire. But the weapons were in the jeep. He ran over to it, took a Uzi, and went back to his stones, firing burst after burst at the wall, providing thereby some cover for Aryeh Golan, who was trying to extinguish his burning clothes.

Alex's jeep was still stuck on the road when a long burst cut through it, killing Yoav Gross and Uri Koton and wounding Alex and Reuven Cohen in their legs. Reuven got out and lay behind the vehicle, using it as some sort of shield, and Alex crawled backward.

The last jeep stood there without moving, with Reuven Schachem lying wounded over the steering wheel and behind him Achinoam the orderly, injured near the knee, and Weiss hurt in the eye. Weiss somehow managed to get away to the rear by himself.

When the commander of the jeep, Uri Leviatan, rushed to the machine gun, he found that it was aimed toward the front while the enemy fire was coming from behind, from the wall. Uri managed to turn the gun, and returned fire at the wall. Then a Jordanian bullet caught him in the face and his jawbone was broken. Achinoam and Reuven got out of the jeep and lay on the street, and Uri dashed across the street to the wall of the bridge, grasped the parapet, and pulled himself over in a second, hanging by his hands, with his legs suspended in the air. The jump seemed to be very high, higher than he expected. But he had no alternative, so he let go and thudded to the ground.

From the heap of stones, Uri Arbel continued to fire and to provide cover for his mates. Then he too was wounded. Reuven Golan had not succeeded in overpowering the enemy fire. It had overpowered him and he stopped moving, although he continued to breathe.

Reuven Cohen felt the jeep beginning to roll onto him, and the back wheel was actually pressing on his ribs when at the last moment he managed to roll away. The tracer bullets died down and it became dark. Reuven began to crawl toward the rear for evacuation. On the street he came across Gabai, who was headed back, and the two supported each other until their comrades ran to meet them and pull them to a place of safety.

Close to the hill, in an area in front of the wall which was protected from fire for the time being, stood the reconnaissance platoons—one behind the other. Most of them had started around the corner when they heard Kaposta call Yishai on the instrument to advise him of his mistake. All along the line, cries and shouts were heard: "Come back! Come back!"

Zelcer, a platoon commander, took his platoon up above. Yoram's platoon, with four jeeps, had already reached down below, near the entrance to Lions' Gate. The area in front of them was being blanketed by Jordanian fire. At the order "Come back," the force turned round and went back toward the Rockefeller.

Dubi, a platoon commander, began to turn the munitions carrier of his platoon, when they reached the first wounded.

From up the street a group of soldiers under the command of Buchman came running, rushed to the wounded moving toward them, and brought them to shelter. Dr. Hadas arrived and began to treat them, and Noam and Dob helped him.

From the bridge came the cries of the wounded: "Medic! Doctor!"

Chovi, another platoon commander, decided to go down to the bridge. A new hail of bullets held him back for a moment. Chovi called to the wounded in a calm voice: "Don't worry! We're coming! Don't worry!"

The tracers went out and Chovi, Shindler, Rami, and Shauli rushed below, Shindler and Shauli put the wounded on their shoulders and returned with them up the street while Chovi and Rami stayed on the bridge to attend to the others.

Shindler came back and went to Aryeh Golan, who was practically unconscious. Shindler tried to take off his burning clothes and badly scorched his hands, but he went on treating him and saying words of encouragement.

Suddenly the Jordanian fire was renewed. In Shindler's hands, Aryeh Golan was hit again, this time mortally. Shindler ran to the wall of the bridge. His burned hands were weak and he slipped down the deep drop and crashed onto the ground. But he got up, undamaged, and began to climb the wall of the wadi toward his mates.

Rami was wounded and turned back to the top of the road while Chovi stayed on the bridge to help the wounded. For some time, it was quiet again and evacuation was organized along the row of platoons. Kaposta instructed every munitions carrier to take two men with stretchers down toward the bridge. Dubi and Yoram went by themselves down the slope of the road to be near the bridge area.

Dubi sent Ilan and Pinchas to see what was happening on the bridge itself so as to decide what to do. When they crossed the street going up to Lions' Gate, enemy fire began again, tracers lighting up the area and bullets cutting across the bridge and its surroundings. Rami appeared on the bridge with a bandage on his head, and when questioned, said, "There is no one on the bridge! I don't know where Chovi is!"

The firing grew weaker and gradually stopped. When Ilan and Pinchas got on to the bridge, they met Chovi, but before they could exchange a word, the firing started again even more fiercely. With a quick leap, the three of them swung over the north wall of the bridge and remained there hanging by their hands. Now Ilan and Pinchas knew why Rami couldn't find Chovi.

"Don't let go," Chovi warned them, "and don't jump. It's deep."

Their legs sought support in vain and their hands weakened, but finally the firing stopped. With the last ounce of their strength, they pulled themselves up and Chovi stooped to evacuate one of the *chevra*.

Ilan and Shauli went back. They had to bring tanks to provide shelter. Otherwise, it was impossible to help the wounded. Shauli stayed next to an electricity pole to maintain shouting contact with Chovi. One of the wounded begged them to finish him off. Chovi calmed him. He shouted to Shauli not to bring down any more men to help. "There are enough! The main thing is to bring tanks!"

Dubi heard him and passed the request on to Kaposta.

Yoram and his men drew near to the wall lining the street facing the wadi. Their idea was to jump in and advance secretly to the bridge. But in the darkness the drop seemed very deep; it looked as if jumping down would end in disaster. Bullets, shells, and antitank grenades were being fired from the wall. Each time they made a noise the firing was renewed. When they kept quiet, the Jordanians stopped firing.

When Rafi had ordered the tanks to stop and turn around, Gilboa, the tank platoon commander, who was standing on the square opposite the wall corner, had turned down on the correct road in the direction of Augusta Victoria. After he had gone down a steep slope and reached the market, however, he realized that he was alone, so, while trying to make contact with Rafi, he brought the tank back up the slope. Once he was on the high road, he did make contact, and told Rafi that he had found the right corner and suggested that they follow him.

A bazooka bomb cut off the conversation, causing the camouflage net to catch fire. Gilboa attempted to control the fire by going outside the tank and trying to put it out. But it began to burn above the gas containers and he was hit. So he told the team to get out and they used the fire extinguishers to prevent a blaze. Then he dispersed the team to other tanks, and he himself was evacuated to the rear for treatment, leaving the tank smoking on the traffic island in the street junction. The rest of the tanks remained standing between the corner of the wall and the Rockefeller, Shaul's tank in the lead.

When Kaposta's voice came to me from the darkness—"Motta, the *chevra* are catching it down there from all sides. We have to go down to them with tanks."—it was clear to us all they had not gone along the planned route, and that there had been a major breakdown in the operation. It was also clear that some of the *chevra* were under heavy fire in a kind of ambush.

"Take the tanks at once and do the necessary."

Kaposta went to Shaul. "Follow me. We have to go down below to rescue the wounded on the bridge."

"Good. I'm coming."

Shaul took the microphone and ordered the platoon to move after him and, without waiting, told the driver, "Go!"

The tank began to move slowly down the slope, Shaul assuming that the others were following him. But in fact they hadn't budged. Some had not heard the order and others were still finishing tasks requested by the paratroopers.

Shaul saw men of the reconnaisance company hugging the wall near the entrance to Lions' Gate. He heard shots from the bridge and saw red rockets fired at it. Shaul turned his tank half-right and fired toward the Old City wall and the cemetery. The paratroopers urged him to keep on firing, for when he did, the Jordanians were quiet. He fired five more shells toward the Gate of Mercy.

Dubi's platoon remained close to the wall. To the left, Yoram's platoon was stretched out next to the railing that provided some protection from the deep drop down to the Kidron Stream. From the right, bursts were being fired at the platoon. On the slope of the hill, the *chevra* identified a machine gun and opened fire to silence it.

Dubi asked Shaul to bring his tank lower down and help in the removal of wounded, so Shaul went on until a mortar shell exploded on the deck, covering Yoram's platoon with shrapnel which hit a few men. Shaul went on shooting. Then he shouted to Dubi, "Sorry, ammunition finished. I have to go."

"O.K. We'll manage by ourselves for the time being," Dubi answered, and Shaul's tank made for the top of the street.

Dubi decided that there was only one way out—to go close to the bridge. He instructed the platoon to be ready to move on foot. The moment it was dark, they rushed across to the other side of the street, jumped over the rail, and went down the slope of the dry bed of the stream.

Round us at the advance command group there was tumult. The noise of the tanks preparing to move clashed with that from the loudspeakers of the communication instruments pouring out orders and conversations.

We were overwhelmed by a feeling of heavy depression. Instinct drew us down toward the *chevra* in trouble on the bridge. But we had to carry on with the brigade's assignment: to conquer the Augusta Victoria ridge. Nothing could be allowed to interfere with this. Kaposta would have to deal with the evacuation of the wounded.

Kaposta was one of the finest officers in the army. He knew every man in his company; they had served together for years. We had been together at the Mitla, and I remembered how brokenhearted he was about his comrades who had fallen. If it was at all possible to do anything, he was the man who could do it. Whatever he asked for had to be given to him. But we had to carry on with our job.

Uzi Narkiss contacted me. I told him about the terrible blunder with regard to the roads, and all our subsequent problems, but added that we had straightened things out and were going ahead with our attack. He confirmed my decision.

We tried to reorganize the tanks by giving them commands over the network, but there was no answer. I called Amos and Arik to me, two staff officers who had been longing to get into more active fighting ever since morning.

"Arik, you put some order into Rafi's tanks that are standing on the street, and organize the evacuation of the wounded. Amos, take Eytan and collect all the tanks that can move. Take them to the Augusta Victoria ridge, according to the plan."

Both of them were pleased. At last they would get into the battle. They ran off and disappeared among the vehicles in the dense blackness of the night.

I had nothing more to do at this stage of the game. Kaposta was dealing with the rescue of the wounded and Amos was bringing the tanks that were left into new positions. The crisis was over. I felt professional satisfaction that we had overcome the hitch in our plans, and that our forces would soon be in fighting trim.

On the other hand, I wondered that I could manage to think with calm detachment and apply military professional knowledge to a situation while my closest friends, sent into battle by me, were threatened by enemy fire. My heart wanted to be with them on the bridge. But I dared not think like this for more than a moment, and, in fact, I didn't; the onrushing military decisions pushed such thoughts out of my mind. I had to think as if I were facing a tactical problem during an exercise, rather than in the middle of an actual battle.

Thus two worlds alternated in my mind: One was full of suspense and anxiety about the wounded, the other considered tactics on a cold and gloomy night.

In the road below the museum, the tanks began to reorganize. Amos went first to Ben-Gigi's tank, in Gilboa's platoon.

"Follow me," Amos ordered.

"Who the hell are you?" asked Ben-Gigi.

"I am Amos, the staff officer. You made a mistake, and I have to lead you."

Ben-Gigi hesitated, not knowing if he should take orders from somebody other than his own officers. Arzi's tank was next to him so he asked Arzi.

Arzi told him to listen to Amos. Then Ben-Gigi raised another difficulty: he had no gunner. "Never mind," Amos urged. "I'll be your gunner." He got into the tank. "Move!"

The tank began to move down the slope and Ariel's tank followed. Amos, in the first tank, reached the corner of the wall where he saw the deserted burning tank at the road junction. They bypassed it, turning sharply to the left, and went down the slope of the street—this time the right street—till they came to the market. They carried on up the slope and approached the Palace Hotel, where Amos stopped and waited for the other officers of the staff.

Arik went to the second group of tanks with the aim of helping Amos to continue the attack. Eytan sat in the turret, his head exposed, and Arik ran up to him and climbed on the tank, tapping Eytan on the head, and asking, "Who is the commander of this?"

"I'm the second-in-command of the tank battalion," Eytan replied. In the brief meeting we had had before the battle, the officers had not had a chance to get to know each other. We had thought that Eytan was a company commander, and all the while he was second-in-command of a battalion. Arik had not even met him.

"Very good," Arik replied, and began to explain the revised plan. He stressed the directions to be taken, warned Eytan not to turn left at the first turn, and not to miss the second turn. "A burning tank is standing there. Turn left. On your right you will see the corner of the wall. There are tanks standing on the slope of the street on the left. Take command of them and go on to the Augusta Victoria."

Eytan gave the order on the communications network and turned to carry out the assignment. Zisman, commander of the next tank, followed him. But Adler and Chuyun did not hear the order, and stayed where they were. Arik went on foot in front of the tanks and directed them. Near the first turn of the street going up to the Wadi Joz neighborhood stood a column of the medical team. To the right were Kaposta and his men. Arik took leave of

Eytan and joined Kaposta to help him with the evacuation of the wounded.

Eytan went on and was fired on immediately from the corner of the wall. When he found the second turn left, he began to change direction, but the turn was so sharp that he was compelled to maneuver backward and forward twice. Zisman did the same.

Eytan started down the slope but Amos stopped them on the street. Eytan got off the tank and Amos explained what was intended. When everything was clear, Eytan tried to set up communications with the tanks of Ben-Gigi and Ariel, but could not, as they were from Rafi's platoon and had different communications systems.

Amos reported to me that the tanks were already organized on the correct slope and would soon be ready to move. But, he said, there was no contact between the tanks, and each order had to be passed personally to the commanders by climbing on the caterpillars. I instructed Uzi to get Battalion 71 ready to move.

We were encouraged by the fact that the Jordanians had not opened fire on us with their artillery. The ridge was silent, but we did not know whether it was empty, or if they were preparing a trap for us. I was prepared to assume this time that they had been immobilized by the ferocity of Ziklag's barrage, that their artillery had been knocked down or had withdrawn. Otherwise there would be no explanation of their almost superhuman restraint. I decided to continue with the attack, even though we only had four tanks now and were without the reconnaissance company. As for the rest of the tanks, some were damaged, some were taking part in the rescue of the men on the bridge, and some were firing straight at the ridge.

Suddenly I was called to the radio. Noah, the radio technician, had heard from Menachem, the commander of the garrison on Mount Scopus, that he had seen the lights of the vehicles on the ridge.

Menachem was an old friend, and it was worth having a personal word with him.

"Menachem, what exactly did you see?"

"On the eastern slope of the woods, we saw sixteen lights of vehicles."

"Stationary or moving?"

"Moving. We had not seen them before."

"Did you hear the noise of the caterpillars of tanks?"

"No. The lights give the impression of being those of cars."

"Right, Menachem. Thank you very much. If you see anything else, get on the network and tell me. See you soon."

I put down the microphone. Amos and Uzi were already on their way. I wondered if I should change the plan because of those lights. We held a short staff conference. This was, in fact, the first real piece of information about the enemy force on the Augusta Victoria since morning. It might be a transport that had just arrived, or perhaps one that had been hidden during the day. We wondered where they were going, and why, and if the lights represented trucks with soldiers or recoilless-gun jeeps. If they were retreating, they would be surprised by our tank attack.

I decided to continue with the plan without any change.

"Arik, make certain that the commanders in the field heard the discussion with Menachem."

Uzi Narkiss came on the air, wanting to know what was happening, and I outlined the position.

Amos reported that the tanks were already on the move.

Ziklag dropped a few shells on the ridge. It was only exploratory fire. His main purpose was to ascertain the accuracy of the hits and to maintain activity without rousing the suspicions of the Jordanians that a major assault was coming.

There was nothing new from Kaposta. Now and then shots and rockets were fired from the direction of the wall. They seemed to be very nervous; perhaps they feared we were going to attack the Old City. Understandably, as during the afternoon, Paikos's battalion of the Jerusalem Brigade had conquered Abu Tur, though unfortunately Paikos had been very badly wounded.

At 2140 Orni came to me: "Motta—Intelligence tells us that tanks are moving from Jericho to Jerusalem."

We went together to the radio, where Arik was asking Command for precise details.

Arik said into the microphone: "Right. Wait." With the microphone still in his hand, he reported to me: "Forty Pattons are waiting to enter the Augusta Victoria from the Jericho road."

Without hearing more, I gave an order on the spot: "Orni, tell Amos and Uzi to stop the advance and to wait where they are for further orders. Get me Uzi Narkiss."

While I waited for Uzi, we tried to assess the information and its significance. "Forty Pattons, precisely forty, and precisely Pattons." This did not sound like an empty rumor. This was a major force from the Jordanian tank brigade, kept in reserve in the Jericho district.

I decided at once that if the information was confirmed as accurate, we would have to stop our attack and bring the Air Force into action. There would be no sense sending four Shermans of two different types, and without contact between them, together with infantry, against a battalion of forty Pattons. It would be better to wait for morning and activate the Air Force. After they had hit the Pattons, we could go on with the assault. To send our men against an unknown military position by night, defended by so many tanks, while simultaneously storming a fortress, could not be considered. Uzi Narkiss came on the line.

"*Shalom.* Have you heard about forty Pattons?"

"Yes."

"Is it accurate, and can one rely on it?"

"Yes."

It seemed that the order to retreat given to the Jordanian forces had been cancelled. Instead, their 27th Infantry Brigade from the Heights of Edom and a battalion from Armored Brigade 60 had been sent toward Jerusalem.

"If so, I recommend that we stop the attack, reorganize in an urban area, and in the morning make use of the Air Force. After that, we can see."

"Where are your forces?"

"We have some tanks at the beginning of the rise, and Battalion 71 is on the slopes of Wadi Joz."

"Perhaps you can reorganize for defense below?"

"No. If the Pattons do arrive, I want our forces to be concealed among the houses. We'll clear the whole row of houses on the outside and hole up in the inner area in such a way that the tanks won't be able to harm us. We'll deploy all the tanks and the antitank weapons available to them."

"Very well. Report developments. *Lehitraot.*"

The staff were standing beside me. From the discussion they understood what was happening. I issued orders: "Moshele, bring back all forces and summon the commanders to me for further orders. Arik, prepare a photograph and, until the commanders arrive, we can plan the organization of the defense and the distribution of sectors."

We were tired and disappointed, but I had no doubt that our decision was correct. Recognizing this, however, did not prevent our hearts being heavy. It was not easy to decide to cancel an assignment.

The time was 2200.

Meanwhile, opposite the corner of the wall stood Kaposta and his command group. Shaul's tank had returned, but since more tanks were needed for the rescue, Kaposta had sent Eli Natan, his deputy. Eli arrived just as we were deciding to cancel the attack. Kaposta went down to the vicinity of the bridge to observe the situation from close at hand.

I gave permission for the tanks to be used to rescue the wounded and Arik joined Kaposta to ensure that the tanks went into action immediately. Adler's and Chuyun's vehicles stood at the bottom of the square. Eli Zelcer, commander of a reconnaissance platoon, came to me; Kaposta had sent him to fetch a half-track for the evacuation of the wounded. I instructed them to give him the command half-track. Forman drove it, and Wiesel and Amikam worked the machine guns. Arik got to Chuyun's tank.

"Who is the commander?" he asked.

"Adler, in the other one," answered Chuyun.

Arik got down, climbed onto Adler's tank, and explained to him that he should go down to help with the evacuation of wounded from the bridge. Adler did not quite understand what was expected of him. Arik said, "There's a bridge down below with a lot of wounded. Go down there to create an iron wall to protect the wounded as we evacuate them." He explained to Adler where the wall was and what was happening down below. Adler asked if the Jordanians were shooting from the wall with antitank guns too. Arik replied, "No, only with light arms." Adler sent him to explain the position to Chuyun, and afterward Arik signalled with a flashlight. The tanks began to move, Chuyun not far behind Adler. As they approached the road junction at Lions' Gate, the Jordanians opened fire from the wall. The tank crews saw the paratroopers of the reconnaissance company next to the wall above the wadi.

When the fire from the wall increased, Adler returned fire. Adler put his head in and told Ben-Ari, his driver, that he should move slowly. He was driving by the light provided by Arab rockets. Adler told Menashe, the gunner, to turn the gun to the right. Suddenly they felt that the turret had seized. He told the driver to stop. They looked inside, but saw nothing wrong. Adler guessed that something had happened outside. The turret would not turn.

Meanwhile, in the wadi, Dubi's platoon marched along the bed toward the bridge. Dubi shouted to the *chevra* on the bridge, but heard no answer. Now and then bursts of fire came from the direction of the wall and bullets straddled the bridge. Some single bullets even came down into the wadi.

Dubi crossed the bottom of the wadi and began to climb up the eastern side.

At that moment Chuyun's tank arrived at the bridge. When Adler realized that the turret of his tank had jammed, he explained the position to the paratroopers next to him and added, "Sorry, but I can't carry on like this."

The paratroopers went up to Chuyun's tank and called to him on the telephone. Chuyun heard and they explained what they wanted. "Pass Adler and go on down. Provide cover for the evacuation of the wounded. Don't stop shooting. As long as you fire, the Jordanians won't. If you stop, they will open fire again."

Chuyun ordered the driver to move. Shauli jumped onto the tank to explain to Chuyun by word of mouth what to do. Yosef, the driver, bypassed Adler's tank and continued down the slope. Meir, the gunner, and Shlomo, the loader-signaler, fired nonstop. The turret swung to the right, to the wall. Shauli, taken completely by surprise, was blown off the deck onto the street below. He crawled to shelter. The rise of the hill and the wall were flooded with fire from the tank and the Jordanians were silent once more.

The tank reached the corner of the bridge. Chuyun stood exposed, with only the shelf protecting him from the direction of the wall. The belt of bullets in the machine gun was finished. The Jordanians renewed their fire and a tracer bullet hit the camouflage net of the tank, which began to burn. Dubi's *chevra* watched what was happening from the wadi slope, and Shauli watched them from his place of shelter on the hill.

Chuyun continued slowly forward. Suddenly he saw that the deck was on fire. He gave instructions to the crew to leave the tank and they turned the gun from five o'clock to eight o'clock in the direction of the wall, so that all the men could get out. They jumped out and ran forward, but were fired upon for the whole length of the bridge, and the light from the rockets was like daylight. Chuyun hid at the entrance, but Yosef and Apollo did not get so far. By the light of the rockets he saw *chevra* lying on the bridge but did not know if they were his tank crew or paratroopers. He was also worried that he had not turned sideways correctly, and that two of his men were trapped in the tank.

Adler went on a little behind Chuyun and then a shell exploded on the tank. With the turret jammed, there was no sense in remaining, so he told the driver to reverse. They entered under the stone wall, traveling in reverse. So as not to fall into the deep wadi, they swung to the side; and now and then they hit the wall. They came to the square above and he heard shots from the bridge and saw fire. His internal communication system was cut off and there was nothing to be done but wait. The team dozed off till morning.

The forces organized for defense next to the Rockefeller Museum. Arik told Eytan and Amos to return, and Amos and Arik came back on foot, Amos to the advance command group, while Arik stayed with Kaposta opposite the corner of the wall. Meanwhile Eytan brought the tanks back on the slope past the market. Ariel's tank skidded sideways and slipped down into the wadi; the team was rescued, but the tank was lost. Eytan went on with only three tanks. When he reached the corner of the wall, he was fired on, but did not return fire. He continued on while Arik signaled to them with a flashlight: forward—back—forward, and the turn was completed.

When the fire of the bazookas from the corner of the wall increased, Kaposta decided to knock out the post. He placed three antitank squads—those of Yuval, Ami, and Zeevi—to hit the bazooka post and cover the passage of each tank. Yuval fired three times and then suddenly a rocket from the wall exploded besides the squad, wounding Yuval. Kaposta took his equipment from him, and the *chevra* evacuated him to the rear.

Meanwhile, in the corridor of the museum we made detailed plans for defense against the Pattons.

Amos spread out the aerial photograph. We assumed that the Jordanians were not likely to attack with infantry, and we planned to prevent men being wounded by distant tank fire while at the same time we struck back at the Pattons. We saw no reason to change the deployment of the battalions, but only the method of spreading them out, so that the units would be hidden from tank fire. The chief problem was to place the antitank weapons at the edge of the built-up area in firing posts that were both efficient and safe.

One Jordanian move had to be considered—a drive to link up with the Old City. The street junction of Azaria—Lions' Gate was still in their hands, as well as the road going up to Lions' Gate. Ziklag was charged with preventing this from happening. He was to find the ranges for his guns to hit key objectives all along the Augusta Victoria ridge and in the Kidron Valley.

Amos marked out the battalion boundaries in red pencil, and we waited for the antitank unit commanders to consult with him before deciding where they would be placed and how they would be used. Foxie had already gone to ask them to join us. In the course of the staff conference, heads dropped and eyes closed. We laughed at ourselves. I began a sentence and dozed off in the middle of a word. The laughter woke me. I continued speaking and again fell asleep. Amos's pencil fell from his hand, his head bent and he lay on the photograph. I heard the sound of heavy breathing; in the end I decided to stop the conference so that we could snatch a little sleep.

Kaposta came in tired and dejected. He wanted to arrange another attempt to get his men out with tanks, and I authorized this. Then Kaposta returned to the bridge and Eytan went after him, ordering the tanks to move and Zelcer's platoon to follow. Eytan's tanks came down from the direction of Rockefeller. Opposite the corner of the wall, he let off two shells and went on. They reached the entrance to the Lions' Gate and the paratroopers stopped. It was still not clear how they were to continue, so the tanks waited.

Kaposta decided to make a last attempt at a quiet approach at the head of Zelcer's platoon. He went down into the wadi, where he met Dubi with his men. Dubi reported: "Quiet below," so Kaposta decided to continue.

They went along the bed of the wadi, Kaposta and Har-Zion looking for an easy ascent to the road. Kaposta climbed up where he could see his four men lying on the bridge, without a sign of life.

Then the tank at the corner was hit; its ammunition exploded and the tank rolled down on the jeeps and crushed them, spraying shrapnel and tongues of fire.

Kaposta realized that the rescue operation had failed, and went sadly back to his men. Eytan received permission to return, and the tanks came back to the museum square. Eytan came in, his eyes bleary, his glasses pushed up onto his forehead. He was obviously exhausted, but I could not let him rest yet; the tanks that we had left from the two companies had to be reorganized into one unit. Rafi was missing. Nobody knew where he was, or even if he was still alive. So only Eytan could do the job of merging the tanks into a single fighting force, sharing out the ammunition, insuring that they had a common communications network.

He went off again to do what I asked, after trying in vain to find out what had happened to the missing half of his company, the half that hadn't arrived in the afternoon. Arik went with him to show him where to place the tanks.

At 0100 we referred our plan for a morning attack on the Augusta Victoria ridge to Central Command for approval, and advised them of the time schedule we recommended. We suggested that zero hour should be 1130, which seemed rather late, but I calculated that it would take several hours of daylight to reorganize the tanks, the reconnaissance company, and the battalions. We also asked for an air attack on the Pattons.

Central Command approved of our plan and schedule and Arik Regev, the staff officer at the command, asked me to decide when I wanted the air strike. I suggested that the first squadron should hit the ridge at 1030, and from that point on the Air Force should act independently and knock out any targets it could find.

It was two in the morning. The various forces were expected to be in their positions by four and we ourselves badly needed a couple of hours to reorganize our personal forces. We dozed off.

The commanders of the antitank units came in and woke me, so I woke Amos, and together we selected the key points to place their weapons to stop the enemy armor, if the Pattons should attack. We covered every post in detail before they returned to their men.

Our plan was that the antitank squads would concentrate on enemy tanks in every sector from the Rockefeller to Mount Scopus and we would also bar the roads against a tank attack by setting up physical roadblocks.

So much for defense, in case we were attacked by the Pattons. For our own attack on the Augusta Victoria ridge, I decided that we would have to change the original plan, designed for a night assault and broken off when we heard about the Pattons. If there were tanks on the ridge, it would be difficult for our forces to go up alone from the Kidron Valley. So we now would have to operate from two sides to make the enemy dilute his forces. This meant that the 66th would have to launch a frontal attack from Mount Scopus, while the 71st went up from the Kidron Valley against an underbelly that might not be as soft as we had once hoped. Yossi arrived and I told him that his battalion would be needed, after all, and explained why and how it would function, and he went back to carry out the arrangements.

At 0220 we heard over the communications system that our planes were bombing the Jordanians beyond the Augusta Victoria ridge. Now and then we saw flares.

Rafi's tank had fallen to the bed of the wadi with a terrible impact. Then, slowly, one by one, the *chevra* had crawled out of the vehicle and, to their joy, found that nobody was injured, although they were all badly bruised. They took out all the weapons and maps from the tank, shut off the fuel, and went into hiding. Not far away Chuyun's team, split in two, was also hiding. Neither team moved for fear of being taken prisoner or encountering heavily armed enemy forces. They also did not know which way to go. In the end Chuyun started out cautiously along the stream bed, and so met Rafi's men, and together they went on until, toward morning, they reached the museum.

At 0400 the next morning I woke up after my short nap to find my staff officers asleep on the floor and the corridor dark. Save for the heaps of people, I could see nothing in the first rays of light which stole in from outside.

I had to get up and issue orders for the day. If the Jordanians really had brought a battalion of tanks onto the Augusta

Victoria ridge last night, heavy fire would descend on us very soon. The square in front of the museum was completely exposed to shells from the ridge, and we had already suffered from the sniping from there. If we didn't hurry, we might be stuck indoors, unable to go out without taking great risks. So I woke the others.

We went outside to find the square already almost empty, although on the slope of the street there were vehicles exposed to fire. Round about there was absolute silence. The sniping from the wall had not yet begun. The sleep had been wonderful—and vital. Now we could think properly again. We started to search for a suitable building for our headquarters, from which to direct the conquest of the ridge. We needed complete observation and at the same time protection from the fire from their tanks.

Not too far from us there was a high building made of white stone, and it seemed to me that its upper windows or its roof would suit us. On our way to it, we gave orders that all vehicles be moved from the road, so Kaposta's reconnaissance vehicles, our vehicles, and also the recoilless-gun jeeps were pushed into a hidden area, and all the rest went into the yards of houses or narrow streets. The drivers and officers, in spite of their great weariness, executed the moves quietly and quickly. Except for occasional shouts to waken those still rubbing their eyes, the tranquility of the morning was not disturbed.

We went into the house selected as our headquarters through an ornamented black iron gate. It had a beautiful garden, in the English wild style. Shrubs and flowers were mixed with each other in a small, charming jungle. In the center of the garden was a pergola of green peppers and climbing vines. Inside the building we found our men, prepared since dawn to receive the enemy.

We went up the stairs to the second floor and crossed to the side that faced east. From the room a door led out onto a half-open balcony. Before us stretched the Kidron Valley, with its two walls; we could see the entire Mount Scopus ridge from French Hill on the north to the Abu-Dis village on the south.

I gave orders that our headquarters be transferred here at once, and went on with my tour of the house. The roof was open, with a railing about two feet high. It was exposed to sniping from the Old City wall and the top storey was also exposed to tank fire from the ridge.

But the excellent observation was more important than perfect shelter. We would have to take care that our forest of antennae did not give us away to the eyes of a keen Jordanian observation officer. We then descended to look for an extra gate through which we could come and go without being exposed to the snipers.

We found one on the south and opened this too, but could not find an extra entrance door to the apartment. We discovered a small road suitable for the advance command group vehicles, the half-track and the two weapons carriers. On the north of the building there was a narrow winding alley. When the operation started, and we wanted to advance to the battlefield, we could drive straight from our building to one of the roads in the Wadi Joz neighborhood, and from there go either to the Kidron Valley or up to the Augusta Victoria ridge.

Meanwhile, the first of our radio technicians arrived and arranged telephonic contacts with the large communication instruments, which remained on the vehicles down below. In this way, we could work from our headquarters but still retain our usual network.

We checked out the nearby streets carefully, to be sure that everything was concealed from a sudden attack.

At 0500 I felt that the Jordanians were also waking up, for they renewed their sniping from the wall and the ridge. Then we heard the thunder of our heavy machine guns returning fire, and here and there a Mag. The tune played by the snipers was familiar from the day before. I knew how a soldier could develop a dangerous indifference to the sound, and we reminded the fighters constantly not to treat it with contempt, but to take care all the time not to expose themselves needlessly.

The brigade doctor was looking for a suitable site for the medical team. Accompanied by Dr. Kahanski and Yechezkel Katan, he came to the Hotel Azahariyah, which seemed eminently suitable. In answer to a knock at the door, a woman appeared.

"Is there anyone here besides yourself?"

"No. There is no one else here."

Despite her assurance, they combed the rooms carefully. After a few minutes, they came down with a police sergeant, armed with a rifle and hundreds of bullets, and three other men dressed in pajamas, also carrying weapons. It came out that these men had been sniping from here in all directions, especially at the Rockefeller, throughout Tuesday. They also found a fifth Arab, dressed in an elegant civilian suit, who ignored the other four, pretending not to know them.

The medical team settled in and spread out the medical equipment.

We went back to our headquarters building to find great excitement, for seven Jordanian soldiers had been discovered in an attic in the middle of the building we had selected for brigade headquarters! The apartment had seemed to be entirely a domestic establishment. Two women, heavily built and rather old, were standing with brooms in their hands. The soldiers, holding their weapons, were moving furniture and carpets from one side of the room to the other, to help the women to clean and to put the furniture where it would not be damaged.

In the hall the prisoners stood facing the wall, with their hands up. The paratroopers pointed up to the attic, and told us how they had caught the Jordanians. The women who were cleaning the apartment had talked to each other in Arabic, not knowing that Moshele understood every word they were saying. Suddenly he had caught a remark: "What if they discover them?" Under questioning, the women had admitted that seven armed Jordanian soldiers were hiding in the attic, but insisted that the soldiers had forced their way in, and that the women had only given them shelter out of fear of being killed.

The seven were called on to surrender, and meekly passed down their arms and then came down themselves. We sent them to a point in the Museum courtyard that had been set aside for POWs.

Our room had already been prepared for a planning session with tables, chairs, and communications. While the staff settled down, I went up to the roof to see what I could of a world at war.

Alongside the railing that ran around the roof were the radio technicians with the antennae of their instruments placed on the diagonal, so that they could not be seen by the Jordanians. Since the main danger from snipers came from the south, I told the radio technicians to go across to the northern side of the roof, where they would be protected against fire and could not be seen.

As there was a chair next to the door, I wearily sat down for a few moments. But I kept worrying about the occasional bullets from snipers and hoped that the boys were not taking unnecessary risks.

It was wonderful, for a change, not to be in a hurry, and to be able to relax and enjoy the view in front of me. The main points of the plan were clear. We had set the zero hour at 1130, but first the planes had to destroy the Pattons. Otherwise the open valley between us and the rise to the ridge might be turned into a valley of death.

When the maps and photographs were ready, I was called below and we started the planning session, all of us in good spirits. At 0530 the telephone rang. It was an urgent call from Uzi Narkiss. Because the telephone wire was short, I had to go across to the window. Uzi wanted to know my plans and I explained that we were going to attack at 1130, and had ordered the planes for 1030.

Uzi urged greater speed, as political pressures were mounting against us and every moment had become precious. We might be stopped by the great powers, as had happened so often in the past. True, there was as yet no authorization to take the Old City, but it was vital that we control the ridge as soon as possible. If we did not enter Old Jerusalem, at least we could surround it and cut it off.

I understood and I promised to do everything possible. I turned to the officers, who realized at once from the look on my face that something had happened. I explained, but before I could sit down I was called to the telephone again by Uzi, who asked if he should put forces from the south of the city into action, across the Azaria intersection?

"No," I asserted, knowing that the intersection was held by the enemy in great strength, and that action in that area was likely to end in another disaster. Besides, I had enough forces to attack in all directions simultaneously. I said, "Don't worry, Uzi. Everything is going to be O.K."

He added that there was a company of tanks on Givat Hamivtar, all armed and ready, at my disposal.

"Great!"

I summed up the new plan we had worked out last night. The 66th would attack the ridge directly from Mount Scopus, in spite of the dangers involved in such a frontal attack.

I sent Amos to Yossi to explain the new plan and the time element, and to coordinate action with Menachem Sharfman, the commander of Mount Scopus.

Then I contacted Yossi by phone and told him to go at once to Mount Scopus, to collect the company of tanks on Givat Hamivtar, and prepare to attack the Augusta Victoria. "Amos is on his way to you with further information. Uzi will also attack from the direction of the Kidron Valley, to make certain of a breakthrough, whatever happens."

I phoned Uzi to come to me, for Battalion 71 headquarters was near us, and I wanted to explain the plan face to face. We would have to coordinate the movements of the two battalions very carefully, so as to make sure that they did not hit each other during the assault. Under our new plan, the tanks of Eytan and Rafi, in one unit and followed by Kaposta's reconnaissance company, would precede the 71st.

We realized that moving through the Kidron Valley by day and going up the hillside would leave us vulnerable to Jordanian snipers and gunners operating from the wall in our rear. It was essential, therefore, that the posts on the wall be silenced by the artillery and tanks before the move.

Moreover, if we did get the order to move into the Old City, the wall would have to be completely neutralized before the 28th could break through one of the gates and head for the Temple Mount. Somehow, I felt in my bones that we would get the O.K. that day. So the artillery and tanks had to smash the posts for them as well.

The 28th could effect a breakthrough in one of two ways. They could either go across from the Rockefeller straight at Herod's Gate, or go around the wall as far as Lions' Gate. Once through there, they could take the Via Dolorosa to the Temple Mount.

So we decided that the artillery had to find the range precisely and bombard the wall before anyone moved. Ziklag pointed out that shelling the corner of the wall, just across the way from the Rockefeller, was very dangerous and difficult—a shell falling short would land among our own men.

But there was no alternative. Uzi would have to make certain that all his men were hidden inside the building, in a wing far away from the wall. The structure was so sturdy that, even if a shell fell on it, nothing would happen to the men inside.

I told Ziklag that his shells must fall right next to the wall, so that the snipers and the other Jordanian soldiers would be forced to flee, and not be able to interfere with the climb to the ridge.

Moshele looked hard at me. All of them realized the gravity of my decision. Leaving the museum during the rangefinding could not be considered, because the Jordanian tanks, which were probably already on the ridge, and perhaps even near the Old City, might take advantage of our absence and retake the museum, losing us our main base for conquering the ridge and the Old City. Furthermore, if we did not shell the wall, we would expose the infantry to attack from the rear at very short range. The memory of last night, when the Arabs mauled Kaposta's company so savagely from the wall, was still all too fresh in our minds. So the rangefinding was vital, even if it might endanger our men near the wall, including ourselves. There was simply no alternative.

"Let me go to help Ziklag," Moshele suggested.

"Why? There is no need. Ziklag is capable of doing it very well by himself."

Moshele did not reply, he just nodded his head as if to say, "Very well. If that's the way you want it . . ."

Then I changed my mind. The operation was vital and Moshele wanted to take some of the responsibility, in case something went wrong. It was good that he, as my second-in-command, should do so.

"All right. If you think so. You go too."

I sent Uzi to his battalion to warn everyone about the rangefinding, and to issue stern orders that all men get inside the building. We decided that Moshele and Ziklag should begin the rangefinding after they had received Uzi's confirmation that all his men had taken shelter.

Ziklag informed us that he was ready to go and explained what system he would use. He was going to begin with a long shot into the Old City, and then would make corrections of twenty-five meters at a time until he reached the general area of the wall. We agreed that the rangefinding would be carried out from one of the houses next to the wall, near the "red house," opposite the museum. The group went on its way and we stayed sitting round the table to complete the last details.

Uzi Narkiss contacted me again and I explained to him that we were working on three possible alternatives at the same time, so that if one didn't work out, another would. Whatever happened, this time Jerusalem would be in our hands.

"When do you think you can attack?"

"I think around nine o'clock, but I'll find out exactly and let you know."

"Hurry, Motta. Hurry. We have so little time. And it will be bad for us if we miss out."

"Uzi, what about the Old City?"

"Sorry. No permission as yet. But there will be. If things go well, authorization for the Old City will come too. I'm sure of it."

He told me that at least three squadrons of planes would be put at our disposal and that we had to get word to the Air Force of our plans.

Delay might be caused by the 66th, which had to reach Mount Scopus, link up with the tanks, coordinate with the garrison stationed on Mount Scopus, and deal with the mines, before it could storm the Jordanian positions.

We contacted the battalion, to hear the good news that some units were already on the move. It was close to seven o'clock and I asked for Yossi. "Can you attack by nine o'clock?"

"With great difficulty," Yossi replied. "I would like more time."

"We'll investigate and let you know," I answered.

Arik advised me, "We have ordered the planes for eight-thirty. Is that O.K.?"

"No," I answered. "It's too early—Yossi won't be ready. Arrange for the first squadron at nine." It was a pity to keep the planes idle, but it was also a pity to go into battle inadequately organized.

Uzi and Eytan arrived and I explained the plan to them before we all went up to the roof. From here we could see the area closely and the whole axis of the advance. Eytan wanted to study the exact path his tanks were to take—no doubt he was remembering what had happened to Rafi. Yesterday's experience had been very bad. I told Giora, of the reconnaissance company, that he should find a way for the tanks to go straight from the Wadi Joz neighborhood to the Kidron Valley, and he went off to reconnoiter.

The Jordanian shelling and sniping continued, bullets whistling overhead. We bent down, running and stooping at the same time, to get across to the eastern railing. From the north corner we could see the whole region, from the deployment area of Battalion 71 in Wadi Joz up to the ridge.

I explained to Uzi: "Yossi will go straight across from Mount Scopus, by way of the road, to the Augusta Victoria grove. You wait till the tanks and Kaposta's reconnaissance company have gone up the road past the Palace Hotel. Then you go up behind them to hit the Jordanian posts near the barracks on the ridge. If, by any chance, we get the authority to attack the Old City, you simply turn back and come down again. Then we'll put the Old City plan into operation—you'll probably go through Lions' Gate."

I told Eytan: "You lead, up the road, with your tanks. I'll only send the others behind you if I see that you don't come under heavy fire. If we get the O.K. to go for the Old City, you also come back down from the ridge, and go through Lions' Gate."

We heard muffled explosions from the direction of the Old City, and it seemed that Ziklag had already begun. But when we

THE BATTLE FOR JERUSALEM

got up to watch, we could see nothing, though we could hear the whistle of bullets. We bent down again.

Everything was finally clear to Uzi. I also had not forgotten Zamush's special request: "If we enter the Old City, I want to be among the first at the Western Wall."

There were more explosions from within the Old City. Suddenly one was heard nearby, and we got up to look. Smoke rose from near the museum, but there were no cries for a medic. We couldn't tell whether it was our shell or if the Jordanians were opening a barrage prior to a counterattack.

I asked them to contact Ziklag, and Arik and Orni, who were with us on the roof, went into action. Arik tried to clarify from Intelligence whether the Jordanian artillery was shooting at us; Orni attempted to contact Ziklag.

Suddenly there was another explosion and, as smoke rose from inside the museum, we heard the heart-stopping cry: "Medic! Medic!" More shells came from the Old City and we rushed from the roof, and with huge jumps raced down the stairs.

My head was bursting with worries. If the shells were ours, I couldn't understand why our men were outside, in spite of the firm orders that they should go into the building.

I ordered the radio technicians to get Moshele and Ziklag, and to tell them to stop firing, but could get no contact. I ran into the silent, empty street, roaring with all my might: "Moshele, stop! Moshele, stop!"

Coming toward me was Katcha, second-in-command of Battalion 28, returning from a reconnoitering mission to place his antitank weapons. He said that a shell had fallen next to him and that he was flung onto the street by the blast, but apart from bruises, was unhurt.

"Motta, they're shelling here!"

"I know," I answered, "but the artillery may be ours. Get

everyone away from here, and help me to find Moshele to tell him to stop."

Katcha turned to two reconnaissance jeeps that were standing at the corner of the road and tried to make contact with Moshele through their instruments. I went on toward the "red house." Moshele was supposed to be operating the rangefinding from there. "Moshele, stop! Moshele, stop!" I shouted at the top of my lungs. The *chevra* in the posts on nearby roofs joined me, and from all sides came the cry: "Moshele, stop! Moshele, stop!"

"Pass it on all round here," I roared in a rasping voice. "Pass it on to Moshele. Stop!"

I went back to the square of the museum; I knew that if these were our shells, any minute another might drop. If they were Jordanian shells, it was even worse, because soon whole salvos would descend on us. On my way down, I saw *chevra* there, and I wanted to get them away as quickly as possible.

I was horrified by what I saw in the square. At the entrance lay a few wounded; in their arms, they held men who were absolutely quiet. Parts of personal equipment and pools of blood covered the square. Among those killed were our own soldiers and some POWs.

Some men were dealing with the wounded, and among them was Orni. "You get away from here! You are the communications officer and I need you," I roared at him.

"Get away from here, all of you, and go into the building!" I shouted at the men with all my strength. "More shells will drop here any moment." The medics looked at me wide-eyed, ignored me, and went back to their work. Also working among the wounded were two doctors, Dr. Kahanski, from the medical team, and Dr. Zemach, a medical officer of the 28th.

"Get away from here!" I screamed again, but to no avail. They refused to leave the wounded. Next to the wall, Rami was lying, his arms and legs dripping blood. "Motta, Motta!" he shouted. "What's going on, Motta? Look what has happened to me!"

"It will be all right," I answered. "Keep very close to the wall. The attack will soon be over."

I heard more explosions from inside the Old City, and a weight lifted off my chest. At least we were not being hit by our own shells. It seemed clear at last that the Jordanians were returning our fire. A third shell exploded in the nearby olive grove and Yishai and Gabai took shelter near the recoilless-gun jeep, which was to be used to repel advancing enemy tanks.

Suddenly a POW jumped up and ran. Gabai caught hold of his leg, but only got the shoe of the man, who was still running, wearing the other shoe. Yishai went after him and caught him. We waited for more shells. Experience had taught us that the Jordanians did not fire according to a plan, so we expected them now to move the fire to another area.

A jeep arrived, followed by a truck. Dr. Leventhal had been sent by Dr. King. The medical men moved the wounded away from the courtyard and treated them.

Orni came back. He had managed to stop our fire. When he had failed to get Moshele and Ziklag on the radio, he made direct contact with Uzi Narkiss, and asked him to stop the firing at once. Uzi communicated directly with the artillery battalions and ordered them to cease firing.

"Very good, Orni," I called out. I almost kissed him. Another shell exploded, again in the olive grove.

Orni told me briefly what had happened. His men had been still moving across to the new command headquarters from the Rockefeller when a communications officer of the nearby mortar battalion had stopped Milman and told him that his instrument was out of order. Milman had answered that he was just going to the new building, and would return immediately to repair the instrument.

When he had reached the building, he had told Danny Oren that he was returning to the Rockefeller to repair the instrument, so Danny Oren joined him. Meanwhile Yossi Shurzenberg had begun to work on the instrument. When Milman had realized that spare parts were required, Yossi went to bring them and returned with Danny Peres and a suitable instrument. Meanwhile in the open square Nathan Schechter, the orderly, had waited, chatting with Yossi. The *chevra* had urged them to finish, for shells were already falling in the area. Then an officer had come out of the prisoners' quarters, and warned them not to remain outside. Danny Peres had urged Yossi to remain with him, and they all had stood at the door, talking. Then from up the road vehicles arrived to evacuate the POW's, and the commander of the guard for the prisoners had ordered the sergeants to bring the prisoners, who were handcuffed, in single file to the vehicles.

Suddenly there had been an explosion, and waves of the blast had blown them inside into the yard. Yossi had fallen, covered with blood, and Rami had been wounded. Amid cries of "Medic!" "Medic!" Nathan had gone to Yossi.

Those who had been unhurt had started to aid the wounded, and other paratroopers had hurried out of the building to help them. Then a second shell had exploded right in the middle of the group, killing Yossi and Nathan as well as several of the soldiers who had gone out to help them: Mordechai Ashkenazi, Gideon Hirsh, Meir Mor, Avraham Frankfurter, Moseh Sternfeld, and Yehuda Shamai. Danny Peres and several others had been seriously wounded.

Danny, Oren, and Milman had remained unhurt, and at once had begun to rush help to the wounded. Milman had run to call Orni, who had come at once. Danny Peres had asked for water, and Orni had given him a bottle. Milman had been particularly upset, as it was he who had persuaded Danny Peres to come from the Brigade Command.

They placed the wounded swiftly on the jeep and the truck and left the dead behind. Within the Old City, the explosions started again and Moshele and Ziklag resumed the rangefinding.

We looked around and saw that the two shells had reaped a blood harvest—we had lost ten of our best men, killed and wounded. I ordered the rest to disperse and take shelter before a new salvo caught us.

While there were still cries of "Moshele, stop!" Moshele, Ziklag and Yossi came out of the building, happy and laughing to report that the rangefinding had gone very well. The artillery was all set. The Moslem Quarter was within the range of all the guns, and the *chevra* in the posts reported that sniping from the wall had stopped.

Only now did they have time to look at our faces and at the carnage about us. They had carried out the rangefinding from the tower of the museum, and had no knowledge of what had been happening outside. We returned to the command post filled with sorrow for our losses.

From the Old City, more explosions were heard. But the Jordanian shelling had moved to another sector, and we wondered if we would have more men wounded there too. Yossi Avidan reported: "There are wounded from the shells. Shells fell in the yard of the monastery near Mandelbaum Gate."

I asked Uzi to find out why men were outside in spite of the strict warning issued before the rangefinding. He was to come to us immediately to receive the order to attack.

Only now did I notice that my voice had become hoarse, almost inaudible. I had lost it shouting to Moshele. On the stairs, Moshele explained to me that they had decided to do the rangefinding from the tower of the museum after they realized that they couldn't see what was happening inside the Old City from the "red house," and would not have been able to correct the ranges. Furthermore, they had wanted to make sure that nobody remained outside, which they did with Uzi's help when they crossed over; Uzi even had gone with them right up to the rangefinding point.

They had also been joined by Haggai. The others had been very useful, because observation from the windows was limited and only through comparing the impression of four people could they cover the whole sector and note every shell. In their opinion, our shooting had been efficient—they had no doubt that the artillery could neutralize the wall.

We went into the command post and took off our helmets and personal gear. Geula, our girl signaler, who had been with us throughout the war, served hot coffee from the kitchen of the apartment. What luxury!

We pulled ourselves together and settled down to work. Arik reported that there was no fresh information about the enemy strength, nor any further news of the Pattons, and that yesterday's report about the tanks heading for the Augusta Victoria ridge had been incorrect. Though the false supposition had made us abandon a battle, this was not the time to try to find out how it had come to be accepted. We were just thankful that it was wrong, and that we could plan according to our previous belief that there were about two companies on the Augusta Victoria ridge and about the same strength in the Old City.

We sampled some of our battle rations, which still tasted like battle rations. Amos was with Battalion 66 on Mount Scopus, so I asked Arik to write out the orders and he took out a piece of blue paper.

The telephone rang and it was Amos Regev, from Central Command, who wanted to know whether we had finally fixed zero hour.

We contacted Yossi, who said it was absolutely impossible for him to begin at 0830—with great difficulty, he might make 0900. Central Command said that any delay was out of the question. The planes had been ordered for 0830.

I accepted the decision, and agreed that our move would start at 0900. It was agreed that at 0830 the first squadron would bomb the Jordanians, and that the second squadron would do so at 0850. After that, we would shell with artillery and then the third and fourth squadrons would go in if called on.

The die was cast, and zero hour pushed up to 0830.

Amos arrived and reported that all loose ends had been tied up on Mount Scopus. Now the 66th was carrying out its last preparations for the assault. But he doubted whether the battalion would be ready before 0900. He took the pen from Arik and went on recording my orders.

Yossi P. appeared, and I told him: "Now that we know that there are no Pattons to worry about, we don't need you to participate in the attack on the Augusta Victoria, unless something goes wrong. As soon as we begin the assault there, you deploy your forces so as to be ready to enter the Old City, either through Herod's Gate or Lions' Gate, the moment you get the word from me to go. We'll place at your disposal all the tanks and artillery we can."

When everything was clear, he went back to his battalion.

I explained our plan to Kaposta. "First the tanks go up to the top of the ridge. As soon as I am sure that they are not encountering opposition from tanks or heavy guns, I'll send you in. You go behind the tanks and clean up the ridge as far as the Azaria crossroads. Go like hell, and keep going, whatever happens. Fire in all directions and hit everything you can. The infantry will follow behind you."

Eytan came in to say that the tanks were ready. He had altogether nine tanks, including some of Rafi's. Rafi had been taken to hospital.

I explained to him: "You travel first up the road. When you get to the Augusta Victoria crossroads, you'll either go left to help take the Augusta Victoria position, or you'll turn right and take control of the Abu Tor ridge. Which it will be will depend on the orders you get from me then. You're our spearhead. I'll send in the reconnaissance company and Uzi's battalion only after we see what fire you draw. To your left, on Mount Scopus, Battalion 66 will attack. They have about eight tanks."

"I know," answered Eytan. "Those are my tanks. That's the second half of my company, cut off from me since yesterday afternoon. They returned at night to Givat Hamivtar."

"That's great news—you'll have no communication and coordination problems with them. That's very important."

Eytan instructed his people to get the tanks together and bring them to the inner road of the Wadi Joz neighborhood. From there they would descend to the Kidron Valley, on the road reconnoitered by Giora. Eytan wanted to examine the path personally, and went off with Giora. I continued writing the order of the day, which I dictated and Amos wrote down. From outside came the sounds of shots and the thunder of explosions. Ziklag was not letting the enemy organize, and dropped shells on them without letup. According to plan, Battalion 71 had to attack the enemy forces south of the Augusta Victoria crossroads as well. For this reason Ziklag was shelling the area and also softening the slope where armored cars and other objectives had been detected last night.

From the room we saw the mushrooms of rising smoke on the dome of the ridge. The fire was concentrated mainly on the pine grove, opposite which Battalion 66 would break through.

Once again from Central Command Arik coordinated the

objectives on which the planes must "come down." We suggested that the central objective should be the area between the barracks and the forest, inclusive. We wanted napalm bombs around the barracks, so that the hutments would be burned and the trenches, threatening the Kidron Valley, covered by fire. We also wanted the pilots to machine-gun any snipers they could see in the communication trenches.

This plan dovetailed with the artillery shelling. We had no air advisor with us, but Arik Regev was working out the plan through the command Air Force adviser. Orni was preparing our communication instruments for contacts with the planes. These had been placed on the balcony facing east.

We heard from below the roar of tank engines and the din made by the caterpillars as the Shermans rolled slowly along. Now and then, as the drivers pulled out the throttles, there were loud backfires, and some people looked around nervously for sources of fire. In war it becomes tremendously important to be able to recognize the different sounds, to distinguish between various noises so as not to panic at every explosion, to work out in a flash who is shooting, at whom, and where. Otherwise, a soldier is in constant suspense, which paralyzes his ability to think and act coolly.

Yossi replied to our nagging that things were dragging out, and he doubted that he could begin at 0900. Much remained to be done, in particular the difficult job of removing the antitank mines between the Scopus garrison and the Augusta Victoria, to make it possible for his tanks to advance.

I was compelled to tell Yossi that the time schedule could not be changed, because the political clock was working against us, that the Command insisted on beginning the attack by air at 0830, and the planes were already waiting to take off. I told him that I was confident that by 0900—under protection of the aerial bombing and artillery fire—we would manage to complete most of the preparations and be ready for the breakthrough.

In dry, matter-of-fact tones, Yossi answered that he would do his best. We returned the microphones to the radio technicians, both of us worried.

In the units, the preparations proceeded at feverish pace.

Eytan's tanks reached the corner of the street from which they would move on to the road going down into the valley near the market.

Kaposta's company began to organize behind the tanks in the street below us. Reconnaissance jeeps, recoilless-gun jeeps and weapons carriers loaded with men and munitions lined up, leaving suitable distances between the vehicles in case a shell should drop among them. They were hidden from the ridge by a row of houses.

Kaposta's briefing to his men was simple. "We go up behind the tanks, spraying fire in all directions; every house and every yard may conceal an enemy post. So fire—fire—fire—the more the merrier! When there is a particular objective, we stop, aim, and knock it out.

"While the tanks may be called north to help Yossi, and Uzi is cleaning up posts, we'll continue south along the Abu Tor ridge till we reach the Azaria crossroads and can block off the area and isolate it."

On Mt. Scopus, the forces of the battalion had been brought forward as far south as possible, to be close to the breakthrough area.

The tank company, now attached to the battalion, organized opposite the National Library. Amram and the other officers of the tank company reported to the battalion headquarters for orders. Since early morning, the demolition sergeant, Engel, and his men had been busy removing mines and marking out a track for the tanks to take, some meters to the west of the street. The Jordanians had also erected a physical barrier of barrels filled with stones across the street, which Amram surveyed scornfully. "We'll squash that like a bug," he promised. Yossi sent Rafi, the explosives officer, to help Engel blow up the mines. It took a long time, but eventually they reported, "We think that the road's clean."

Recoilless guns, 20-millimeter guns, and heavy machine guns took up positions in the firing posts on both sides of the street.

Yossi called together his company commanders, and completed the main points of the plan.

When the air and artillery bombardments were over, the tanks would move forward and lead the attack. When they reached the saddle of the hill, they would spread out a little. Some would then go straight on, others would provide close cover for the infantry.

The forces and assignments in the Battlion were: D Company, Giora's—to move first and attack positions west of the street. A Company, Gabi's—to move behind it and attack positions on east of the street. B Company, Dudik's, and behind it C Company, Dadi's—to constitute the reserve, and keep behind A Company.

A last briefing from Battalion 28 explained that D Company and the support company would assemble near the Rockefeller. Vehicles would be sent to A Company to bring them to the area, if needed. What little intelligence material was available about the gates in the wall and the anticipated lines of advance inside the Old City was made available to the officers.

Then, at 0804 Uzi Narkiss called and insisted that I come in person to the microphone, however busy I was. I took the microphone: "This is the commander—over!"

Through the earphones, I heard Uzi's voice, very excited: "This is it! Permission granted! You are to take the Old City."

"Thanks very much. Will do."

"Can you set aside one tank company for a direct break-through into the Old City?"

"Sorry. All the tanks are already in action. It would throw the whole attack out of gear. But we will manage, don't worry."

"Right. Good luck, Motta."

The faces of the paratroopers around me flushed with excitement as I turned to them after putting down the microphone. I didn't need to talk: They could see the message on my face. We were to liberate the Old City. At long last Jews were to return as free men to the Western Wall.

At such a moment there seemed to be no room for outbursts of emotion. I asked Amos for paper. This was a command I would write out myself, in my own handwriting. I wanted the order for the conquest of the Old City to be mine, entirely mine. I sat down at my ease on a chair to frame the order of the day.

At 0820 the time had come to go out onto the balcony, from which we would direct the operation. This balcony had a great advantage in that, apart from providing good observation of the battle sector, it was also protected on three sides from fire, which made quiet, comfortable work possible. The radio technicians were already there. Uzi, the operations officer, was on the roof of the Histadrut House, serving as our contact with the Air Force.

In front of us, on the ridge, shells were falling amid black mushrooms of smoke and dust rising up among the trees and buildings. The crowding was pleasant and the excitement great. Everyone felt that a great day lay ahead of us. I took off my jacket and rolled up shirt sleeves.

The planes were due to arrive in a few minutes. Ziklag instructed all his units to stop firing lest their shells endanger the planes when they dove down to attack. The Kidron Valley was quiet.

We heard the thunder of the planes, and turned our heads to look for them in the skies. We knew that they should come from the south, and Yossi tried to contact them to direct them to the objectives endangering his force, but the planes did not answer. They were connected directly with the air adviser at the command, and our efforts to enter that channel and to have direct contact with them failed.

The planes passed quickly over the Augusta Victoria ridge, turned west, and streaked upwards. We knew that the moment had come. In a few seconds they returned right over the houses of the Abu Tor ridge and approached their targets at great speed.

It was 0832. The first napalm bombs dropped from the planes and flew forward and diagonally down. They struck among long barricades, from which now rose a terrible flame, which went up and up, accompanied by a cloud of black smoke, heavy and thick.

Again, the planes came in to attack. This time they performed a nosedive to fire their machine guns.

We followed them, detecting the flash and smoke of the shooting, hearing the thunder of the fire and the explosions of the shells. But the hits disappeared among the buildings and the trenches.

Each squadron had two runs. I felt more elated than I had ever felt before in my life. Eli Landau was standing next to me. "Eli, write down every command and every word that's said. They will be of historic importance. He took out pen and paper and began to write. But I was not satisfied. I took a pen out of my pocket and asked for paper, and began to write my own record of this most momentous of all days.

By 0850 the second squadron of planes had entered the attack. Again mushrooms of fire and smoke billowed up. I instructed the tanks to move forward and go onto the road, and from the olive grove they went out onto the street, got into formation, and began to travel. Last evening and this morning, sniping from the wall had worried Eytan, so his guns were half-back, facing the wall. They advanced in single file: Eytan's platoon, with Zisman and Adler. Arzi's platoon, with Ben-Gigi and Bruno. Shaul's platoon, with Mazliach and Moshe. When they came near the houses, Eytan realized that the wall was quiet. He ordered the tanks to swing their barrels forward and to open fire. The rows of houses near the street, and their closed yards, were flooded by salvos of fire and shells. Then Eytan ordered them to stop and wait for the end of the air and artillery attacks. Five minutes later the battalion on Mount Scopus was ready to go. Giora's men had taken off their haversacks so that they could go faster; they reckoned they would need much less equipment. Baruch Tenne cleared a captured Land Rover, laden with booty, of everything on it so that it could be used to evacuate wounded.

The plan was that the company would move on foot behind the tanks, and when they reached the grove they would turn right away from the street and spread out, the platoon of Reuven Mimin on the right of Buki, on the left; and of Zvika, behind and in the middle. The Mags were next to Giora, in the middle.

The 81-millimeter mortars were in two sections. As Hermoni, the platoon commander, began to fire, the heavy machine gunners prepared heaps of sacks and some of them took up positions on the balcony, some in the hall. The tanks, recoilless guns, and heavy machine guns opened flat-trajectory fire.

At 0900, zero hour, as the second squadron of planes concluded its run, a heavy pall of thick black smoke hung over the ridge. As soon as I ordered Ziklag to launch the preliminary barrage, the first shells dropped on target.

The tanks were climbing up the hill on the street from the market to the top of the ridge. Eytan came as close as he dared to the zone where our artillery shells were falling. He contacted Ziklag and asked him to move his fire eastward and southward, and Ziklag obliged.

I saw that the enemy fire on the tanks was weak, so I ordered

Kaposta: "Go! Follow the tanks!" Within seconds we saw the weapon carriers and jeeps "galloping" down into the Kidron Valley and then up the hill on the far side.

I ordered Uzi to get going, and soon we saw his men moving through the olive grove. The attack was in full force, and explosions thundered in the air, while the ridge was covered with clouds of dust and smoke.

The tanks began to move forward slowly, all the while pouring out fire, and the battalion command followed close behind. Now that the aerial blow and artillery shelling had cut down the reactions of the enemy to a minimum, our aim was to get in fast, before he recovered.

Amram, the tank company commander, told his second-in-command, Bar-On, to turn a little to the right with the tank, and to provide cover for others. Bar-On did so and opened fire while Amram followed with the rest of the tanks. After he had gone a few meters a mine exploded beneath Amram's tank, covering Yossi, who had been standing close to it, with shrapnel and soot so that his exposed limbs became completely black. Apparently Engel had not found all the mines. The tank stopped and the gunner and machine gunner opened fire on the Augusta Victoria grove. The other tanks also opened fire.

Amram told Jackie to pass him and to advance, but as Jackie turned half-right and moved forward, he also went over a mine. Rafaeli's hand was crushed and Boogi was thrown out with such force that he split the helmet of Micha, the operations officer. Jackie left the incapacitated tank and went back to Maccabi's vehicle, which continued to shoot and to provide cover.

Feivush was in command of the fourth tank. When Giora saw that the first one had hit a mine, he called Feivush on the back telephone: "Hello—can you hear me?"

"No," Feivush answered, "Can't hear. Put a token in!"

Giora laughed. "We'll leave the line open for you. Go right along the track marked in white."

Yossi noticed that the enemy forces were silent, not reacting to the attack. On the other hand, the mines had held up the assault. The concentration of men behind the tanks made them an excellent mark for enemy fire from afar, even if the Jordanians had fled from the front-line positions opposite. The situation therefore was potentially dangerous. And he was worried about the time factor. He decided that the tanks could give cover from where they were, and that the plan should be changed then and there, sending the infantry ahead of the tanks.

"Follow me!" he roared, rushing forward with his staff along the road.

Giora, who was directly behind him, ran ahead of him. "Pardon me, Yossi, my privilege. Let me pass."

"D. Company, Forward!" Giora shouted. Yossi continued to run next to him.

The entire company came after them on the double, trying to keep formation. The pinning-down men picked up the speed of their shooting. Amram jumped out of his tank, ran to Maccabi's, and told Jackie to take his vehicle away to the right of the street, and only later to get back onto the road; he hoped by this maneuver to bypass the mines.

Jackie sent Maccabi to take over his tank, while he himself stayed in Maccabi's. He turned right, where the track was marked out, and advanced. After about twenty meters, he again turned left, returned to the road, and continued south.

Giora's company advanced on the field to his right, all along the road. There was a roadblock opposite and, prodding his driver, Jackie raced past the paratroopers and crashed through it. While running, Yossi and Giora saw the forces of the 71st going up the ascent of the ridge on the west. Yossi made contact will Uri to coordinate both movements and fire, so as to make sure that they did not hit each other.

Even while he was running, Yossi decided on a change of plan. He contacted Gabi, commander of A Company behind Giora, and told him: "Instead of moving to the eastern objective, stay on the road. Enemy resistance is nil. I want you to get deep into the enemy formations as fast as you can."

Giora reached the edge of the wood and found on the right a stone wall and a barbed wire fence. "Follow me!" Giora shouted, and turned to the right. The covering fire from the tanks behind him hit a nearby enemy position. Giora worried that the tanks might hit our own men, so he sent a message back to Feivush to stop shooting. Feivush confirmed. "Reuven right!" Giora shouted to his platoon commander, "Be careful of mines!" As the *chevra* followed him, a hail of bullets came from the grove and Giora, in the van, was an inevitable target. He fell. Ganz bent over him and shot into the grove to cover his stricken company commander.

The *chevra* rushed on, firing furiously with every weapon they had. Micha, Giora's second-in-command, spurred them forward, shouting, "Keep going! Farther! Go on!" They came against the barbed-wire entanglement and a "spider." Shiloach, who had been wounded yesterday but had sneaked away before they could get him to hospital, and had rejoined the *chevra*, shouted for a wire-cutter. Avishai searched for one, but before it came, Shiloach had found a breach.

Up above the grove from which came the murderous bursts was a bunker. Nissan stopped and fired a bazooka shell, which was a direct hit, and Shiloach went through the breach only to be wounded a second time. He went to the rear for treatment as the rest of the *chevra* rushed on, shooting incessantly in the trenches and outside them. Yamkovson tried to help Shiloach. "Leave me. Nothing has happened to me." Avishai was also wounded, but could go on.

Giora's fall had struck them like a sledgehammer. Fury gripped them and their throats were choking. Someone would have to pay a heavy price for shooting Giora, their beloved leader. They fired round after round at the flashes from the wood aimed at them.

The assault continued. Opposite them stood a building with a red crescent, indicating it was a clinic. Mottka's squad entered and Reuven and Simon led the advance toward the central building, allocated to them, until they met men of Mussa's company—Battalion 71. "Stop!" came the command, passed on at once from man to man, and the companies merged and went on together. Mussa, the commander with longer service, took control of the force and ordered Nissan to shoot a bazooka shell into the building. Nissan did so and the two forces went ahead in the trench.

While Giora's company advanced in the wood, cleaning it up, Jackie went on with the tanks along the road until he was near the hospital. Two recoilless-gun jeeps had been brought there by Dan. He had already cleaned up the hospital and was ready to organize the next move.

When Feivush received Giora's order to stop, he told his gunner to cease firing. He said to the driver, "Take care. We are going through mines. Travel only in Jackie's tracks."

The tank went on until suddenly there was a thud. Feivush thought he had been hit by an antitank shell. But the driver knew better. A mine had exploded under him and he was wounded. Well trained, he called over the network: "Driver killed!" and the tank stopped.

Amram got on another tank, Ducher's, and directed it in Jackie's tracks. When there was an explosion under this tank, Amram ordered it to continue. It turned out to be only a personnel mine, so the tank passed on up the road.

* * *

A bunker was revealed opposite the crossing and Shoham aimed a bazooka shell at it, but the shell went too high. Arzi put in another, but it hit a tree. The *chevra* threw in a few grenades and with sudden momentum the platoon reached the big central building—a stone house at the top of the hill—the company's objective.

Dan Arzi placed explosive next to the entrance door. As soon as he detonated it, the door flew off and he ran through a maze of rooms, systematically throwing grenades and firing his Uzi.

From across the road, Yonatan, the intelligence officer, shouted "Stop! Stop!"

Gabi's company galloped forward on the road, toward the hospital.

Dani, the battalion medic, knelt down beside Giora's body. Then Giora's men brought up the Land Rover, lifted his body tenderly, and placed it gently on the vehicle.

At 0900 the tanks and reconnaissance company went up the slope of the road. The fire from the enemy was weak; only here and there shells were dropping and bullets whistling.

Two companies spread out in the olive groves. On the south was B Company, Eilat's. He had two platoons forward, Gadi's on the left and Oded's on the right. Amit's platoon was at the back and Eilat was in the middle, next to the Mags.

In the north was Mussa's D Company, with a similar formation—Golman's platoon on the right, Izmirili's on the left, Arnon in the rear, and Mussa and his second-in-command, Reuven, in the middle with the Mags. Their objective was the Jordanian position in the pine grove.

Uzi and his command were between the two companies, and Dan, with a recoilless-gun jeep, was on the road with the tanks and with Kaposta's company.

The companies advanced swiftly. The area in the Kidron Valley is like a plain, and one can march in it without difficulty. They wanted to "get at the enemy" for, a few minutes before, when they had been waiting, a number of shells had dropped between the companies. A few had exploded uncomfortably near and shrapnel had hit the men. No one had been seriously wounded, but two shells had rolled, like soccer balls, in the direction of the force. Every eye had followed them, dreading the damage they would cause. But they had not exploded and still remained in the field.

Other shells had exploded in the yards of the houses and in the Wadi Joz neighborhood, close to the rearguard companies, and between them and the fire bases. Fire had come from the buildings and the *chevra* had returned it. Then the enemy had quieted down, although now and then there was still a shot.

It was best to advance, to get out of the zone shelled by the enemy. Near the Hotel Palace, they stopped, waiting for the completion of the artillery barrage and permission to go on.

The mortar platoon fired quickly. But its shells landed too close to our own infantry for comfort. "Stop!" came the infuriating command, after they had fired only thirty shells.

The artillery barrage stopped and the men resumed the advance. From the road came the noise of tank engines and caterpillars, and the recoilless-gun jeeps and the jeeps of Kaposta followed. The companies advanced and climbed in the open area. The slope was steep, rocky, and covered with fences. Slowly but persistently, the men of the first lines climbed, conserving their fire, waiting for the command to shoot or for an encounter with the enemy. Uri and Yossi coordinated the actions of the two battalions.

They reached a fence and Mussa ordered Gershon, a platoon sergeant, to lie on it. Gershon did so, and all the men crossed it, using him as a bridge.

Mussa's men leapt into a trench, while Eilat's men broke into some barracks, where they found no one. The enemy had fled, leaving behind signs of their having been there that very morning. Mussa made contact with Giora's men in the 66th, and they joined in the action together.

Eilat's company went into the barracks, where they found beds and mattresses as orderly as though for morning parade. The jeeps, with Dan, arrived at the crossroads and turned left toward the hospital.

In the Kidron Valley, Chabal, the regimental sergeant major, collected a column of vehicles to follow in the wake of the assault, and Dr. Yigal, the doctor, and his band of medics cleaned up the Palace Hotel room by room to get it ready for the wounded. They prepared cars in the yard to evacuate wounded to hospital.

By 0910 all forces were attacking, and meeting little resistance. I felt this was the time for our brigade's advance command group to move, so I gave the order that we should join the forces. Our excitement knew no bounds. We took great leaps down the steps and rushed to the vehicles.

At my side, in the driver's seat, sat Ben-Zur. I had asked for one of our own drivers, for my experience with outside drivers had not been encouraging. Our party consisted of the half-track and two weapons carriers. Giora, the reconnaissance officer, drove his own jeep. We reached the street that went up to the ridge and saw, before us, columns of tanks and jeeps spread out, shooting in all directions.

On our left the men of the 71st were climbing a steep white hill, and the first tanks had reached the road junction. Yossi reported that the advance was being carried out swiftly. I estimated that very soon the two battalions would enter the fortifications area, and feared that they might injure each other.

Enemy fire was almost nil, so I commanded the two battalions: "Stop!"

We drew near the road junction. The tanks and jeeps had gone off to the south and we heard fierce firing from there, but the noise of shooting to the north had died down. By 0920 Yossi reported to me: "The Augusta Victoria ridge is in our hands."

Chapter VIII

THE OLD CITY

By 0930 it seemed incredible that only thirty minutes had elapsed since zero hour: Tanks, jeeps, infantry, and staff were all racing along now, at headlong speed. We saw almost nothing of the enemy, except for a few Legionnaires fleeing in the distance, and soon we reached the great Intercontinental Hotel on the top of the hill, above the ravaged Jewish cemetery, on the crest of the Abu Tor ridge.

Arik Regev called from Central Command, and told Arik, our intelligence officer, that he had an important order for me from the Chief of Staff. Arik repeated the command: "You must enter the Old City at once and conquer it."

Just like that. "Right," I answered. "Confirm receipt of the order, and tell him we'll execute it right away."

Everyone was swept up, as if by storm, by the thought of taking the Old City! Going up to Jerusalem—even though physically it lay below us. (According to a tradition as old as time, one could talk only of going up to Jerusalem, never down.) We were going to turn that spiritual ascent into a physical reality for the Jewish people.

We looked below us at the Holy City—the Temple Mount, the

gold dome of the Mosque of Omar, the silver dome of El Aksa, the wall, the gates, the arches, the minarets, the spires, the towers. It was difficult to move our eyes away from the breathtaking vision; we could have stayed here enraptured forever. But our driver, Ben-Zur, was apparently less romantic than we: He pressed his foot hard on the accelerator.

The street wound down the hill with sharp turns. A tank blocked the way and we were forced to stop. In front of us was a mixed column of tanks and jeeps, heading for the Azaria crossroads, which they had been ordered to capture as soon as possible.

Suddenly, after passing the first turn on the slope of the Mount of Olives, Eytan saw three Pattons. It seemed to him that they were abandoned, but there was no point in taking any risks. He fired a shell and hit one, but there was no enemy reaction. The Pattons were really unoccupied.

The tanks went on and reached the Azaria crossroads. "Zisman, take up blocking position, facing Jericho," Eytan commanded.

Eytan himself went down the slope of the road to the right, to the north. On his left the wall of the Old City reared up. Eytan ordered the force to open fire with all weapons at all positions along the wall, taking care not to hit the mosques. The tanks climbed up onto the sidewalk with one caterpillar, turned the turrets left, and opened fire from cannons and machine guns. They wall began to "dance."

I told Ben-Zur to wait. I still had to draw up the command to attack the Old City. From my present position, I could not observe the whole area well. True, I had often given orders while traveling in a half-track, but this time my message had to be different, unique. I instructed Ben-Zur to turn around and go back to the garden of the hotel, where I could see the Old City well. It was a suitable setting from which to issue so memorable a command.

"What has happened?" the staff officers wondered. "Why are we going back?"

"To give the command for the conquest of the Old City from an appropriate place," I answered them. "From a place from which Jerusalem is revealed in all its beauty and glory." The *chevra* smiled at my nonsense, rather patronizingly but affectionately.

So we turned around and went back. Soldiers traveling in the opposite direction wondered what had happened. We smiled and waved reassuringly. When we reached the entrance to the hotel, we turned on the path immediately in front of it and I looked westward at Jerusalem. But it seemed that we were too far from the edge of the ridge, and could not see the whole valley. So we crossed the flower garden on foot, and went to the very edge of the road below the hotel.

This was the ideal place from which to issue my order of the day. At our feet was the garrison of Abu Tor, and behind it the Mount of Olives. At its foot wound the road from Jericho, reaching the twist at the bridge, and from there climbing again in a steep incline to the wall of the Old City with its famous seven gates.

We sat for a moment and looked. There was the Temple Mount and to the left, along the wall, a road went up to the Dung Gate; on the right another road went to Arab Jerusalem; above the bridge, on the left, was Lions' Gate; beyond was the corner of the wall and the museum.

The smoke of our shelling interfered with good observation. Thick black-gray smoke collected over the whole Moslem Quarter so that the cemeteries close to the wall were almost invisible. Beneath the curtain of smoke, we could not discern our objectives, so I instructed the artillery to stop shelling.

Exactly opposite us was the Gate of Mercy, closed and "protected" by graves. The tanks on the street across from it were shooting at it.

I asked all commanders to come to the communications

instruments. The staff officers were wild with excitement and nobody tried to hide it. My mind was a mixture of tactical plans and choice phrases. I decided that the tanks should move ahead of the infantry, and at the same time selected words for the order.

I took the microphone. The smoke was melting away and the wall was now clear along its entire length. The words had to suit the moment. I did not need to be too shy to use lyrical phrases for I would be forgiven if I indulged in nonmartial emotion. All the officers were watching me intently, and listening to every word I said.

"Parachute Brigade 55," I began, and there was a ripple of amazement, for I had broken security by breaching the rigid rule against identifying a unit. But I was not going to send a code name to liberate Jerusalem. It was Parachute Brigade 55 that was making history.

"We stand on a ridge overlooking the Holy City. Soon we will enter the city, the Old City of Jerusalem, about which countless generations of Jews have dreamed, to which all living Jews aspire. To our brigade has been granted the privilege of being the first to enter it. Eytan's tanks will advance from the left and will enter Lions' Gate. The 28th and the 71st will move to that gate, with the 66th in reserve behind them.

"Now—on, on, on to the gate! We will hold the passing-out parade soon on the Temple Mount!"

My staff officers were shocked by my breaching security, but they were also pleased—in fact, delighted.

Yossi reported that there were still some Jordanians near them at the Augusta Victoria. I told him to leave a small force to deal with them and to make his way down to the gate. "Get your tanks to fire from the ridge at the wall."

Yossi answered, "It is difficult from here. The range is great, and smoke obscures the target. Would it not be better for my tanks to move to where you are?"

But I wanted fire at the wall, plenty of it, right now. So I answered, "No! Let them fire from where they are. Now!"

I told Kaposta to move to the Azaria crossroads and block it off.

The voice of Rabbi Goren blared over the instrument: "Motta, Motta, Motta, I have good news for you. Where are you?"

I answered immediately. "Go to Lions' Gate."

"I am coming at once."

Eytan's tanks were advancing along the street, and the first was already on the bridge.

Yossi ordered Battalion 66 to form two columns on either side of the road and instructed Amram, the tank commander, to attach a tank to each company, so as to cover the passageway between the houses. The companies formed a sort of avenue and the tanks went between them and took up positions at the head of each company.

From one of the houses in the Wadi Joz suburb the Arabs opened fire. Chaim's tank returned fire and the enemy was silent.

Battalion 71 was deployed on the slope near the Palace Hotel. Zamush's A Company, which had purposely been left behind as reserve, would now constitute the spearhead to break into the Old City, just as I had promised Zamush. The men in Yair Levanon's platoon, detailed to enter Lions' Gate, were already sitting on their half-tracks. Yigal Shefer, a section commander in the platoon, was to lay demolition charges and blow up the gate. Immediately after the explosion, Yair's half-track would go through while men in Zamuch's half-track provided cover for him, and then entered behind him.

The other companies organized all along the street. Uzi mounted the command jeep and joined Zamush's campany. Dan Ziv, his second-in-command, left the battalion recoilless-gun platoon and returned hurriedly to the battalion command jeep. Yitzhak, sergeant of the recoilless-gun platoon, advanced with two recoilless-gun jeeps to the head of the line to help with the demolition of the gates.

Battalion 28 was at the Rockefeller Museum. The shells of the artillery were falling on the Moslem Quarter and on the area at the corner of the wall. The men waited for the artillerymen to move their targets. As soon as the infantry were safe from our own shells they would move around the wall to Lions' Gate.

As soon as I had issued my order of the day, Ziklag's artillery resumed the barrage, shells exploded among the buildings of the Moslem Quarter, tanks smashed the stones of the wall and the thunder of explosions reverberated once more through the hills.

"To the vehicles!" I sat down next to Ben-Zur and pulled out the day book. "Has anyone written down the order?"

There was no response, and I stifled a curse. It was understandable that everyone had been so worked up that they had forgotten to do this, but it was an unfortunate lapse.

The tank platoons advanced in turn, one moving forward as the other provided cover. They approached the bridge, Arzi's platoon in the lead. On the bridge was a ghastly relic of the previous night's disaster: a burned-out tank and the jeeps it had crushed, black with soot. Along the length and breadth of the bridge were scattered pieces of metal and munitions. Arzi crossed the bridge first, and climbed in the direction of Rockefeller. The steep ascent made progress difficult, and it was not pleasant to have to move so slowly while fire was being poured down from the high wall a few meters to the left.

The tanks sprayed the wall with shells and bullets, and Eytan ordered the first one to secure the north side of it, so Arzi went past the turn to Lions' Gate and on as far as the open space opposite the corner of the wall.

Ben-Gigi's tank stopped opposite the street that went up to Lions' Gate, and faced the wall, exactly opposite the gate. There was a bus on the right side of the street, not far from the gate.

Chaimowski, the gunner, set it alight and then systematically pounded the gate and its surroundings. After a few rounds, Ben-Gigi instructed Sharon, the driver, to advance. The Arabs fired at the tank with bazookas and machine guns, from the embrasures of the wall.

Eliyahu shot in all directions with the machine gun and Ben-Aharon, the leader-signaler, supplied Chaimowski with shells at a crazy rate.

The tank advanced slowly and approached the burning bus. Immediately behind this was the Lions' Gate.

My driver pressed down the pedal and we were on our way. I instructed Kaposta to continue to Abu-Dis and to block the Jericho road against any Jordanian reinforcements that might come from the Heights of Edom or the Jordan Valley. I felt very sorry that the reconnaissance men, who so deserved the honor, would not be first to enter the Old City. But there was no alternative. The road from Jericho had to be blocked; at the moment, they were the best people to do this.

We moved on. The barrage was continuing in full force. We hoped that the smoke would not keep the gunners of the tanks from finding their targets.

Arik Regnev contacted us from the command: "It is important that we take Abu-Dis."

"To hear is to obey," we answered. "Abu-Dis is already ours."

He found this hard to believe. Only a few minutes had passed since he had given us the Chief of Staff's order to attack the Old City. He asked us to repeat and we confirmed.

Hundreds of times we had studied the minaret of a mosque at Azaria crossroads with field glasses and planned how to conquer it from the south, from the west, and from the north. Nobody had thought of taking it from the east, as we were now doing. Before us stretched a two-lane highway. Eytan's tanks were advancing in the western lane and shooting at the wall.

We repeated a previous order. "Be careful not to hit any holy places. Shoot only around Lions' Gate or to the north."

But we needed only to snatch a quick glance through the skylight of the half-track to confirm that the tank crews were being scrupulously careful. The company was maneuvering, firing, and moving; some of the tanks were stationary and shooting; others were moving and advancing.

We passed behind the tanks on the east lane and sped down the slope. We had entered the race quietly but with enthusiasm. Amos called to Eytan to move faster. I made notes in the diary.

Zamush's company advanced up the rise of the street from the market to the corner of the wall, Yair Levanon's platoon on half-tracks, the rest on foot.

Ben-Gigi's tank advanced to Lions' Gate. On both sides of the road were steep walls, and every shot and explosion sounded like an earthquake.

The tanks came up to the bus enveloped in flames near the gate. Ben-Gigi figured that the fire, with its leaping tongues of flames, might set the tank alight, so he ordered the driver to reverse slowly, downward, and to take up a firing position. The team did this and Chaimowski continued to fire upward. At the crossroads, Ben-Gigi stopped, still firing at the gate and all around it.

Zamush's half-tracks arrived from the rise of the road, and stopped for a moment next to the tank. Zamush exchanged a few words with Ben-Gigi as shells fell near them. The *chevra* were tense and excited. Uzi's jeep sped on its way to them.

The advance command group of the brigade continued to advance. We approached the bridge. To the right was a wonderful church, a riot of colors and spires. On the bridge we saw the sad reminder of yesterday—the burned tank and the crushed jeeps, ravaged and black with fire, and the advancing tanks stopped, not wanting to harm the bodies of the men hit in last night's battle.

I wrote in the diary and instructed Ben-Zur to press on. Moshele, in the weapons carrier behind us, also did not stop. Behind him were the radio technicians in another weapons carrier, and behind that the van of supplies.

We were sheltered by the sides of the half-tracks, while they were exposed, but they kept close to us, only a few meters away. To our right was the steep drop to the bed of the wadi; to our left the black bridge. In front and above us towered the wall of the Old City. General Chaim Bar-Lev, the Deputy Chief of Staff, called and asked what the position was. I answered: "Fine. We're going in soon."

"Good. Very good."

The half-track slowed down. The slope was steep, so Ben-Zur changed gear. To the left—next to the turn to Lions' Gate—stood Ben-Gigi's tank. Opposite, close to the wall of the hill, were the half-tracks of Battalion 71. The entrance was almost blocked up.

"Ben-Zur," I ordered, "go past the tank on the left. Don't stop. Forward."

With an effort, Ben-Zur swung the wheel to the right—changed gear—and pulled again to the left. To the left was the tank, to the right the half-tracks, in front a steep rise to the wall, which was covered with smoke and dust. We heard shells exploding and bullets whistling overhead. Soon we would come under fire from our own artillery and tanks.

"Ziklag," I ordered, "cease firing. Stop!"

Ziklag passed the order on to the units and we carried on.

Soon we would be inside. To the right of the street, just in front of the gate, a burning bus blocked more than half the road. Traveling in first gear, head bend down between the shoulders, thinking that any minute "something" might enter the half-track, I made notes in my diary.

The men in the half-track and weapons carriers were ready to fire. Everyone looked in every direction, and anybody seeing a target shot. It was difficult to tell if the Arabs were shooting from the wall at us, or if we were only seeing ricochets from our shots and stone splinters and shrapnel from our own shelling. Tank shells passed above us. The wall trembled, and stones fell down. Then, above Lions' Gate, the stones of the arch collapsed. The burning bus gave off black smoke and flames shot out from it every now and then, narrowing the passage.

The gate came nearer and the wall got higher and higher. We approached the bus, and wondered if they would throw hand grenades at us from above. Behind us were the open weapons carriers.

We reached the bus. "Pass," I said to Ben-Zur, thinking as I did so that the heat might explode the fuel tank. Ben-Zur made for the narrow passage, then the left wheel bumped on the sidewalk and waves of heat struck us. Then we were through and the gate was opposite us.

The right part of the gate was half open; the left completely open, with the door lying on the ground. On top of it lay the fallen stones of the archway. They were large, and heaped up so high that I wondered if we could get past.

"Ben-Zur, go on!" Ben-Zur pressed down the pedal and we were in the gate. We butted hard against the right door, and the half-track slipped and slipped from side to side. Just opposite us was a wall, and on the left a gate. We were half a meter from the wall. Ben-Zur swung the steering wheel to the right and made it, then swung to the left, just missing the house in front of us. Before us was the Via Dolorosa, narrow, long, with high walls.

We were in the Holy City! Ben-Zur changed gear. To the right an Arab hid in a doorway. He could have been holding a grenade in his hand, but didn't throw anything. Along the Via Dolorosa, lovely, small stone bridges overhead linked the houses. A half-paved road went off to the left; I remembered the route from the aerial photograph.

"Ben-Zur—left!"

Ben-Zur pulled at the steering wheel. The *chevra* from the half-track looked about them in wonder as they fired their weapons.

To the left there was a tall mosque, and between it and us an open stretch. We were on the winding road and I found I remembered the route by heart. Now the mosque was on our right and just opposite us was the Temple Mount area. We continued on and turned left again. Opposite us was the wall of the Old City, but now we were looking at it from the inside. Two-thirds of the way up were bazookas and piles of shells. Our *chevra* shot in every direction to make sure nobody would fire at us. Near the wall we pulled right again. To the south, opposite us, was the Gate of the Tribes. From here we went to the open area of the Temple Mount, where we found the gate and in the middle of the gate a motorcycle. Behind it was a Jordanian military camp—yellow tents and stones painted with whitewash in straight lines. We did not know if there were any Jordanian soldiers in the camp, or if the motorcycle was mined, but there was no time to investigate.

"Ben-Zur—go on!"

Ben-Zur ran over the motorcycle and we shut our eyes, half-expecting an explosion. The half-track rocked—but only from the collision. We heard the noise of the motorcycle being dragged along under our wheels.

Right in front of us was the golden dome of the Mosque of Omar. We advanced along a well-cared-for pathway, with greenery and trees on both sides. We had reached the end of the road, and were on Temple Mount. To our right were the broad steps, the pillars, the arches. It was hard to believe.

"Stop, Ben-Zur, stop!" The door was already open and the *chevra* jumped off the half-track and the other vehicles. We went up the broad and splendid steps and were on the open square. Opposite us—just opposite us—next to us—was the Mosque of Omar.

There was no shooting here. This was a holy place.

It was 1000. I asked for the instrument and Senderowitz came up to me. I took the microphone and ordered: "Cease fire—stop shooting, everybody! All forces, stop!" And a few seconds later, again: "All forces, stop! Cease fire!"

We were on the square of Temple Mount and ran to the center, next to the Mosque of Omar. Again I took the instrument, and sent a message to Central Command: "Temple Mount is in our hands. Temple Mount is ours! Temple Mount is ours!"

Uzi Narkiss came on the network, and said, speaking with great emotion: "Message received. Great show! Great show!" Then he added, "Mop up enemy nests in the Old City!"

I confirmed and he added: "There is nobody like you. At the Mosque of Omar! I'm on my way to Lions' Gate. See that there is someone to meet me."

I confirmed and he repeated: "I'm going full speed to Lions' Gate. Out."

Here and there shots were still heard. I repeated the command to the units: "Stop firing. All forces cease firing. Over!"

Everyone wanted to hurry to the Western Wall, particularly Moshele. But I asked him to wait, as I had promised Zamush that he would be among the first and he should reach us any minute.

Several *chevra*—Foxie, Vaksi, Nitzan, and Aharon from the Brigade Headquarters—came running from the direction of the eastern steps. The tank had blocked their way at the gate, so they had jumped out and run the rest of the way. Here came Zamush and Levanon's platoons, who hugged each other, shouted, laughed, yelled, and embraced again. Some were so bewildered that they did not credit what they saw; they were like men in a dream. But Moshele urged them on—he wanted to get to the Western Wall. From inside his shirt Zamush produced a flag. They looked at me, and I nodded—Moshele started running, everybody started running with him. The *chevra* vanished. Temple Mount meant the Western Wall. The consummation for which we had fought so hard—Mount Moriah, Abraham and Isaac, the Temple, the Zealots, the Maccabees, Bar-Kochba, the wars against Romans and Greeks. Thoughts of our long history churned in our minds. We were at the Temple Mount. The Temple Mount was ours.

A great crowd from the Brigade Headquarters and from Zamush's companies collected around Moshele as he ran westward. On the wide steps, they descended in front of an open space. Opposite them was a long, high wall, and in it were archways, with large doors, locked with bars. Close to this wall stood a Jordanian truck. Two Legionnaires emerged from the right and took up firing positions behind it, but an antitank gun quickly liquidated them both.

Moshele turned left, but didn't know how to find the entrance to the Western Wall. He stopped to ask a scared woman standing there, but she was struck dumb.

Moshele turned right. Into the street came an Arab, well dressed, with a red ribbon on his sleeve.

"Where is the Western Wall?" the *chevra* asked him.

Without emotion, the man answered in fluent Hebrew: "Come with me I'll show you." Happy but impatient with his slow pace, the *chevra* stepped out behind him. The Arab pointed to a small gate.

"From there," he said, "you go down to the Western Wall."

"Thank you," Moshele said, and started running again. Bending their heads, they went through a narrow, low gateway and an equally narrow passage. On the left was the wall of a house; on the right, an iron fence and some very narrow, steep steps. They had to go in single file. Suddenly there were ecstatic shouts: "The Western Wall! The Western Wall."

Everyone stared, their eyes devouring the Western Wall, stone by stone, gigantic blocks with shrubs growing out of them, the Wall of Prayer, the Wailing Wall.

"Where can we hang the flag?" somebody asked.

The wall was high and smooth and there was no place for a flag. But the flag was important. Over the wall—on the northern side—they saw an iron grid which they could use.

"Turn back!" Moshele commanded.

They turned round and went out of the gate where, again, they were in an open space. They ran to the left, looking for a door until they reached a gate and broke through it. Opposite them appeared a young man, his arms around two girls, one white, one dark. He was a Jew who had become a Moslem. "What are you looking for?"

"We want to get to the top of the Western Wall." He told them to follow him, and they entered his room and went out onto the roof. On it was an iron trellis and they looked down on the wall.

Zamush pulled out the flag and other hands opened and spread it until it was flying. Kotik produced a square bottle of whisky. As ordnance officer, he had thought of all vital supplies well in advance. Ben-Zur opened the bottle and they drank and shouted, *"Lechayim! Lechayim!"*

The bottle passed from hand to hand, from mouth to mouth and everyone drank. *"Lechayim!* To the State of Israel and the Western Wall!"

* * *

The open square of Temple Mount was quiet. The men of the advance command group sat next to the wall of the Mosque of Omar, our eyes never sated as they caressed every stone.

Soldiers poured into the square from every corner, every opening. Odd shots were heard from the direction of the city, and sniping continued from the north. Then shots were suddenly heard from the south as well. Uzi Narkiss's advance command group, including the Deputy Chief of Staff, General Bar-Lev, was approaching the Temple Mount. On the slope of the street, among the soldiers, the chief chaplain, Rabbi Shlomo Goren, marched, a Scroll of the Law in one hand and a Shofar to his mouth.

Meanwhile, Mussa's company was advancing swiftly down the road from the corner of the wall. Other forces turned right, toward Lions' Gate, but they continued going around the wall to the south and entered Dung Gate.

On their right was the wall; below, in the valley, were the grave of Zechariah and Absalom's monument, and before them was the village of Shiloach. Even while preparing for battle, they took time off to marvel at the enchanting view.

They went up the street, shooting at any point from which fire was coming. The street turned west, and all at once, they saw Mount Zion opposite them, with its towers and its turrets, and on the right the silver dome of El Aksa. The ascent was steep, the houses close to the street on the left. They were drawing near to a blank wall where, in front of them, a street ran right and left. A slight turn right, and the *chevra* were standing at the Dung Gate, which was closed. Dan went up to it and saw that it had a sliding door. His Uzi hanging from his shoulder, he placed both hands in the middle of the door, and with a slow movement pulled the two sections apart. When the door was opened, they saw that the road went on and up. They heard odd shots, but kept on going.

Now D Company was inside the Old City. Their eyes darted in all directions looking for the Western Wall, the Jewish Quarter, the famous old synagogues, the way to Temple Mount.

On the right was a locked gate, and behind it the El Aksa Mosque. Mussa broke through the gate and they moved north. Suddenly they saw figures on the top of the golden dome of the Mosque of Omar and they fired—and then saw the Israeli flag, so they stopped. Dan contacted Uzi and told him where they were and Uzi, already at the Western Wall, rushed to him and brought him in. Thus we had come through still another of the gates.

The street leading up to Lions' Gate was thick with people. The road must have looked just this way two-thousand years ago, during the spring and autumn harvest festivals, when pilgrims went up to Jerusalem on foot.

Mixed forces of Battalions 28 and 71 lined both sides of the street, and between them traveled the vehicles of General Bar-Lev, Deputy Chief of Staff, and General Uzi Narkiss. Above the crowd, borne aloft by Rabbi Shlomo Goren, was the Scroll of the Law.

Suddenly shots were fired from the north side of the gate, and Katcha ordered his men to return fire immediately. A fierce salvo covered the embrasures of the wall and its firing slots. The men ran to the north. Above the Lions' Gate, a little to the right, Jordanian soldiers rose, their hands up to surrender.

Rabbi Goren carried on as if nothing had happened. Yossi P. tried to persuade him to keep close to the wall lest he should be hit, but it was impossible to talk to him. As the Rabbi walked between the lines, his singing became louder, and in his enthusiasm he swept many soldiers along with him. They answered his singing with roars of excitement and enthusiasm.

"Rabbi, you're interfering with the fighting," called Yossi P., who asked Kuchuk, the operations officer, to see that the rabbi went to the rear. But when Kuchuk tried to stop him, the rabbi said angrily, "Don't be impudent." Kuchuk shrugged and went on his way. He knew when he was licked. The rabbi turned to Yossi P.: "You'll never make me go to the rear!"

General Bar-Lev smiled and said that they should leave the rabbi alone. Rabbi Goren put the Shofar to his lips, and a long paean was heard through the streets of the Old City, a sound which had not been heard there for many years.

Suddenly there was sniping from the minaret in the tall mosque at the corner of the Temple Mount. Without any command, the *chevra* returned fire: rifles, submachine guns, machine guns, bazookas, recoilless guns. In the thunder of explosions the order "Stop!" was not heard. After a few minutes the firing died down.

Adler's tank took up a position in the open area opposite the mosque. Shots came from one of the archways above the street, and the tank returned fire. Then there was quiet and Arab citizens gathered around. For them, the war had finished and they had come to watch a show.

I could not help thinking that never had any brigade had such an address for its headquarters: Temple Mount! We got an order from Central Command to hurry the mopping-up operations and to open a route as quickly as possible from Nablus Gate to the Western Wall for Prime Minister Levi Eshkol. In a special order, Uzi Narkiss emphasized that no holy places were to be touched, and that the civilian population must not be harmed.

At 1027 a medley of people came up the northern steps, Rabbi Goren at their head, the Scroll of the Law in one hand and the Shofar in the other. From time to time, he stopped, raised the Shofar to his lips, and blew a blast.

The group, among them General Bar-Lev and many high-ranking officers, came nearer, all smiling, laughing, shouting. We went out to meet them. A handshake was not enough: pats on the shoulder, hugs, embraces, even kisses, even tears. My throat was choked. Soldiers gathered around and then we heard the cry,

"There's our flag above the Western Wall!" Somebody called for three cheers, and the hurrahs reverberated, as blasts of Rabbi Goren's shofar rent the air. Our pent-up emotions, which could not be expressed in words, found some release through these cheers and the sound of the trumpet.

A radio journalist, Raphael Amir, pushed a microphone into my hand, and said, "Here is the commander of the conquering forces, General Motta."

In a hoarse, strained, emotional voice I shouted into the microphone, "It is impossible to express what we feel in words. We have been waiting for this moment for so many years. We paratroopers were thrilled when we were given the assignment to liberate the Holy City. We have executed it. The Holy City is ours." Chaim Bar-Lev interposed: "Forever." I went on, "Ours forever, as Chaim Bar-Lev says. For always and always."

There was a roar of cheering from the soldiers.

I went on: "Only a little while ago we looked down on the Old City from the Augusta Victoria ridge and marveled at the sight from above; now we are marveling from inside. We are hoarse from our cries of enthusiasm and excitement. When we entered, our advance command group on a half-track broke through the gate, crushed a motorcycle, passed through a Jordanian camp. We were the first to come straight here to the Western Wall. Moshele, my second-in-command for many years, at once and with some of the *chevra*, hoisted the flag above the Western Wall. Arik, our operations officer, and Orni, our communications officer, hoisted another flag on the Mosque of Omar.

"And now the whole of the Old City is in our hands. We are very, very happy."

Once more there were cheers from the lips of hundreds of soldiers. Uzi Narkiss took the microphone: "On the eighteenth of May, 1948"—Rabbi Goren interposed: "The month of Iyar"—"We succeeded in breaking into the Old City! Today we are at the Temple Mount. So wonderful an experience has never happened before to anyone standing here today." Uzi's words were swallowed up in Shofar blasts and more shouts.

Hundreds of soldiers began to sing "Jerusalem of Gold," and everyone was exchanging experiences. The singing mounted, then suddenly Rabbi Goren called out: "To the Western Wall! To the wall!" and rushed there, followed by a large crowd.

But we still had work to do. Uzi Narkiss repeated his order for us to clean up the whole of the Old City, at the same time treating all holy places with great respect and doing no harm to the civilian population.

And then Yossi P. came toward me with a group of Arab civilians, among them the Governor of Jerusalem, the Chief Khadi, other officials, and priests. We shook hands and the governor, tall, bespectacled, wearing a dark suit, asked me for permission to speak. His command of English was perfect and his enunciation clear.

"I have come to submit to you the surrender of the city and to express our wish for peace. Since midnight, the soldiers of the Legion have abandoned the city. This enables me to promise you, in my name and the name of all the population, that we have decided not to resist, not to fight back. It is possible that irresponsible people may not comply with the official decision, but I ask you to regard any breaches as exceptional."

"You know," I answered, my voice hoarse, "that if I instruct my forces not to shoot, this may place my soldiers' lives in jeopardy, if they are attacked at all."

"I know," replied the governor. "What I have said to you, and what I have promised, I have done in the name of the whole population. There will be no resistance in the city."

"I am very glad. In this way, we shall avoid destruction and bloodshed. I shall give the appropriate order to our units."

"And now, what must we do?" he asked anxiously.

"You are all free to go home," I answered.

"Pardon?"

"You can go back to your homes and families," I repeated.

"But if—"

"Don't worry." I calmed them down. "Everything will be in order. You can safely return home."

"Perhaps his honor the commander will give us an escort, or . . . perhaps we'll stay here in the offices?"

"There is no need for an escort. No harm will come to you. If you like, for my part, you can stay in the offices. But you can also go home. Don't be afraid."

I saw in their eyes that they still did not believe that they would be allowed to return home in safety. Again we shook hands, and they turned around and made for their offices, which were at the corner of the courtyard of the Temple Mount.

I told Yossi P. that he must have the route from Nablus Gate to the Temple Mount open and safe by noon, and that he must place units along the route, at crossings and possible danger points, for the Prime Minister was to come that way.

Gadi's company, from Battalion 71's B Company, mopped up a Jordanian post at the Gate of Mercy, and two Jordanians who resisted were killed in hand-to-hand fighting.

On Temple Mount the courtyard filled with paratroopers and I studied their faces, their eyes, as I walked among them, and chatted to them.

"*Nu*—how do you feel?"

"Wonderful. Just wonderful!"

Their eyes shone as they looked up at the flag above the dome and smiled. Their helmets were pushed back onto the tops of their heads and the chin straps loosened. Their feet dragged from exhaustion.

"Satisfied?" I asked. "Any complaints?"

"Of course not."

But suddenly there was a question. "When are we going to attack Syria? The war can't finish without their getting the lesson they deserve. Why, it was really they who started all the trouble."

There were cries of agreement.

I looked at them in wonder. In spite of the bitter hand-to-hand fighting for nearly two days; in spite of being shelled and shot at for so long; in spite of the dead and the wounded; in spite of the supreme emotional experience of liberating the Temple Mount, they didn't want to rest, they wanted to know when we would attack Syria.

It was a privilege to lead such men.

"Their turn will come too. Don't worry."

We got reports that snipers were still firing from the wall between Lions' Gate and Herod's Gate, so I asked Giora's reconnaissance men to mop up the area.

A jeep appeared on the northwest side of the courtyard, and I was shocked that someone had dared to come up to this holy place on a vehicle. I saw that it was the regimental sergeant major of Battalion 71, Chakal, on his way to the battalion. "What's this?" I asked him angrily. "With a vehicle, on Temple Mount?"

Chakal, at the peak of enthusiasm and joy, was perplexed and drove away from the courtyard. I issued orders to prevent it happening again.

The Via Dolorosa was such a narrow street that only two people could move side by side along it. Platoons of the 28th were delegated to clean it up. At the head of a spearhead squad marched Dani, Dror, the platoon commander, and Eli, with Leon and Hagai behind them. They felt relaxed, at ease, for the shooting had almost ceased and the streets were empty. At every intersection a squad remained behind to guarantee safety. The men moved quickly, for the distances were short and there were no people. When the spearhead squad got near to the broad steps going up to Damascus Gate, bursts of machine-gun fire suddenly struck at them from the opening of a nearby lane. Dani, walking on the right, immediately threw a hand grenade. Shuel, a little behind, put his submachine gun in action and covered the lane with fire. He detected fleeing Jordanians and aimed at them. The lane was full of smoke from the explosions, and the Jordanians managed to get away, leaving behind them Bren guns, which the squad took as spoils.

The steps were free and the men went up them to the gate. Eli opened it and the spearhead squad went to the open area of the gate and to the bridge that connected the gate with Arab Jerusalem. Then they wondered if they had the right gate. They had been told to take Nablus Gate—yet on the gate was written "Damascus Gate."

An Arab standing there told them of another gate to the west, and offered to take them there. This in fact was the New Gate, opposite the Notre Dame Church. Nablus Gate is really just another name for Damascus Gate, and the first gate was the correct one. But they did not know this.

The Arab walked first with Leon. Behind them were Dan, Dror, and Eli. The path took them into a narrow lane where all the shops were closed. Suddenly a grenade was thrown at them and Eli detected two Jordanians in the middle of the lane, standing and shooting. Dan was hit by fire and the grenade exploded, hitting Eli. The Arab leading them began to run forward toward the Jordanians, and Leon shot at the three of them and hit the one that brought them there, but the two others got away.

Now he turned to deal with his two wounded comrades. Suddenly a second grenade exploded between them, and Leon too was wounded in the legs. "Give me the bazooka," shouted Haggai, the company commander, who was just behind them. The Jordanians had disappeared. Meir, the adjutant, together with

Rafi and Shechter, ran to alert a doctor. On the way, an old woman with a white flag stopped them, crying in Arabic, "My son! My son!" Meir forced her to go into her house. Dan and Eli were evacuated but Dan died on the way to the casualty clearing station.

The spearhead of D Company was replaced and the others went on. New Gate was seen against the background of the Notre Dame monastery. They advised Yossi P., who sent us word: "New Gate is in our hands." Now it was clear that the gate where they had been before was the right one. Yossi P. added quietly: "Nablus Gate is in my hands. The road is secure."

Suddenly they heard a child crying. Close to one of the walls, a little boy was sitting alone, weeping. Meir remembered the Arab woman who had spoken to him earlier, and stopped to pick up the child and carry him back to the woman's house. He knocked at the door, but the Arabs were afraid to open. When Meir forced the door open, the family looked up, terrified. Meir held out the child and the family couldn't believe their eyes.

"Come in, come in," they invited him, through a deluge of blessings. "No thank you, some other time," he answered hastily, and went back to the battalion.

They cleaned up some snipers' nests between Damascus Gate and the Jewish Quarter of Musrara and took twenty prisoners. Yossi P. reported again: "Connection has been made with Jewish City. The way to the Temple Mount through Nablus Gate is secure."

Mussa's D Company headed for Jaffa Gate by alleys that were very narrow, at times crooked. There were no people in the streets, and they did not encounter any resistance even at the Kishele, the Turkish prison. Along the wall there were already men of the Jerusalem Brigade, who had come through the Dung Gate.

Suddenly a shot was fired at them from the wall, near Jaffa Gate, and they fired a bazooka shell in reply. A Jordanian came out, his hands up, and when the *chevra* went inside they found a dead Jordanian.

They climbed to the top of the Citadel, David's tower, the symbol of Jerusalem in so many pictures, and word was flashed back to us: "The Citadel is in our hands!" In the fortress they found two drums which they began to beat with great gusto. They went to the top of the tower to drum the great news of the victory to the citizens of Jewish Jerusalem. Israelis came out of their houses one by one, and soon the area filled with a great crowd, singing and dancing to the beat of the drums.

The lane was narrow and on both sides there were high buildings and tall stone walls. On the left, toward the wall, was a building with an iron gate, ornamented and beautiful, which was St. John's Hospice.

B and C Companies were cleaning up the area when they heard a shot and Aryeh Weiss, at the corner of the building, fell. Aryeh was an antitank man who had only joined the company at Temple Mount. Although not one of our men, he could not bear the fate that had fallen to his lot—to miss the ultimate battle. Having friends in Eilat's company, he had joined them in the front line.

It was difficult to identify the source of the shooting. The echo of the shot reverberated in the narrow street, and it seemed that in every window and behind every shutter there might be a man with a gun. The *chevra* cast looks in every direction and somebody noticed the barrel of a rifle in one of the grilles. "Fire!" he cried, "Fire at that grille opposite!"

Baruchi and Gil emptied their magazines, and David Natan fired a bazooka shell which shook the wall with its thunder. As the smoke cleared they saw the shell had made a hole in the wall.

Other men ran up as the Jordanians went on fighting. The building had to be mopped up, room by room, and six Legionnaires were killed.

Aryeh Weiss died before they could get him to the hospital.

Opposite the New Gate, in the monastery of Notre Dame, just across the road, but on the Israeli side of the old frontier, were the soldiers of the Jerusalem Brigade. When they saw the paratroopers at New Gate, they shouted joyously across to them and the paratroopers asked them to send regards to their homes, so the men from the brigade telephoned the messages.

Mussa and Zamush reported: "Jaffa Gate and the Citadel are clear." Yossi P. reported to me: "Mission accomplished. New Gate and Jaffa Gate are in our hands. We have one killed."

The reconnaissance company crossed the Via Dolorosa and set out to clear the area around Herod's Gate. It was from posts in this zone that so much heavy fire had poured down on the Israelis near the Rockefeller and around the wall on the way to Lions' Gate. But now they met no resistance.

They found stores of equipment and weapons in a school. Then they also discovered a doctor attending to two wounded Jordanians. The doctor asked for water and Yigal, wounded in the hand himself, gave the doctor his canteen, and also some food. The wounded men revived and the doctor dressed Yigal's wound.

Giora instructed the men to evacuate the wounded Jordanians to the hospital and to turn the school into a base for the company. Meanwhile Arab citizens came out of their homes and began to walk about, and Giora reported, "Herod's Gate is in our hands!"

At Dung Gate and Zion Gate men of the 66th linked up with forces of the Jerusalem Brigade and encountered virtually no resistance. Yossi reported to me: "Dung Gate and Zion Gate are in our hands!"

By 1230 the courtyard of the Temple Mount was almost empty. Now and then a group of people went past us—both soldiers and civilians. All were streaming toward the Western Wall. They stopped to greet and thank us, before going on.

Kaposta's reconnaissance company was still at the Azaria crossing. Eytan had placed his tanks there, and also on the way up to the Intercontinental Hotel. His men were busy with repairs and stores and all was quiet.

The reports from the units came in to me one on top of the other. The gates were in our hands, the Old City was in our hands, all Jerusalem was in our hands. The time had come to go to the Western Wall ourselves.

We left a reduced advance command group to deal with any problems that might arise, and headed there ourselves. On all sides I saw the *chevra*, displaying signs of shock and utter fatigue as well as deep satisfaction. Now that the intense excitement and emotion of victory had passed, other feelings, suppressed during the fighting, came to the surface: sadness, pain, resentment of the folly and cruelty of war. Now they thought of their comrades who had fallen, whom they would never see again.

We came to the narrow little gate, known as the Mograbi, and lowered our heads to duck through it to the top of the gloomy, crooked, steep, narrow stairs. We heard the sounds of praying as we went down the steps. The space in front of the wall was packed with people. Soldiers were praying, some swaying devoutly as if in synagogue, although they were still wearing their stained battle dress.

To our right and above us was the wall: huge blocks, gray, bare, silent. Only shrubs of hyssop in the cracks, like eyes, gave the stones life. We saw that somebody had set up an Ark, brought from a military synagogue, and that in front of it stood Rabbi Goren praying in a hoarse voice. He had been praying nonstop now for two hours.

The site, the prayers, the great victory, the thoughts of the fallen seemed to release the paratroopers from their armor of iron and many of them wept unashamedly, like children.

Somebody called for "Hatikvah," the national anthem, and

the vigorous singing of it—broken with tears—united all present. The soldiers stood at attention and the officers saluted. Before the last strains of the anthem had died away, Rabbi Goren began the Kaddish, the prayer for the dead. He intoned: "In memory of the slain who died in the Name of the Holy One, for the Liberation of Holy Jerusalem!" One's throat was choking.

Rabbi Goren, General Narkiss, and General Bar-Lev kissed each other before all present, and General Narkiss said briefly: "This is an extraordinary experience, impossible to describe."

Rabbi Goren again said the Kaddish: "Let us say Kaddish in memory of the martyrs who fell in liberating Jerusalem, the Temple Mount, and the Western Wall."

Sounds of weeping intermingled with the words of the Kaddish.

"Now we shall have a memorial prayer," Rabbi Goren cried, "in memory of the slain of the Israel Defense Forces, who fell in this war against the enemies of Israel.

"God, full of compassion . . . in the exalted places among the holy and the pure." Weeping choked the Rabbi's voice. The memorial prayer went on as tears flowed. "Who fell in this war against the enemies of Israel and who fell in the Name of the Holy One, for the nation, and the Land, for the Liberation of the Temple, of the Temple Mount, of the Western Wall and of Jerusalem, City of God . . ."

Toward the end of the prayer the tears prevailed over the words. The living and the dead were united in this moment of time—the spirits of the fallen seemed to hover over Jerusalem, reunited, reborn!

At 1211 the rabbis began the midday prayers.

Rabbi Stiglitz, the paratroopers' chaplain, read the Prayer of Supplication, but Rabbi Goren interrupted him: "Let us rather sing Hallelujah!"—the Song of Praise, of Thanksgiving.

"I cannot, Rabbi," answered Rabbi Stiglitz, "I have been busy among those collecting the dead—I cannot say Hallelujah—I will say the Supplication . . ." So each rabbi said his own prayer.

I drew near the crowd of soldiers praying, and when they noticed me they indicated I should go to the front. I thanked them but stayed at the back.

Despite the great congregation, I had to undergo my own private experience. I did not listen to the prayers, but raised my eyes to the stones and looked at the paratroopers praying, some with helmets on their heads and some with skullcaps. I scanned the buildings closing in on us from three directions, which gave the square a very intimate character.

I remembered our family visits at the wall. Twenty-five years ago, as a child, I had walked through the narrow alleys and markets. The impression made on me by the praying at the wall never left me. My memories blended in with the pictures that I had seen at a later age of Jews, with long white beards, wearing frock coats and black hats. They and the wall were one.

I came back to reality. Some distance away from the community of soldiers stood a man as though joined to the stone and part of the wall. He wore a long brown coat and on his head a black hat with a brim; beneath it strayed his long white hair. Nothing moved, neither his head nor his hair, body or legs. His two arms were bent, with the palms spread out flat, affixed to the stones as if they wanted to penetrate them.

I could not take my eyes off him. I was joined to him from afar, as he was joined to the wall from close to it. Through him I felt the wall, and through his half-paralyzed body I felt the beat of the heart of the Jew joined to these stones.

So we stood bonded together for a few moments in time—he, I, and the wall.

I asked Amos to arrange a meeting with the battalion commanders.

We were back in Jerusalem.

Monday, June 12, 1967—Fourth of Sivan, 5726

Paratrooper brigade 55 was in parade formation on the Temple Mount. All the wounded who could be moved were present.

I addressed them:

"Paratroopers! Conquerors of Jerusalem!

"When the Temple Mount was conquered by the Greeks, the Maccabees liberated it. When the Second Temple was destroyed, the Zealots and Bar-Kochba resisted the Romans heroically but in vain. For two millennia, no Jew could enter the Temple Mount . . .

"And then you came, you paratroopers, and you restored the Mount to the bosom of the nation. The Western Wall—the heartbeat-of every Jew, the place to which every Jewish heart yearns—is once more in our hands.

"Throughout our long history, many Jews have risked their lives to reach Jerusalem, and to live in it.

"Innumerable songs of longing voice the yearning for Jerusalem deep in the heart of every Jew.

"During the War of Liberation, mighty efforts were made to recover for the nation its heart—the Old City, the Western Wall. These efforts failed.

"The great privilege of finishing the circle at long last, of giving back to the nation its capital, its center of sanctity, has been given to you.

"Many paratroopers, among them our closest comrades, our great friends, the nation's finest sons, gave their lives in this bitter battle. It was a fierce and very difficult battle. You crushed all opposition, and you never counted the cost, never hesitated because of the wounds you suffered. You went on.

"You made no complaints, you presented no accounts, you lodged no claims. For you it was enough that you drove forward and forward—and you conquered.

"Jerusalem is yours—forever!"